AFTER DEATH

AFTER DEATH

A New Future for Human Consciousness

DARRYL REANNEY

WILLIAM MORROW AND COMPANY, Inc.
NEW YORK

Library of Congress Cataloging-in-Publication Data

Reanney, Darryl.
[Death of forever]
After death : a new future for human consciousness / by Darryl
Reanney.
p.   cm.
Originally published: The death of forever. Melbourne : Longman
Australia, 1991.
Includes bibliographical reference.
ISBN 0–688–14420–9 (alk. paper)
1. Death—Psychological aspects.   2. Fear of death.   3. Future
life. I. Title.
BF789.D4R43   1995
129—dc20   95–13186
                                                          CIP

Printed in the United States of America

First U.S. Edition

1 2 3 4 5 6 7 8 9 10

BOOK DESIGN BY JUDITH ABBATE

We speak of ourselves as "human beings," despite the image that the word "being" conjures up—a fixed thing, a stable state. Yet we live in, and are part of, a universe that is endlessly fecund, inventive, everchanging, ever transforming itself. It would surely be better if we abandoned the term "human being" and replaced it with "human becoming."

This book is dedicated to two human becomings who are special to me, my children, Justine and David. May they inherit a future I can only dream of.

ACKNOWLEDGMENTS

Many people, wittingly or unwittingly, have helped me create this book. I wish especially to thank Dr. David Bathgate for his gently constructive criticism of various ideas in the book as they struggled to take shape, and for drawing my attention to several seminal authors whose works subsequently influenced the texture of my argument. Thanks are also due to Dr. Jeff Pressing, who collaborated with me in the early 1980s to develop some of the concepts expressed in Chapter 9 and who generously read a draft of the book in its formative stage. Similarly, I am grateful to Professor Geoff Opat for checking Chapters 2 and 7 for accuracy and Dr. John Jenkin for performing a similar task with respect to Chapters 1 to 5.

Finally, it is a pleasure to acknowledge my appreciation of, and indebtedness to, Robert Coco and Stephen Kime of Longman Cheshire. The helpful criticisms of the first helped me to improve significantly many sections of key chapters, while the enthusiasm of the second supported me through the process of revision and beyond. Both combined a necessary capacity to criticize weaknesses in individual sections of the text with a strong belief in and commitment to the book as a whole. The final form of this book owes much to their encouragement and advice.

The publishers wish to thank the following for permission to reproduce copyright material: Chapman and Hall, London, for the diagram, Fig. 2.6, from *Accuracy in Molecular Processes* by Kirkwood et al., London, 1986, p. 22; Mrs. Elizabeth Dexter, for the diagram, Fig. 6.3, from *Endurance of Life* by MacFarlane Burnet, Melbourne University Press, 1978, p. 133; W.H. Freeman and Company, Publishers, New York, for four diagrams, Figs. 7.1a–c, 7.2, from *Black Holes and Warped Spacetime* by William J. Kaufmann III, copyright © 1979, pp. 183–85; Faber and Faber Ltd., London, for extracts from the poems "Little Gidding" and "The Hollow Men" from *Collected Poems 1909–1962* by T.S. Eliot; David Higham Associates, London, for an extract from the poem "Do Not Go Gentle into That Good Night" by Dylan Thomas from *The Poems;* Jonathan Cape Ltd., London, and the Estate of Robert Frost for an extract from the poem "The Road Not Taken" from *The Poetry of Robert Frost,* edited by Edward Connery Lathem; George Sassoon for the poem "Microcosmos" by Siegfried Sassoon from his *Selected Poems,* Faber, London, 1968; David Syme and Co. Ltd., Melbourne, for extracts from *The Age Monthly Review,* Vol. 2, August 1982, pp. 8–9; Transworld Publishers, London, for the diagram, Fig. 7.3, from *A Brief History of Time* by Stephen J. Hawking, Bantam Press, copyright © 1988, Space Time Publications, all rights reserved; Weidenfeld and Nicholson Ltd., London, for the diagram, Fig. 3.3, from *The Double Helix* by J.D. Watson, London, 1981. We have also used diagrams from *The Tao of Physics* by Fritjof Capra, Fontana, London, 1983, p. 201 (Fig. 23), and *The Mind Machine* by Colin Blakemore, BBC Books, London, 1988, p. 190 (Fig. 4.1).

CONTENTS

INTRODUCTION

THE ROAD
TO GIZA

In 1980 I traveled around the world as part of an Australian Broadcasting Company (ABC) camera and production team to film sequences for a television series on genes and evolution. Our itinerary was extensive, taking us from Calcutta to Cairo, from New York to Rome. We also traveled widely in Australia. Three memories of that journey are particularly clearly etched, and I want to set them down because, from many points of view, they were the seeds from which the ideas for this book grew.

Toward the end of 1980 the ABC team and I traveled into a remote region of western Australia called the Pilbara. We were able to drive up the Western Australian coast from Perth by car, but the final leg of the trip took us into inaccessible country, and we had to use a helicopter to get to our destination. It was a spot called Marble Bar, where I had to record a voice-to-camera sequence. For once, I got it right without too much fuss, and the "take" was finished in about half an hour. Three members of the team, including the cameraman, left in the helicopter to get some wide-lens shots of the region from the air, leaving the sound recorder and myself behind.

What I remember so clearly is the sense of solitude that possessed me as I watched the dwindling speck of the helicopter vanish into the sky. That and the silence. In a city, and even in the country, there is usually a background medley of noise to distract the ear and occupy the mind. Here, however, was the nearest thing to a sound vacuum I have ever experienced in the open air, with no noises made by man and none by nature, apart from the thin piping of insects among the rocks.

What gave the moment its magic was the feeling of genesis. The flat, timeless Australian landscape had often given me an uncanny sense of déjà vu, as though I was seeing a familiar image in a strange context that somehow prevented me from recognizing it for what it was. In this part of the Pilbara I suddenly found the words to fit the image. The weathered landscape looked just like the seabed, drained of its water and dried in the sun. Which is exactly what it is. This region, like so much of Australia, was once under water. The buff-colored rocks around us were marine sediments. What we had just filmed were curious striated humps that appeared to have been formed by layering successive "leaves" one upon the other. These laminated cones were, according to the experts, remains of stromatolites—distinctive structures formed by the action of tiny living things. The point of it all lay in their age. These relics, like the sediments around us, were three and a half billion years old. We were at the navel of creation, one of the places where, in the unthinkably remote past, life had begun its long march toward man.

Some months later I was able to see whither that long march had led, when I came to the second event that remains etched in my memory. That took place in another remote part of Australia, a cave called Koonalda on the edge of the Nullarbor Plain, arguably the largest expanse of flat desert in the world. The entrance to Koonalda is fifty or more feet below the surface of the plain, and to reach it we had to clamber down a rickety metal ladder. After a briefing session we armed ourselves with torches and powerful lamps and began our descent into darkness.

I will never forget the netherworld that engulfed us as we moved farther and farther underground, into a silence so profound that we hushed our voices, while the the lights of our torches cut deeply into an alien realm with the dimensions of a cathedral and the atmosphere of a tomb. Several members of the crew began to show signs of claustrophobic nervousness, conscious of the increasing weight of earth above us. I know just how they felt.

Somewhere during this fumbling descent the thought came to me: If this experience is awesome for educated sophisticates in the twentieth century, what must it have been like for the first Stone Age intruders into this stygian gloom, their way lit not by the sharp-etched brightness of electric lights but by the flickering glow of burning brands? What did they think as they watched the uncertain shadows pick out strange shapes in the changing zones where the light stopped and the dark began? In a cave like this it was easy to see how the *underground* could become transformed in the human imagination into the *underworld*, a place of fear, peopled by demons and gargoyles and haunted by the spirits of the dead.

The spirits of the dead. Standing in the subterranean darkness of Koonalda, I began to sense how primitive people could come to populate places of underground burial with the shades (the word itself is evocative of its origin) of the departed. The evolution of ancient underworld concepts like the Greek Hades and the Hebrew Sheol became easier to understand.

This sense of going back in time was a fitting preparation for what awaited us at the end of our journey. Some three hundred meters inside the cavern, deep under the ground, we found a soft rock face into which long-vanished hands had gouged enigmatic, crisscrossed, parallel markings. This "macaroni" artwork is arguably one of the oldest aboriginal engravings in Australia and is strikingly similar to the earliest cave art found in southern France and Spain. It is dated as approximately twenty thousand years old. To put that in perspective, the men who made this imprint had died over fifteen thousand years before the pharaohs built the pyramids at Giza.

They have left some trace of their sojourn on this planet to live after them. If they made the marks with an unconscious sense of doing so, of communicating a feeling for something greater than the span of the individual life, then these faint tracings may represent early evidence of a religious rite. Here, strangely preserved in its own underworld darkness, may be one of the first footprints of faith.

At Koonalda, then, was another possible Genesis, the dim, misty Genesis of religious awe: some faint consciousness of time and death, the hallmarks of the human state.

This brings me to my third memory. During the course of filming the series, the crew and I visited Egypt. Like all tourists, we headed to Giza to see the pyramids.

Most photos give the impression that the pyramids stand in the middle of a desert. In fact, they are built on a plateau, which overlooks the modern city of Cairo. Nothing prepares one for that first unhindered glimpse of the Great Pyramid as one's car starts to climb the plateau. The ascending slope of the hill lifts the eye upward until it catches and follows the ascending lines of a structure so stupendous that it nullifies one's preconceptions and numbs one's sense of criticism. For a fraction of a second, the pyramid seems the work not of men but of gods. As it was meant to.

The facts about the Great Pyramid are well known: It was built in about 2720 B.C. by the pharaoh Cheops. It contains over two million quarried limestone blocks whose average weight is two and a half tons. The scale of the structure is such that it poses a challenge to time itself. Here is a house that was meant to survive the ages, a dwelling for eternity. That is why, for just under five thousand years, human beings have come to this place to stand, as I did, awed into silence. That is why they will continue to come. The lure of the Great Pyramid is its being the most powerful symbol of the ancient human longing to live forever; it is the greatest, if not the first, of man's attempts to defy death.

The attempt was partly successful. Almost fifty centuries on, the pyramid still stands, ravaged, ruined, but there, contemptuously indifferent to the ants that crawl around its base. And the name of Cheops is known to this generation, as it has been to all the generations that have come and gone since his reign, and as it will be to all generations that call Earth home. But, in terms of the intention of its builder, the pyramid is a gigantic monument to failure, a poignant witness to the futility of human hopes. While the pyramid still stands, the frail body it was meant to protect has vanished without trace.

For an added sense of the paradox involved, one has only to go to the Cairo museum, to see the mummified remains of a pharaoh like Ramses II, which did survive. On one level, the mummy is a magnificent testimony to the skill of the ancient Egyptian burial priests and the art of embalming;

Ramses could look upon his mummy today and undoubtedly recognize himself. But the very success of this attempt at eternal life turns the dream of immortality into a caricature. As I said later, in the television series *Genesis,* "If the onlooker is moved to a sense of awed unease, it is because these shrunken remains speak not of the divinity of kings but of the mortality of men."

My journey to Giza was a milestone in my life and, from many points of view, the beginning of my own journey, a journey of which this book is a record. Nothing I experienced before (or since) brought home to me more powerfully the way human psychology is colored by two features unique to our species: a *fear of death,* the primal terror; and a *longing for immortality,* a yearning to live forever—the dream of life eternal.

This is what it means, at root level, to be human. A primary characteristic of the human mind is its yearning to outlive the perishable construction of flesh and bone and water that houses it. From this yearning for forever spring most of humanity's greatest achievements in art, music, literature, and science. Paradoxically, it is the very awareness that life is fleeting on the wings of time that directs human activity toward the creation of artifacts that possess the durability their creators lack—images in carved stone and marble, words written in books, beauty woven from sound, ideas captured on film. Most of civilization is a by-product of the quest for immortality.

If my experience at Giza was a major signpost on the road that led me to this book, so, too, were my experiences at Koonalda and Marble Bar. In some strange way, each deep-etched memory became a focus for ideas, images, and information centered on an issue that fascinated me more and more as time went by, the interlocking themes of mortality and immortality. In trying to understand the basis of the human longing to live forever, I had to map a backward path to the ancestral Dreaming of the human mind, which will always be symbolized for me by the descent into the haunted underworld of Koonalda cave. And in trying to pin down the basis of human mortality, I found I had to follow life itself back to its roots in the ancient seas that nurtured the Marble Bar stromatolites, to understand the mechanism of genetic memory, the encoded image that endures while its creations perish.

My initial concept of this book was a brief, science-based investigation into the biology of human mortality and the psychology of the human longing for immortality. But, inevitably, the scope of the project widened. I could not discuss death without discussing time, and I could not discuss time without discussing relativity and quantum mechanics. Moreover, I had to view things from an unusual perspective to examine not the physics of time and the biology of life, but the physics of life (Chapters 2 and 3) and the biology of time (Chapters 4 and 5). So what started out as a tightly focused essay on genetics and the fear of death grew into a preoccupation with the whole issue of mortality in its physical, biological, and religious aspects. And the task of writing this book, meant to take no longer than six months, has taken ten years.

This extended timescale is important, and it is necessary to comment on it. When I began the book, I was forty. Today I am fifty. Thus I wrote this book during what American author/developmental psychologist Gail Sheehy has called "the deadline decade" of the human life cycle. Those years correspond to the most profound changes I have undergone as a human being, at least in my own self-assessment. Inevitably, therefore, the way the chapters of this book unfold mirrors the way these changes came about. The person who wrote the end of this book is not the same person who wrote the beginning. When I reread the words of Chapter 1, I feel that they were written by a stranger—which, in an important sense, they were.

A "good scientist" faced with this apparent inconsistency might be tempted to rewrite the entire script. I have resisted this for a special reason. My life has brought me into contact with a lost generation in our society: people in their middle years who yearn for some sense of deep meaning to life, but who are prevented from growing toward it by the very tools they use to seek it out—their education and their intelligence. Not for nothing did Goethe, in *Faust*, depict Mephistopheles as the cynical intellectual.

To such people I can say truly, "This book is for you," for my experiences over the past two years in particular have taught me that the latter half of life necessarily consists of unlearning much of what has been learned in the youthful years. As I wrote this book, I began to change the way I saw truth, and consequently the things that projected a certain "image" when examined from my viewpoint in earlier chapters sometimes looked quite different when examined from the perspective I had developed by the later chapters. I have let these differences of emphasis stand because it is only by leaving this story in the sequence in which it happened that I can preserve an authentic record of the process that has led me from the mechanical models of science to that sense of sacred reverence that alone can restore wholeness to life. It is my ardent hope that I have been able to see this process through to its end without compromising the legitimate logic of science on the one hand, or lapsing into simplistic religious solutions or spiritualistic mumbo-jumbo on the other.

Before I begin, I would like to comment briefly on the techniques I have used. Most scientists acknowledge that any attempt to translate scientific concepts into nonscientific language involves some degree of simplification, but they demand a commitment to the same standards of "objective" scrutiny they themselves use when they publish material in technical journals. However, the ability of a human being to see things "objectively" has come under attack recently from science itself. Quantum physics has shown to the satisfaction of most physicists that the reality we observe is strangely altered by the act of observation. Consciousness seems not an observer but a participant in the workings of the world: mind and matter, subject and object, are no longer separate; somehow, subtly, they interact.

It is important to stress this because so many people, especially in the social sciences, demand of authors an unrelenting commitment to "objectivity," revealing a belief that truth is somehow separate from the mind that sees it. This is not a position that science can validate. I believe authors should have a fierce commitment to honesty, but I am skeptical of the principle of objectivity, which, in my experience, is often simply the currently popular viewpoint in disguise. People who insist on "objective statements" admit to an ignorance about what physics says and is.

I have not followed the standard procedure, which is to present all the competing theories in the various fields I cover. My treatment has been selective; any writer is selective because the attitudes and assumptions he starts off with influence the choices he makes. I have selected the theories that, after careful scrutiny and comparison with other alternatives, seem to me to fit the available facts best, to offer the most promising window into the future. Wherever possible, I have had the accuracy of my interpretations checked by experts in the various fields covered.

It is in the light of this personal approach that readers should interpret my use of the masculine gender, i.e., of the term "mankind," rather than non-gender-specific equivalents like "humanity." My experience in life has taught me that men and women, for whatever reason, usually approach matters from different perspectives, based on different attitudes and values. I am a man, and I have no doubt that my gender has colored my perception. I have let that "bias" show openly in this book by choosing the words and images that best convey the thoughts I am trying to express. It is also worth noting that I agree with American depth psychologist Richard Tarnas that "the crisis of modern man is an essentially masculine crisis."

John Fowles, author of *The French Lieutenant's Woman*, made the interesting comment that, after he had got halfway through the text, the characters started "telling him what to do." I can relate to that, because the story I have set out in the pages that follow is not the story I intended to write. The "plot" has developed a mind of its own, taking me into unexpected areas of experience and almost compelling me to consider issues I might never otherwise have thought important. In particular, my view of death has been stood on its head. I urge readers not to be put off by the fact that the first half of this book probes so deeply into that buried darkness we all dread, the thought of dying. Greatly to my surprise, I find I have written a story with a happy ending—and one that does not violate the scientific ethos in which my thoughts have lived their life.

This is a safari along the risky frontier where scientific knowledge and personal experience meet—an adventure. I invite you to share it with me.

The span of a man's life—that is nothing. But what a man makes of that span—that is something. A man must make his own meaning for life—meaning is not automatically given to life. Do you understand what I am saying?
—A FATHER'S ADVICE TO HIS SON, FROM *THE CHOSEN* BY CHAIM POTOK

1

ON FACT, FAITH, AND FEEDBACK

May the gods be with you,
in those secret places
you must walk alone.
—ANCIENT EGYPTIAN SAYING

When he was in his mid-sixties, my father developed lung cancer and, after a fairly long illness, symptoms of pneumonia. One afternoon my stepmother tucked him in blankets in his favorite chair and went into the kitchen to prepare some food. When she reentered the lounge, my father seemed to have fallen asleep. He was very peaceful, very still. He was not asleep. He was dead.

Death is unique. It is the one aspect of reality humans cannot look full in the face. Death is the ultimate paradox: It exposes a fundamental contradiction between the legacy of our genes and the legacy of our experience. That is why man is a flawed and divided creature.

Most people deny that the fear of death plays a negative role in their psychology. "I never think about death" is a common comment. But the underlying reality is different. One has only to watch the face of a man who has just been told he has AIDS to see how the mere suggestion of death shakes the pillars of life. Foreknowledge of imminent death invades the most personal part of us, threatening the sanctum of our very identity, the self, with extinction.

1

The pitiless reality of death is aptly captured in these unforgiving words by James Russell Lowell:

Console if you will, I can bear it,
'Tis a well-meant alms of breath
But not all the teaching since Adam
Has made Death other than Death.

Communion of spirit! Forgive me,
But I, who am earthly and weak,
Would give half of my income from dreamland
For the touch of her hand on my cheek.

Death presents us with a logical absurdity, which our day-to-day thought processes conveniently disregard. We say a well person is "alive," while a terminally ill person is "dying." Yet each and every one of us is dying. The process of dying begins with conception; all that differs from person to person is their relative distance from the same finality.

It is often said that the young are "subjectively immortal" in the sense that they never consider death as something that can happen to them. That is true from one point of view and false from another. Some time ago I was walking through my garden with my two children (then aged ten and twelve) when we came upon a blackbird that had evidently broken its neck by flying straight into a window. The reaction of my children to this image of death in another creature was immediate: Both showed signs of distress and walked quickly past, eyes focused elsewhere, demanding that I "get rid of" the evidence. I feel certain that the children did not consciously relate the bird's death to their own; but the sight of a dead creature upset them "instinctively"—it was an image they wished to avoid.

A doctor once said to me, "Most people die beautifully." That is often true: Nature is kind to those privileged to die in bed of old age. As life winds down, the brain reacts less powerfully to things that threaten it. But a more accurate biological indicator of our reaction to death can be seen where a relatively fit person is warned in advance. Then the reaction often takes one of two forms: terror or outrage. The same doctor who told me people usually died beautifully later told me of an exception. During the

Second World War, when Allied soldiers were preparing to cross the Rhine on their way into Germany, an American GI was brought into the field hospital mortally wounded yet fully conscious, and he remained conscious to the end. He was, in the doctor's words "very angry." The word "angry" was obviously an understatement; even in telling the story the doctor became agitated. I was reminded of the words of Dylan Thomas:

Do not go gentle into that good night, . . .
Rage, rage against the dying of the light.

We can ignore death only because we have sanitized its image and hidden its victims in hospitals and cemeteries. We have restricted our contacts with it to those few shocking occasions when it springs upon us unbidden. But the shadow is there, always. This is the terrible price nature exacts from us for the privilege of consciousness.

To find a "model" of our fear of death it is useful to look at other deeply rooted fears in the sense that they relate to biological survival. Three common phobias are vertigo, claustrophobia, and agoraphobia. I believe that all these are exaggerated forms of fears we have inherited from our vertebrate ancestors. The progenitors of the human species were tree-dwelling creatures that evidently moved down from the trees onto open savanna country during that critical period of evolution that shaped the characteristics of our kind. An almost instinctive fear of falling is a natural element of the psychology of a tree-living mammal. Fear of being "shut in" is natural for any creature threatened by predators, because it means the creature is trapped in a situation from which it may not be able to escape. That may be the distant origin of claustrophobia. Reciprocally, fear of being "out in the open" is also natural to a threatened animal because, in a totally exposed situation, it has nowhere to hide. This may be the distant origin of agoraphobia.

I can speak about agoraphobia from personal experience as I have suffered from it since I was eighteen. It has almost no effect on my everyday activities; it is effectively invisible to others, but it sets precisely defined limits, what physicists would call "boundary conditions," to my life. If I step beyond those boundaries, my distress is immediate and, in extreme cases, devastating. Like most phobia victims, I get through life with the help of mental security blankets. I overcome the fear of being alone in strange places by fixating on a belief that friends are always nearby. This fixed belief is an illusion most of the time, but my ability to act out a normal life is totally dependent on it.

A phobia like this provides us with an acceptable metaphor of our "death phobia." For all of us, fear of dying is ever present, but it is also normally unacknowledged, invisible, and "offstage." Significantly, our ability to live purposefully in the face of death has been critically dependent on a security blanket that, despite its varied forms and colors, has been universally present in most human cultures for most of history—*the illusion that life does not end with death.* Two of the founding fathers of modern psychoanalysis see this belief as a taproot of human psychology: Sigmund Freud calls faith in a future life "the oldest, strongest and most insistent wish of mankind," while Carl Jung says that the idea of "rebirth (i.e., another life beyond the grave) is found at all times and in all places." A key element in my argument is that the decay of this taproot belief, which has occurred in Western society over the past hundred years or so, has led inevitably (how could it not?) to manifold anxieties, to escapism, in short to what I call the *gap at the center.* I recognize that there have been other, powerful factors operating; my point is simply that the fear of death contributes, in my view, pervasively and insidiously to the modern angst.

I am not speaking as a sociologist or a psychologist, but as a biologist. My thesis is that the decay of religion threatens us much more profoundly than we have appreciated up to now. To see death as it really is, we must look at it from an evolutionary standpoint. That means we must examine the biological mechanisms that preserve life in the face of death.

A living creature is a complex chemical machine. Its survival is governed by the laws of chemistry and physics. In particular, key elements of the "life machine" are constructed around an engineering principle called a *negative feedback loop.* Its essential characteristic is that any disturbance that threatens to upset the system typically provokes precisely the response needed to restore the system to its original condition. A domestic thermostat is a familiar example. If the gauge is set to a reading of, say, 72 degrees Fahrenheit (22 degrees centigrade) a drop in air temperature below that level will automatically cause the gas flares to pump more heat

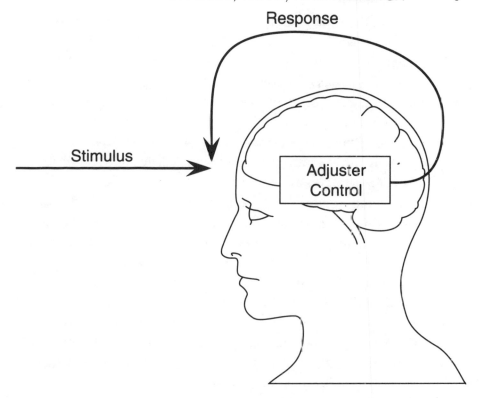

FIGURE 1.1

Life and feedback loops. In human beings, the governor that senses the incoming signal and adjusts the outgoing response is located in deep brain structures such as the hypothalamus, which determine the pattern of our behavior under the stress of environmental change. For example, the temperature of our deep body organs has to stay close to 99°F (37°C) if we are to survive. If the outside air gets too hot, we sweat, which cools us down. If the outside air gets too cold, we shiver, which warms us up.

into the distribution system until the status quo temperature is reached again. Then the system shuts off. In biological language, the drop in temperature corresponds to a *stimulus*, the resulting turning on of the gas flares to a corrective *response*.

Negative feedback loops are a "life motif"; they occur at the level of cells, the individual units of life, all the way up to the level of large animals. Our concern here is with "behavioral feedback loops" (see Figure 1.1). Consider, for example, the behavior of a grass-eating creature like a deer when it is threatened by a meat-eating creature like a cheetah. The appearance of a cheetah (the stimulus) results in a panic flight to safety (the response). This avoidance reaction is governed by a special substance called adrenaline, which triggers a kind of chemical override in the animal's body, catapulting it into an emergency status. When the danger has passed, the production of adrenaline drops, and the system returns to its original condition (see Figure 1.2).

In the case of this flight response, the nature of the danger is, in an important sense, irrelevant. Whatever the immediate stimulus, what the animal is really trying to escape from is a threat to its existence. Quite literally, it is running away from death. But man, alone among creatures, knows *he can never escape from death.* This foreknowledge is a denial of the basis of his biology, of the foundation of his genetic preprogramming for 3.5 billion years of evolution, which absolutely requires him to adapt to any threat to life in a corrective, self-preserving way. Religion was the only way out of this dilemma. By inventing gods and investing them with the power to preserve life indefinitely, man restored to himself the necessary ability to act purposefully in the face of death. For while he could not outrun death, he could perform goal-oriented actions—rituals— which, according to his traditions, would enable him to survive beyond the grave (see Figure 1.3).

People reared in the Judeo-Christian tradition take the link between death and the afterlife for granted, even though they may no longer believe it. It is important, therefore, to appreciate the psychological impact on individuals in this life of the Christian promise. Listen to what Paul says in 1 Corinthians:

> The trumpet shall sound and the dead will be raised, incorruptible, and we shall be changed. . . . When the corruptible frame takes on incorruptibility and the mortal immortality, then will the saying of Scripture be fulfilled: "Death is swallowed up in victory." "O grave, where is your victory? O death, where is your sting?"

Any mind truly accepting this statement as fact would exist in a relatively stable feedback loop, since the fear of death would be annulled in the long term by the accepted promise of ongoing life. The fact that few Westerners take the biblical promise literally anymore must not blind us

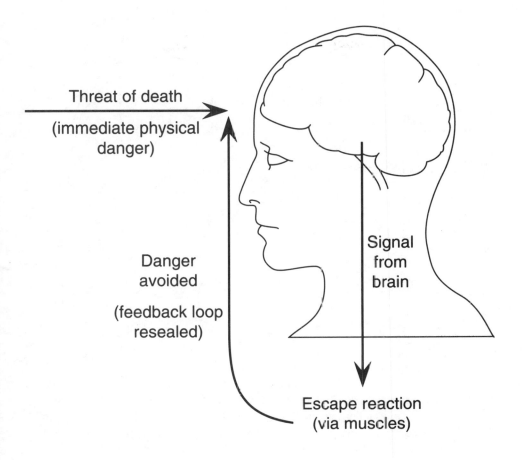

Threat of death

(immediate physical danger)

Danger avoided

(feedback loop resealed)

Signal from brain

Escape reaction (via muscles)

FIGURE 1.2

Feedback loops and the threat of death. Our reactions to things that threaten us are based on the negative feedback principle. For example, if we step off the curb in front of an oncoming vehicle, our eyes rapidly send an alarm signal to our brains; our brains respond by causing the muscles of our legs to contract in such a way as to cause us to jump backward. After such a "close shave" we will find that our hearts are thumping, our palms sweating, etc. This is due to the release of the "fight or flight" hormone adrenaline into our blood. Adrenaline puts our bodies onto emergency status, triggering a series of chemical changes that prepare our bodies for a crisis.

However, that crisis response can also be triggered by dangers that we foresee in fancy before we confront them in fact. Such "projected" threats typically arouse a feeling of diffuse, unfocused anxiety (or in extreme cases phobia) rather than a genuine panic sparked by and focused on some immediate, real danger.

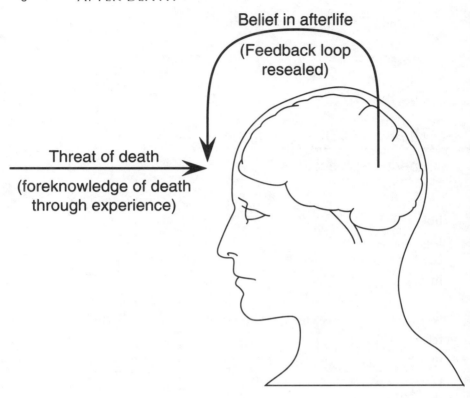

FIGURE 1.3

Belief in a hereafter can be an essential element in the psychological feedback loop. Our fear of death is a projective fear; i.e., we can foresee death long before it happens. Belief in an afterlife corresponded to a "compensatory response" in the framework of the feedback loop. However, modern man in the West has largely abandoned faith in life eternal. He has created a culture in which death has ceased to be a visible feature of the mental landscape; death has been sanitized, hidden in institutions, and fictionalized by TV. Whereas the traditional belief in a life beyond the grave was an effective response to the threat of death, generating a stable feedback loop that lasted for millennia, the contemporary denial of death is a short-term, blinkered strategy that, in effect, sidesteps the threat by pretending it doesn't exist.

to the fact that, for at least a millennium, society lived securely in this stable loop.

While the belief may have faded in the twentieth century, it tended to return in moments of crisis. When the *Titanic* was sinking, an English priest, Father Byles, walked among the crowd hearing confessions. It is recorded that many people sank to their knees and recited the familiar invocation to the Virgin Mary: "Holy Mary, mother of God, be with us now and at the hour of our death."

The point of all this is that, for any creature constructed on the basis of self-preserving feedback cycles, inactivity in the face of imminent death is an intolerable stress on the system. Religion supplies a "formula for action" that relieves this stress. While it may not preserve life, it fulfills the crucial role of maintaining the fiction that it is preserving life. Without this release valve, a future-oriented organism like man could succumb to a deep-seated psychosis that would destroy life by robbing it of purpose.

This explanation for the genesis of aspects of religion may be intriguing, but it is still superficial. Most modern biologists now accept that living things are, in an important sense, survival machines for the genes they contain. Thus really to understand the origins of the human longing for immortality, one has to dig down to the level of the genes themselves.

All living things are creations of their genes. Genes are a blueprint from which the characteristic form of any creature is assembled from raw materials in the environment. Genes are also a memory, ensuring that the image they encode is transmitted more or less faithfully from one generation to the next. From the point of view of this book, the important thing about genes is that they are "immortal." I had a vivid and unforgettable demonstration of this on the journey that took me to Koonalda and the Pilbara. After leaving that part of the Pilbara where the sea once was, we moved to the coast of Western Australia to a place called Carbla Point, situated in a huge tidal inlet called Shark Bay. There we visited a lonely beach whose shoreline is covered with what seems to be white sand but on closer examination turned out to be millions of tiny white shells. And just beyond the shoreline, in the tidal shallows, stand odd-looking "rocks." They look odd because they are odd. They are not rocks. They are living stromatolites, evidently very similar in structure, hence presumably in formation, to their ancient relatives in the Pilbara.

The Pilbara "fossils" are about three and a half billion years old; the cosmos itself is about fifteen billion years old. Thus the genes that survive at Carbla Point in the microscopic creatures that are architects of the Shark Bay stromatolites have preserved their encoded image of life for approximately a quarter of the age of the universe.

This "immortality" of genes is based on their ability to copy themselves.

The ability is *open-ended;* under the right circumstances, it can go on "forever." Because of the chemical patterns remembered in genes, the delicate veining on a butterfly's wing can endure down the ages while seemingly imperishable rocks are worn into dust.

The genes that have survived these enormous time spans are those that have won consistent victories in the battle for life. The legacy of this unrelenting struggle is that the "software" of competing genes is 100 percent oriented toward their own unfettered self-survival. Human genes, like all other successful genes, have inherited this same no-limits survival imperative. But human genes have a problem not faced by the genes of any other creature. The body they create contains a brain. And the brain in question has the unique ability to foresee its own end. *This brings the open-ended compulsion to survive forever (the legacy of the genes) into direct confrontation with the foreknowledge of death (the legacy of experience).*

This is the human paradox. A creature programmed to survive by its *genes* yet made aware that survival is impossible by its *brain* is an evolutionary contradiction. If it accepts death, its will to survive may be fatally weakened. If it does not accept death, it must turn a blind eye to an obvious feature of the real world. It is a no-win dilemma.

The answer has been the invention of a necessary fiction—the idea of an *after*life. In this way, the problem death poses to the psyche is solved by giving life beyond the grave the open-ended continuity denied to the individual in this life. In my view, this is why almost every human culture, from the depths of prehistory to the present time, has been wedded to the concept of life after death.

Like all generalizations, this statement needs to be put in perspective. There is good evidence that primitive man regarded postmortem existence with fear. Far from being a desirable haven, the next world was often seen as a shadowy substitute for this one in which the individual continued to exist as an insubstantial image of his living self. These departed "ghosts" were commonly believed to be hostile to the living; hence rituals were evolved to placate them.

How does one reconcile this dread of the afterlife with my hypothesis that belief in an afterlife was psychologically essential to normal living? The answer, I believe, lies in the widely accepted assumption that prehistoric man had an average life expectancy of only eighteen years. In this hunter-gatherer phase of human evolution, a lingering death due to old age was rare or nonexistent; death was typically a violent phenomenon, due to attacks by wild animals or accidents like falling from high places or drowning. In other words, death came suddenly from without, not slowly from within—men did not die, they were killed. Given this situation, it does not seem strange that archaic man could not even begin to grasp the fact that human life has an inbuilt and inevitable limit. To the primitive mind, death was the work not of nature, but of evil spirits, working their vengeance on the living, and their malevolent influence could be avoided only by reciting magical spells and wearing protective talismans. In his own inner world, archaic man, like a modern child, was subjectively immortal.

Prehistoric man never doubted the continuation of life after death. If this afterlife was regarded as threatening, it was because life was threatening, and life in the unknown was, almost by definition, fraught with peril. Evidence for this prehistoric belief in an afterlife comes from a variety of sources. One of the things that separates man from other animals is the fact that he usually buries his dead. Anthropologists often explain burial in positive terms, as a preparation for the next world. This is very probably true, but I think there is an additional and darker explanation. If a newly dead corpse is left where it lies, it will decay. Few natural phenomena arouse such abhorrence in human beings as decay, especially when it affects the familiar image of one's own kind. Burying the dead underground or hiding them in caves is, in my view, part of the avoidance psychosis that characterizes man's uneasy relationship with his own mortality.

This is speculation. What one can say with some confidence is that human burial is the oldest recorded human activity, apart from the making of tools. Aboriginal remains have been found in the dry moonscape of Lake Mungo in southeastern Australia, disposed in a way that suggests ritual burial. They are believed to be about thirty thousand years old. In the Shanidar caves in Iraq, the bones of Neandertal men have been found amid evidence (including the laying of a body on a bed of flowers) of funerary rites. They may be up to sixty thousand years old. Evidence for the burying of the dead goes far back into prehistory. This suggests that the urge to avoid images of death and corruption has been a powerful influence on the human mind from the beginning of its evolution.

Turning from prehistory to the present day, there is suggestive evidence that belief in an afterlife remains a potent subconscious influence, even among people who have abandoned religion as such. I find it significant that most human beings, in moments of extreme danger or fury, invoke images of either religion or sex—"Oh God!" "Jesus!" "Christ!" "Hell!" "Damn!" on the one hand, "Fuck!" "Bugger!" on the other. While we learn these images from our cultural inheritance, the fact that we produce them "instinctively" in moments of crisis hints at their close association with the survival imperative we inherit from biology. In the context of my argument, the linkage between religion and sex should not surprise us; religion invokes in us our (imaginary) passport to the future by way of the afterlife, while sex invokes in us our (real) passport to the future by way of our children. The common feature in both cases is the urgent recourse to our yearning for immortality; when a crisis threatens *life,* we automatically invoke incantations that deny the possibility of *death.*

If these ideas are broadly true, the concept of eternity is an inevitable reaction to the transience of life. From the foreknowledge of death comes one of the most evocative words in our language—*forever.*

How often we use that word: "I'm going to live forever!" It represents the other side of the human paradox. It is not enough that, for most of history, we have clung to the idea of eternity as a counterpoise to our own mortality. Even now, we live life as though it will never end. Our survival as purposeful, goal-oriented creatures is indissolubly pegged to our psychological feeling of foreverness. It is a cornerstone of our "dreaming"— the illusory rock on which we build our certainties.

While there may be many reasons for this, one stands out. Our brains build models of the world from experience. From childhood on, the most commonly repeated experience, the most repetitive "memory" is that night follows day in uniform sequence. Indeed, the day/night rhythm is chemically governed by a hormone (melatonin) produced by a small gland that sits on top of the "stem" of the brain. When the day/night cycle is disturbed, as, for example, when we cross time zones in an airplane, we feel a marked disorientation called jet lag.

We *never* experience a shutdown of this serial sequence, since when we die our brains are not able to record the stopping of the clock (by definition we cannot remember our own deaths). The self-reinforcing process that says there must be a tomorrow because there have been thousands of yesterdays programs the brain to think of tomorrow as an inevitability. Hence our brains come to regard the future as open-ended, going on forever. That is especially true when we are young.

People who reject formalized religion often see eternity as a comforting myth and the idea of an afterlife as the kind of reassuring fairy tale parents tell their children to make them less afraid of the dark. But all of us accept without thinking the notion that physical time—real time—goes on "forever." To think otherwise would be to challenge the basis of our thought processes.

The process of biological evolution is built around the requirement that physical time goes on forever. If that statement isn't self-evident, bring it back into familiar territory by applying it to human reproduction. Reproduction is nature's answer to the shortness and fragility of life. Our bodies may grow old, but the sperm from the male and the egg from the female have the ability to build a new body—that of a child. To put this in a personal perspective, when I have died, two sets of genes from my body will, I ardently hope, still be reproducing—those from the two sperm that went into the construction of my two children.

Our children, then, are time capsules, which carry our genes into the future. Consequently we are programmed by natural selection to care deeply about a future we will never live to see. Which brings us face-to-face with the crucial point: In the longest perspective, this attitude makes sense only on the assumption that the future is as open-ended as our yearning to continue into it.

Until quite recently, this axiom of biology was also an axiom of physics. Mathematicians made us familiar with numbers that went on "forever," like pi, the unending number obtained when the circumference of a circle is divided by its diameter. Models of the universe were built on the assumption that it was static; i.e., the cosmos was believed to be eternal. And, certainly, real time stretched ahead in an unbroken line into infinity. Popular songs might sing of a love that lasted "till the end of time," but no one seriously considered if, or indeed how, something like time could ever "end."

This reassuring view of things began to soften around the edges when

Einstein published his theory of relativity in 1905. From the beginning, the so-called new physics seemed to unsettle commonsense notions that had been part of the mental equipment of every human generation since our species evolved. This applied especially to our concept of time. Relativity shows that clocks run at different rates according to the speed at which they are moving relative to some point of observation.

That was only the beginning. Powerful attacks on common sense also came from experiment. In 1965, two scientists working at the Bell Laboratories in the United States detected faint traces of radiation in the sky; this "cosmic microwave background" lacked a defined source—it was coming from all directions at once, filling space uniformly with its enfeebled whisper. What was it? Or rather, what is it? The answer still arouses an awe that transcends science. The scientists were listening to the after echo of an event that occurred perhaps fifteen billion years ago—the beginning of the entire cosmos in the so-called big bang—genesis itself!

The discovery of the cosmic microwave radiation demonstrated that the cosmos had a beginning. And that enabled scientists to foretell its end. Measurements show that the cosmos is expanding, or rather that the space between the galaxies is "stretching," causing these huge star clusters to move apart like spots on an expanding balloon. If the sum of all the matter in the cosmos exceeds a certain critical mass, then eventually, in the remote future, the force of gravity will slow down the cosmic expansion, then reverse it. As the universe contracts and the density of the matter it contains rises, its temperature will escalate upward on a swiftly rising scale. Eventually the contracting cosmos will become so dense and so hot that gravity will overpower everything, and the universe will implode into the ultimate "black hole."

What happens if the amount of matter in the cosmos is not enough to stop the outward flight of the galaxies? On this scenario, the cosmos will ultimately wind down: The fires in the stars will die out and the temperature of space will drop until it reaches, or almost reaches, absolute zero, the baseline temperature at which all atomic motion ceases. In this terminal state, the cosmos will be absolutely dark and utterly cold—a titanic morgue littered with the corpses of the suns that once gave it light.

My concern here is not with the question of whether the universe will end in fire or in ice. My concern is with time. Either scenario confronts us with one of the strangest predictions of science—the idea that, one day, time as we know it will cease to exist. I will describe this anti-intuitive notion in a later chapter. What is important now is psychology, not science. We human beings are goal-oriented, forward-looking organisms. Our dependence on the idea of life eternal is a direct consequence of four billion years of evolution, since the hallmark of evolution is the open-ended copying of genes. Now, we of this generation see something no one else has ever seen: that the assumption of an open-ended future is denied by the laws that govern physical reality. In real time, there is no forever. There never was.

Up to now I have been using terms like "our fear of death" loosely. I am acutely aware that that will cause problems for the large number of people who can look into their own psychology and say, quite honestly, "I'm not afraid of death." This brings me to a complex issue, which I deal with in depth later in this book. But because the apparent widespread disregard of death challenges my argument head-on, it is important that I give some evidence to support my views in this opening chapter.

The first point to make is that the human fear of death is not a psychological constant—it changes enormously throughout the normal course of the human life cycle. Thus, while there are wide variations, it is often true that healthy young people are so preoccupied with living that the thought of death seldom settles deeply into their consciousness. By contrast, older people are unavoidably aware that aging increasingly affects their mental and physical functioning as the years go by; from about the age of fifty onward, our bodies send us, with increasing frequency, unmistakable signals of their mortality.

Our ability to shrug off the thought of death has another, different root. A person who is able to say "I'm not worried by the thought of death" has usually had little, if any, direct experience of the phenomenon he affects to disregard. By "direct experience" I do not mean the occasional sight of a dead body caused by a car accident, or even the sight of a dead relative in a mortuary chapel—I mean an extended and intimate association with a known person through the phases of dying, up to and beyond the actual moment of death itself. To a degree that our ancestors would have found quite amazing, death has, in our time, been taken "offstage," hidden in institutions and concealed behind closed doors. Most of us go through life and never see death. When we say we are not frightened of death, we are, to a significant degree, describing our reaction to an event we have not witnessed, passing judgment on something we do not know.

The contemporary ignorance of death shows up in clearer focus if we compare it with the sociology of death in times past. In preindustrial societies, people in the main tended to be born, grow up, marry, and die in the same locale. In this kind of small community environment, the death of the one was usually intimately felt by the many. The close bonding that occurred was especially pronounced in families. Only a century or so ago, it would have been unthinkable for children not to be present at their parents' deathbeds. In today's mobile and transitory society many (most?) young adults live in different suburbs or even different countries than their parents. The death of one generation is thus something that, increasingly, occurs in the absence of the next. Moreover, death is no longer a solemn rite of passage; increasingly it is an unpleasant interruption to "normality," something to be got out of the way as soon as possible so that everyone left can "get on with their lives."

The contrast between the modern attitude and past attitudes to death gets sharper as one goes farther back in history. Over four hundred years ago, death was a common spectacle at both ends of the human life cycle; people died when they were young as well as when they were old. While hard statistics are not available, few authorities would dispute that as many as one child in four might die at birth; also, many women died giving birth (records suggest that approximately 24 mothers per 1,000 births died in the late sixteenth century in London). Moreover, old age, as we know it, was uncommon; as late as 1841, in England and Wales, the average life expectancy was only forty years.

Going still farther back, in ancient civilizations ritual death was an accepted part of the social experience. In Jewish society during the rule of Rome, according to Thomas Godwyn's 1672 account, the death penalty could be invoked for eighteen different transgressions. The modes of execution included stoning (*lapidatio*), burning (*combustio*), beheading (*decollatio*), and strangling (*suffocatio*). They were public spectacles. In the Roman world, institutionalized slaughter was a normal part of popular entertainment. Even in England, public hanging was abolished only in 1868.

Superficially, the phenomenon of ritual death seems flatly to contradict my argument, as it demonstrates that, far from fearing the sight of death, humans have enjoyed it. This view is based on a misunderstanding of what I am saying. What the biological imperative requires is that the individual fear his or her own death; the death of someone else, someone who is not a blood relative, who does not share genes with the individual, may be a matter of indifference or, where sport or ritual is involved, of actual enjoyment. The excitement derived from watching men die is a quite different psychological phenomenon from the fear of personal death; it springs, I believe, from our genetically unforgotten animal legacy, which may predispose all human beings to a form of subliminal cruelty. This is, in the mythic language of the *Star Wars* trilogy, the dark side of the human psyche; it is still very much alive today, as a glance around the shelves of a video library demonstrates.

All this leads me to a simple but, I think, irrefutable conclusion: The generation born in the so-called Western world after the Second World War has had, on the average, less personal experience of death as a major factor in life than any prior generation in the history of the human race.

Paradoxically, the reality of death has also been diluted for modern man by the very machine that brings death and violence into his home every night—television. An average couple in the forty-five to fifty-nine age bracket spends over fourteen hours in front of the television each week. The point here is that television brings experiences, including death, into our lives secondhand. We can experience, vicariously and in total safety, dangers that would have caused an immediate personal response in past generations. Television fictionalizes death, weaving the act of dying into a world of fantasy in which the sight of a dead individual has about the same emotional impact as the sight of an advertisement for toothpaste. The result is that death becomes, in a crucial sense, unreal as an experiential factor in the psychology of the viewer. This view is supported by a study of suicide among American teenagers, which suggested that television and video may have created in the minds of the young victims a sense that death—even their own deaths—was somehow a make-believe thing they could disregard.

Thus, I think, I could easily defend the proposition that this generation is uniquely separated from its biological roots. If readers cannot relate to a fear of death, it is almost certainly because they have had much less direct "hands-on" experience of it than their forebears. But the "death paradox," as I have described it in this chapter, remains a central feature of human life. *Each one of us will die at some time;* that is virtually the only prediction we can all make with absolute certainty. I believe the fact that so many of us turn our backs on this unwelcome reality and lose ourselves in the myriad diversions our technological culture offers merely demonstrates the depth of our hidden psychosis, the buried fear that death provokes in us, its future victims.

In this introductory chapter I have tried to awaken in the reader some feeling for the pervasive power of our fear of death, for the subliminal way it influences our lives. It is now time to begin the journey this book describes, a journey into the reasons for and consequences of our mortality. We must look hard at three crucial issues: why we grow old and die; why we long to live forever; why we deny death. Because we are part of the universe, this human perspective is intimately tied up with the fate of the cosmos, so we must also examine another issue: why the universe itself is mortal, or, to put it another way, why science is able to see the idea of forever not as a feature of the real world but as a projection onto the world of man's oldest and most poignant longing.

These questions throw up other searching questions. What is it in us that longs to survive death? Is it our sense of identity, the part of us that says, "I am"? What is the consciousness whose extinction we dread? Does science, from its dispassionate perspective, deny the possibility that some part of our being may survive death?

These are not abstract or philosophical questions. They affect, in the most intimate way possible, our thinking and doing.

It is time to start the journey. To do so, I ask only that you look down at your wristwatch, the instrument that measures time, Time, the moving finger that counts out the tally of our days.

2

SOD'S LAW AND THE ARROW OF TIME

So sad, so strange, the days that are no more.
—LORD TENNYSON

In the Hindu epic the *Bhagavad Gita,* a mortal (Arjuna) confronts God (Krishna), not as a creator but as a destroyer. Shaken, he asks the dark god the question: "Tell me who you are?"

And receives the answer:

> I am come as time, the waster of the peoples ready for the hour that ripens to their ruin.

Death and time are indissolubly linked.

We do not know when man "first" became aware of the passing of time, but in an important sense that point of understanding marks the origin of our species. Animals are not aware of time. Man is. Man, moreover, has a strong sense of personal identity. He is not only aware of his surroundings; he is aware of himself. More particularly, *he is aware that he is aware.* From this ego comes the potential for morality. An animal lives in a state of innocence; it cannot be guilty of killing another creature because it has no sense of self to which a sense of blame can be shifted

TABLE 2.1
Average Number of Hours of Life

	Males	Females
At birth	639,480	692,040
At 25	420,480	473,040
At 35	332,880	385,440
At 45	245,280	297,840
At 55	157,680	210,240
At 65	70,080	122,640
At 75	0	35,040

back. By contrast, self-conscious man sees a relationship between his actions and their results: He has, or can develop, a sense of responsibility.

Awareness of time passing, a sense of self, a loss of innocence—these are related aspects of a "phase transition" that, thousands of years ago, changed us from beast to man. Echoes of this change persist in our myths. A deep-rooted myth tells us that our primal ancestors, Adam and Eve in the Judeo-Christian tradition, wandered through the ancestral jungle, the Garden of Eden, like animals, without shame at being naked, until their eyes were "opened" by some shift of focus.

What was that shift of focus? In the King James Bible, God says to Adam and Eve: "But of the tree of the knowledge of good and evil, thou shalt not eat of it: for in the day that thou eatest thereof thou shalt surely die."

Awareness of death means awareness of time. It is only when human beings structure their thoughts in time, extending back through memory and forward through prediction, that they can foresee their own mortality.

The myth of the Fall has many layers of meaning, and in a number of surprising ways it foreshadows insights that science has reached only recently. It is no accident that scientists like the astronomer Carl Sagan (in *The Dragons of Eden*) and the biochemist Ken Wilber (in *Up from Eden*) use the myth of the Fall as a metaphor to illuminate some of the deepest issues in evolution. I shall return to the parable of the Fall many times in the course of this book.

Time. Today we are immersed in a time-obsessed culture. The reality of life, as we commonly see it, is that we are allotted a number of hours of life at birth (on a probability basis). Each passing second reduces that number. The span of our lives is like a one-time investment that diminishes, continuously, inexorably, with the ticking of the clock (Table 2.1).

After this, your account is running out of credit, and you can expect the banker to close the ledger when it is empty.

This creates in us a terrible sense of time pressing in, hounding us with a feeling of "Be quick, before it's too late." As the Persian poet Omar Khayyám says:

One Moment in Annihilation's Waste,
One Moment, of the Well of Life to taste—
—The Stars are setting and the Caravan
Starts for the Dawn of Nothing—Oh make haste!

Everything, then, turns on time. But what is time? If we ask this simple question, we are focusing on what, to me, is the strangest issue in science.

Superficially, time is something we create when we measure it, dividing it into seconds, minutes, hours, days, etc. Which brings us up against the first illusion. Our experience of time is of something that moves, that sweeps us on its breast like a river forever moving at a constant rate from past to future. To put this in concrete terms, look at your calendar. Suppose today's date is sometime in the year 1995. If anyone asked you, "How long must you wait before you reach the year 2000?" you would automatically answer, "Five years." However, that answer is a simple statement of human limitation, not a statement of fact. One of the most anticommonsensical axioms of relativity theory is that time slows down as material bodies approach the cosmic speed limit, the speed of light. Thus voyagers on a space odyssey in a ship traveling close to the speed of light might clock the length of their journey as a mere six months, while back on earth a century might have passed. When the voyagers returned home, they would have aged but little, whereas all their loved ones would be dead. It follows from this that we could reach what corresponds to the year 2000 on earth in three years (or one year, or six months) if we built a spaceship capable of traveling at speeds sufficiently close to the velocity of light. This is the famous Einstein "time dilation" effect.

Such time warps do not mean that we can extend the span of our lives by moving closer to the speed of light. We carry around with us our own biological clocks, most noticeably the heart. This biological time setter keeps the same internal time no matter how fast we travel, so our personal ages, as we ourselves measure them, are not affected by speed.

We measure units of time by units of space. Since light travels at a finite speed, when we look outward in space, we look backward in time. If our sun were to vanish now, we would continue to see the solar orb for eight minutes, even though it wasn't there. That is simply because the sun is so far away it takes eight minutes for its rays to reach us.

This suggests that time is interlocked with space—which it is. Einstein showed that space and time are different aspects of one underlying reality—space-time. In the physics of Isaac Newton, gravity is an attractive force that operates between bodies across space. In the physics of Albert Einstein, gravity becomes "geometry," that is, "the force" becomes transformed into a deformation in the structure of space-time itself. This is often visualized by using the analogy of a trampoline top. If one rolls a billiard ball over the smooth surface of the trampoline, it travels in a straight line. According to Newton, that is because no force is acting on it. However, if we position a heavy weight in the middle of the trampoline, we depress the stretchable fabric to form a cavity. Now, when the billiard ball is rolled across the surface, it will be deflected from its straight line and will curve inward toward the heavy object. In Newton's world picture, this curving means a force is acting on the ball. In Einstein's view, the departure from linearity is because space-time itself is "warped" by the presence of the matter it contains. The greater the object's mass, the greater the space-time warp it generates.

The switch from the concept of an invisible force to the concept of a warping of space-time is not easy to follow. A deeper insight can be gained from Figure 2.1. It shows a two-dimensional universe, called Flatland (the two dimensions are length and breadth), represented by the flat sheet, intersected by a tubular semicircle that possesses another dimension

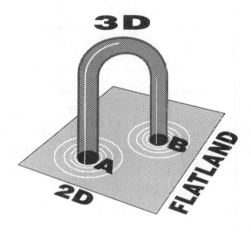

FIGURE 2.1

(width). Now try to put yourself in the mental position of an intelligent inhabitant of two-dimensional Flatland trying to "understand" the reality of the three-dimensional tube. He would see two *separate* circles, apparently quite unconnected. However, he would notice that whenever he disturbed A, he caused some corresponding disturbance in B; hence he would deduce that a force was acting to link A to B.

From our more privileged three-dimensional perspective, we can see that the Flatlander's "force" is the simple result of the fact that A and B are part of the same structure. The principle that emerges is fundamental to our understanding not just of gravity but of reality. Things that seem separate on one level of being emerge as united parts of a single reality when viewed from higher levels of being. Our feeling of the separateness of things is a direct function of the limitation of our vision. *The more limited our vision, the more we see as separate things that are really one.* This principle will be seen to hold true through the course of this book.

We divide time into three tenses: past, present, and future. The present is a human fiction. If you look at your watch and say, "It's ten past two *now*," what you are saying is that it *was* ten past two a fraction of a second ago.

The division between past and future, however, is no fiction. It is, in many ways, the crux of the matter—that quixotic shadow-line that separates what is fixed from what is uncertain. Two analogies may help us to understand the distinction between past and future. Imagine you are sitting in an airplane at the end of a runway at night. The engines rev up, and the plane moves forward. While you remain on the ground, you see the lights at the edge of the runway flashing past in linear sequence: 2,3,4, etc.—just as you experience time in successive intervals: 3:20, 3:30, 3:40, etc. But once the plane has gained altitude, you can look down and see all the lights "at the same time." The impression that the lights were flowing past in a fixed order was an illusion created by your particular position in relation to the thing you were observing.

The second analogy (see Figure 2.2) places you in a plane, this time looking down on a desert landscape of hills and plains. The landscape represents time, past and future. You observe a camel train moving across the landscape. The tracks in the sand show where the train has been. That is its past, fixed forever by the fact that it has happened. However, the driver has come to a fork in the road. Which way will he go? Which future will he opt for?

Here is the essential point. The driver will make up his mind, and the route he chooses will determine *his* future. In the landscape of time, the route he didn't choose remains just as much a part of reality as the route he did. Both routes are equally valid—we can't erase one track from the universe just because a solitary human being chooses not to follow it. In a literal sense, the future that stretches ahead of us is as real as the past that lies behind us. The future is indeterminate because it is by our choices, big and small, that we pick our idiomatic paths through the four-dimensional space-time landscape.

The camel driver example raises an issue central to this chapter and this book: the issue of *choice*—choice that leads to action. Choices between

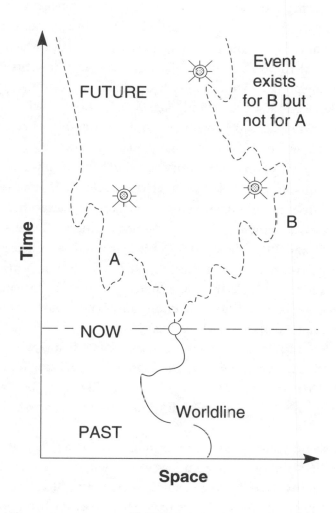

FIGURE 2.2

The distinction between past, present, and future (symbolic). The tracks in the sand show the camel's past history—the "worldline" it has followed through space-time. The dot represents the point where the driver has stopped, i.e., the present, where he ponders which route he will follow, A or B. If he chooses A, the worldline through B will not exist for him even though it is real. The converse is also true. We think of the future in terms of possibilities, i.e., of things that are not "real" until they have happened. But in the landscape of space-time, all future events are equally "real." It is our choices that determine the events we will encounter, i.e., those that will become "real" for us, and the events that we will never know. For simplicity of representation, only one space dimension is shown.

options are such an everyday feature of life that we never stop to think how strange they are. One of the most important branches of physics is called quantum theory, because it deals with the tiny packages of energy (quanta) that comprise the subatomic microworld. Light, which we normally think of as an electromagnetic wave, can also be visualized as a stream of tiny particles—quanta—called photons. Conversely, subatomic entities like electrons are commonly considered as tiny particles, but under certain experimental conditions they exhibit a wavelike character. This wave/particle duality is a cornerstone of quantum physics.

The bizarre side of quantum theory comes to light when we try to figure out what a quantum particle like an electron actually is. One thing it is not is a particle in the ordinary sense of a speck of matter that occupies both a defined amount *of* space and a defined position *in* space. Physicists in the 1920s and 1930s discovered that it is impossible to determine the position and the velocity of an electron at the same time. This is not a flaw in technique. The electron, in a fundamental sense, does not *have* a specific position and velocity. The uncertainty is an inbuilt feature of the real world, not a fault of our instruments.

A deeper understanding reveals the quixotic fact that a particle like an electron has only a certain mathematical *probability* of being found in any one spot. That probability has a ripple or wavelike form, but it is more like a "crime wave"—a statistical distribution—than a physical undulation.

The basis of matter, then, when examined intimately, dissolves into a ghostlike intangibility; the quantum wave is a mathematical wraith, a ripple of possibility. Here is where choice enters the picture. The quantum wave has this wraithlike character only when it is not being looked at. When an observer intrudes, when a scientist, for example, tries to measure the properties of an electron, the ghostly wave function collapses. The particle becomes *real*. It can now be specifically assigned a fixed location, with a probability of 1, i.e., a certainty.

This is a staggering conclusion. It means that consciousness is not an observer in the dynamics of the universe; it is an active participant. Consciousness, literally and factually, creates reality, by summoning forth material particles, definable certainties, from the elusive quantum wave. Objective "reality," in this perspective, falters on the brink of a profound ambiguity. Subject and object, mind and matter, are not separate; they interact and interlock. To discuss time truthfully, we have to discuss the mind.

The quantum world is so strange that any attempt to interpret it in terms of familiar models or examples is doomed to failure. The paradox of the quantum wave is often described in terms of a riddle, thought up by the physicist Erwin Schrödinger, whose mathematical formulation of the quantum wave remains, to this day, a cornerstone of physics.

Schrödinger invites us to imagine a closed box inside which are a cat, a poison capsule, a lump of radioactive material, and a Geiger counter. The radioactive material is what links us to the quantum realm. Radioactive decay occurs when an atom disintegrates, but, in a manner typical of the quantum world, that decay is utterly unpredictable. Over time, we can estimate the average probability of a given decay event, but the genesis of the event itself lies buried in the fuzzy uncertainty that is the core of the quantum.

The Geiger counter links the quantum world to the world of the human observer; it will record any radioactive disintegration when it occurs. The box is set up in such a way that any such disintegration will break open the poison capsule, releasing enough poison to kill the cat; in the time interval allowed for this "thought experiment" there is an exactly fifty-fifty chance that the atom will or will not decay.

This is the basis of Schrödinger's paradox. The observer outside the box cannot know whether an atom inside the box has decayed unless he looks (opening the capsule and killing the cat). The condition of the cat (alive or dead) is therefore a litmus test of reality itself. According to the strict interpretation of the quantum wave, in the absence of observation, the cat in the box is neither alive nor dead but in some indeterminate, wavelike in-between state. It is only when the consciousness of an observer enters the picture that the complex ripple of possibility that is the indeterminate "alive and dead at the same time" quantum cat crystallizes into one of the two possible real outcomes: Either the cat is alive (no atom has decayed), or the cat is dead (an atom has decayed).

In short, it is the observer's decision (his choice) to open the box that summons forth a real cat, dead or alive, from its ghostly quantum state of nonbeing.

Many physicists, shrinking from the implications of the cat paradox, have tried to rescue reality from this apparent trick state. One escape route has been tried successfully, but, to most physicists, the price paid to regain reality is higher than the cost of the original dilemma. In the 1950s, the physicist Hugh Everett "solved" the cat paradox by suggesting that both possibilities (a live cat and a dead cat) are equally real, but they exist in different universes. At the moment of choice, when the observer opens the box, the entire universe splits into two identical copies, alike in every detail except that in one the cat dies, and in the other it lives.

It is critical to recognize that this "many universes" concept applies to the world we live in, not just the paradoxical example of the cat. If it is true—and it is completely consistent with all the evidence—then, whenever we make a choice, whenever, like the camel driver, we decide between two options, the act of observation cuts the twine that binds the two alternative realities together, creating two separate universes, each having its own time and its own space, and each containing its own copy of the consciousness of the human observer.

The "many universes" theory has both advocates and critics among prominent physicists. While I cite the many-universes concept at relevant points in this book, that should not be taken to mean that I believe it to be "true" (I don't). I use the theory as an evocative metaphor, which offers an alternative symbolism to the conventional representation of the quantum wave.

The English physicist/author John Gribbin has summed up the role of human decisions in determining the future we experience in a nice phrase: "All things are possible, and by our actions we choose our own paths through the many worlds of the quantum." I ask readers to remember this point. The issue of choice, the paradoxical nodal moment when we stand poised between two alternatives, two realities, is something that we will come back to repeatedly in later chapters.

This detour into the strange world of the quantum wave has not been a detour at all. As we seemed to be getting farther away from time, the argument has in fact been bringing us back unswervingly to the camel driver at the fork in the road. We can now see that his "choice" of route was more than a mere left/right movement. It was, in the quantum view, a decision that created his future. In the many-universes perspective, his world split in two at that node: In one universe he went left, in another right. Two entire universes were the consequence of that single choice.

Thus, whatever interpretation we place on the quantum wave, everything that can happen has already happened in the landscape of time. All possibilities are already mapped out. However, we will "remember" only that one unique "worldline" we ourselves elect to follow because of the succession of choices we make, experiencing only a single selection from the almost infinite spectrum of potential futures through the distorting window of our senses and brains.

The feeling that time "flows" is arguably the most basic illusion of the human mind. It is not so much time that moves; it is our own sense of an individual self voyaging, by virtue of the choices it makes among the hills and valleys of a future that is already there.

French physicist Louis de Broglie summed up the relativistic view of time aptly when he said:

In space-time, everything which for each of us constitutes the past, the present and the future is given en bloc. . . . Each observer, as his time passes, discovers, so to speak, new slices of space-time which appear to him as successive aspects of the material world, though in reality the ensemble of events constituting space-time exist prior to his knowledge of them.

American physics author Fred Alan Wolf described the "many universes" view of time this way:

Gone by and yet to be are simply reference points based on our sense of now. They are simultaneous with us in the parallel worlds view of time.

I began this section of the chapter with a discussion of relativity, and I will end it in the same way. Particles of light (photons) travel at a constant speed, which we measure at 186,000 miles per second or 2.997929×10^{10} centimeters per second. At this limiting speed, time stops.

In the beginning, says the Bible in Genesis, "God said, Let there be light: and there was light." You are using light to read these words. Ordinary, everyday light. However, from the perspective of each photon that is reaching your eyes at this very second, all the time that has elapsed since the big bang does not exist. Likewise, for the photon, the end of the universe is already here. The photon is a timeless entity. It knows neither birth nor death, neither past nor future; it exists in an everlasting now; it just is.

This is not metaphysics. This aspect of light is an axiom of relativity. That fact alone should tell us humans that, from the perspective of a "higher reality," our curious perception of time as being fractured into past, present, and future, is strangely flawed, unreal, wrong!

If the future is, in some sense, "already there," can we foresee it? When that question is raised, the discussion usually turns to the topic of precognition and to a dissection of the cases where foreknowledge of the future has been claimed to be documented. Such debates usually generate more heat than light because most (all?) instances of precognition rely on anecdotal evidence that fails to meet the rigorous criteria science requires of genuine "proof." My view is that the debate is irrelevant, because it is easy to demonstrate that human consciousness "foresees" future time.

Consider the situation in Figure 1.2. A pedestrian steps off a curb in front of an oncoming truck. Both pedestrian and truck driver foresee the consequences of this action and take corrective action, the pedestrian by jumping backward, the truck driver by causing his vehicle to swerve sharply.

The commonplaceness of this situation hides the deep message of the physics it encodes. In the absence of consciousness, the "worldlines" of the two entities, the driver/truck and the pedestrian, would have intersected. Consciousness quite literally creates a reality that would never have existed but for this "presence of mind."

People may object that I'm splitting hairs. They will say, "Of course, one can foresee the future in the sense you describe; but the whole point of your example is that the 'accident' *does not* happen: I.e., the world it describes remains a mere possibility, not a reality." Such people should think their own criticism through. The reason it doesn't happen is that consciousness foresees a future event and, by avoiding it, creates an alternative reality.

This predicative ability is intimately bound up with the issue of choice. A choice represents a node of uncertainty when two alternative realities hang in the balance. It is the intervention of consciousness (via a "decision") that fleshes out one option into a "reality." *Consciousness operates in space-time by means of its ability to foresee the future.*

This ability is not restricted to man. An animal like a dog, put in the same position of danger, has the similar capacity to take the same predicative avoidance response. The ability to foresee the future is a universal correlate of consciousness.

The impact of this can be appreciated if the issue is put in an evolutionary perspective. Before life evolved, there was only one space-time "map" of the planet Earth. Such movements as occurred—the falling of stones, the upswelling of water—were determined only by physical laws of motion. When the first cells came into being, matter became, in the dimmest of dim ways, *aware* of its surroundings. Primitive cells could "sense" the presence of toxic chemicals, or sunlight, and adjust their behavior accordingly. Even these primitive avoidance reactions have the taproot feature of consciousness—by "foreseeing" the negative consequences of certain encounters, they created space-time "maps" that would never otherwise have existed. As awareness became more powerful, this taproot feature of consciousness spawned more and more alternative realities, based on its ability to read future time. With the advent of human consciousness and predicative cognition, alternative realities multiplied exponentially. We all live in worlds *we* have created, in so many ways.

Quantum waves. Time-independent photons. Space-time landscapes. These abstract concepts are remote from ordinary life, so let me keep the promise I made at the end of the Introduction, by marrying scientific concepts to personal experience.

Some years ago, I revisited the city in which I was born (Auckland, New Zealand) after an absence of half a lifetime. I went for the usual nostalgic reason: I wanted to make a journey into the past, to rediscover the sights and scenes of my childhood. It was a mistake, of course. Where once there were open paddocks and familiar homesteads, now there were densely packed anonymous houses. The boundary of Auckland had expanded until it had obliterated the country village of my early memories.

My sense of disappointment was enormous. The world of my boyhood had gone. I could no longer walk down the tar-sealed road into the small township, past the shops my uncle had built, over the concrete bridge and up the verdant hill that led to the small wooden church where long ago my mother and I had once taken refuge from a herd of cattle that numbered several large bulls. I realized keenly the force of the saying, "The old order passeth." One can never recapture the past, and its traces remain only in the coded crystals of memory, frozen snapshots of things that have gone forever.

But have they? Here is the unfamiliar reality. In the perspective of physics, the past does not cease to exist simply because our awareness moves beyond it. Somewhere in time's landscape the village of my boyhood still survives as a physical structure. The old road still winds up to the old church, and giant macracapas still cast their shade on sun-browned paddocks edged with blackberry bushes. My grandmother is still sitting at her window seat, waiting to welcome a boy with awkward bangs and ingenuous eyes, who today I would have difficulty in recognizing as myself.

What is true of my boyhood several decades ago is true of any point in the past. Somewhere in the corridors of time, the young Hannibal is still setting out on his epic journey across the Alps to challenge the might of republican Rome; somewhere else the dinosaurs still rule the world.

Science dislikes what it calls "privileged frames of reference." The present matters to us only because we happen to inhabit it. In the wider scheme of things, today is no more real than any of our yesterdays.

I have often wondered about this from a moral point of view. We all do things we're ashamed of. One of the most reassuring things about the passage of time is that it bleeds these memories of their sharpness, dampening our sense of guilt. It is unsettling to contemplate the truth—that each and every act we regret, everything that has lowered our self-esteem, is indelibly frozen into the space-time fabric of the cosmos.

The issue of morality again raises the question of choice. The me I am now, and all the me's I have been, result, to a significant degree, from the choices I made along the time track of my life. I am a self-created reality, in every sense. Whether those choices made me into a still-existing worldline in a space-time landscape, or whether my choices created a near infinity of other "me's" that hover near me now, in multiple, still-existing, side-by-side universes, I do not, cannot, know.

Time then is far stranger than we think. Stranger perhaps than we ever thought we thought. The thing to remember, for it forms the base on which the rest of this book will rely, is that the moving finger of time is essentially a figment of our imaginations. The laws of physics have no inbuilt time asymmetry. They work just as well in the future-to-past sense as the past-to-future sense.

We see this clearly when we look at the quantum wave. The wave is a ripple of possibility, not a real thing. It has neither past nor future; it can be described as traveling forward in time and backward in time with equal validity.

That is true not just of the quantum wave. Subatomic particles exhibit the same disregard for time. In the last half century, physics has unearthed a garden of so-called fundamental particles—mesons, positrons, neutrinos, etc. For each of those particles of ordinary matter, there exists an antiparticle of equal mass but opposite "charge" (antimatter).

Figure 2.3(a) shows a particle of ordinary matter colliding with a photon. The particle absorbs the photon, and that raises it to an "excited" state. The photon is later reemitted. The details of the interaction are not important for our purposes. All we need notice is that the particle is moving forward in time.

But is it? The only reason we say this is that all our experience tells us that time only flows "forward" from past to future. Mathematically, however, the interactions in Figure 2.3(a) can be just as well described by saying an antiparticle is moving backward in time, from the future to the past. This preserves the symmetry of the interaction and is a perfectly valid description of the physical process it describes. Figure 2.3(b) shows the corresponding mirror situation where particles are replaced by antiparticles.

According to modern physics, both the quantum wave and the physical particles that constitute matter are symmetric with respect to the direction of time. The space-time landscape, at least as far as quanta are concerned, can be crossed in either direction with equal ease.

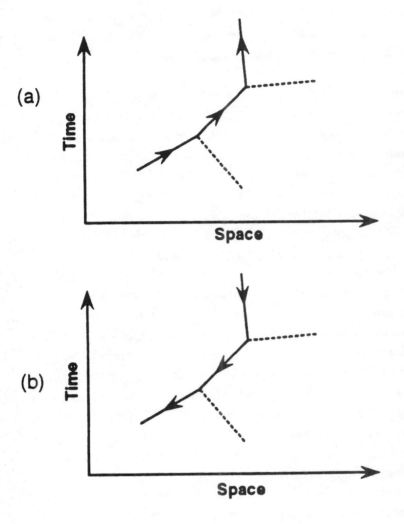

FIGURE 2.3

Particles moving backward in time: Arrowheads in the above diagrams are drawn according to the rule that they signify a particle when the arrowhead points in the same direction as the process under consideration and an antiparticle when it points in the opposite direction. A photon has a unique status: Being its own antiparticle, it needs no arrowhead; i.e., it can simply be represented as a line. In a time-forward process, i.e., from bottom to top of the diagram, (a) depicts a particle/photon interaction while (b) shows an antiparticle/photon interaction. Mathematically, however, it is also permissible to view these processes in a time-reversed sense where, by reading the diagrams from top to bottom, (a) depicts an antiparticle/photon interaction and (b) a particle/photon interaction, with both proceeding backward in time. (From Fritjof Capra, The Tao of Physics.*)*

It is a hallmark of the human condition that we do not see this time-symmetric behavior. We feel a strong sense of time passing. And to our sorrow, we grow old and die.

Why does that happen? Since mind and matter interact, through the quantum wave, we cannot resolve the problem without looking at the question of our sense of self, our consciousness. Only then can we validly attempt an authentic answer to this oldest of human queries. At this stage, we can simply give the conventional explanation that lies in the scale at which the observations take place. At the submicroscopic end of the scale (the realm of particles), interactions are usually time-symmetric. At the macroscopic end (the realm of people), they are not. Why? Because nature deals in statistics. If one chooses to focus on a tiny number of particles to the exclusion of the rest of the universe, one may see time-symmetric behavior. However, on our human scale of observation, we never see small numbers of particles—we see trillions, and large populations of particles exhibit a pattern of collective behavior that does not apply to their individual units.

That sounds esoteric, but it's not. If you want a clear-cut illustration of why we experience a one-way flow of time, go to the cupboard and take out a clean glass. Fill it with water. Then add a drop of ink. Now photograph the glass, just as the drop of ink is beginning to uncurl. Call this A. Next, leave the glass for an hour. When you come back, the ink will have diffused uniformly through the glass. Photograph that and call it B. You now have two photos of the same glass in different states. Give them to a friend and ask him or her to tell you which one came first, A or B?

There is only one answer. If the time sequence of the two photos was B before A, it would mean that all the molecules of ink that were distributed throughout the water in B had somehow gathered together to form one drop in A. That is not impossible but it's highly unlikely, for it would require a population of randomly moving molecules suddenly to experience a joint movement toward a common center in the absence of any force. Therefore, we can be confident that B came after A.

This answer seems surprisingly simple for a question that addresses the root causes of time. However, simple things are often deep things, taking us farther into the heart of an issue than surface subtleties. So it is here. In frame A, all the dye molecules were packed together. In frame B, they

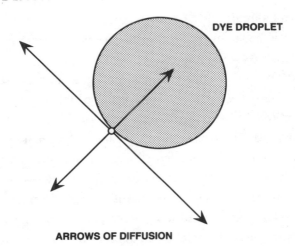

DYE DROPLET

ARROWS OF DIFFUSION

FIGURE 2.4

Time's arrow: why time flows in one direction. Consider a single particle of dye at the edge of a droplet of dye in a glass of water. All particles in the glass (water and dye) are in a state of constant, jiggling motion called Brownian motion. That movement is random; there is no preferred direction. Because it is positioned at the edge of a tiny drop of dye in a large volume of water, most random movements of this particle will take it out into the surrounding water, not back into the droplet. There is thus a gradient of probability from the center of the droplet to the surrounding water, which ensures that the dye molecules initially concentrated in the droplet will gradually spread out until they are evenly distributed through the container. This gradient of probability defines the arrow of time.

were evenly spread. But in both frames they were moving at random. A randomly moving dye molecule in a concentrated state is much more likely to move out into the surrounding water than it is to move back into the dye droplet. In Figure 2.4, I have schematized this by showing four arrows along which any dye molecule at the edge of the droplet can move; only one takes it back into the droplet, the other three all take it out into the water. Thus, by pure probability, most dye molecules will diffuse away from their original center. When they are uniformly spread, the number of dye molecules moving in any one direction is balanced by the number moving in the opposite direction. At that point the spreading process stops; the system has reached a state of equilibrium.

This seemingly pedestrian observation is intimately related to the question of why we grow old over time. In its original state, packed together in a single drop, the water/dye system was in a highly ordered condition—water clearly separated from dye. In the equilibrium state, the water/dye system was maximally disordered—all mixed up so that no (large scale) element of the glass was significantly different from any other. Physicists have a special name for the degree of disorder of any system: They call it *entropy*. What the water/dye example shows is that *entropy always increases with time*. Entropy, then, points the direction of time. To use Sir Arthur Eddington's famous phrase, entropy is "time's arrow."

Many people, in my experience, fail to grasp why entropy points the arrow of time in one direction only. "Why," they will say, "can't you reconcentrate the dye molecules, re-creating frame A from frame B? According to the argument, this would mean that time is running backward."

The point is, of course, that any reconcentration process requires an input of energy from outside the system, which increases entropy somewhere else. A good illustration is provided by a smooth sandy beach at low tide (frame A). If I walk over the beach, I leave a line of footprints (frame B). Superficially, it seems that I could re-create frame A by filling in all my tracks and remaking a smooth sandy surface again; i.e., I could go backward in time by reconstructing the physical setting of the "earlier" image. However, to do that, I would have to dig up sand from another part of the beach, and that would simply create more holes somewhere else. If one looks at the whole picture rather than concentrating on some selected part of it, one can see that, overall, entropy always increases—invariably and without exception.

Entropy is a subtle, slippery concept, because it depends on probability. Consider the example of a jigsaw puzzle. There is only one way all the pieces can be correctly fitted together, whereas there are thousands of jumbled states. Clearly, then, if one starts off with the one correct alignment, any change is likely to "randomize" the pattern. Conversely, if one starts off with all the pieces jumbled together, the statistical chances of getting them to reassemble into the unique, correct pattern with one "throw," while not impossible, are exceedingly remote.

Drops of dye in water, jigsaw puzzles, are helpful guides in our search to come to grips with entropy, but they fail us in one important respect. Both are one-time examples; they do not address the deeper question of how entropy affects repetitive processes, processes in which an image is re-created, again and again, over time, processes that copy.

The question of copying is central to the themes of death and immortality that run through this book. To untangle this issue, pick out three examples of personal possessions that are precious to you and think how you might try to preserve them by making copies of them. First, find a photo of yourself on some remembered occasion in the past—your only tangible memory of a special moment. Take it to an office that has a commercial photocopier. Make a copy of your original print. The chances are that it will retain almost all its clarity and definition. Your face will look back at you, clear, sharp, and identifiable. Now make a copy of the first copy you made. Again, the image on the sheet will be familiar. Now use the third-generation print to make a fourth generation copy, and so on. As the copying process proceeds, the image will become smudgy; the features will blur and fade. Eventually, all trace of your identity will vanish, leaving only a random graininess.

Next, take a page containing your favorite poem or quote and give it to a typist to copy. The typist must copy exactly what is on the page without in any way editing the text. The first copy is likely to be perfect. However, as with the photocopy example, as each copied page is reinserted into the typewriter to be copied again, mistakes are bound to creep into the script. Words may be misspelled, letters jumbled, lines wrongly spaced. Because the typist will blindly copy only what is on the most recently typed page, the mistakes will be reproduced along with the sense elements of the message. While there is a faint chance that a second-generation mistake may fortuitously correct a first-generation mistake, the overwhelming probability is that errors will progressively accumulate as the process of blind copying goes on. Eventually, the original message will have vanished utterly, leaving only jumbled nonsense.

The same thing will happen if you attempt to copy your favorite piece of music—say, Vaughan Williams's *Fantasia on a Theme by Thomas Tallis*—by a process of repeated copying in a tape transfer machine in which each later copy is made from its immediate progenitor. The first copy will preserve the music in almost the full majesty of its power, but as the process of copying proceeds, the level of background static will increase. Eventually, all trace of rhythm will be blurred out of existence, and all that will be left will be noise.

These three examples show that unedited copying invariably reduces recognizable patterns—be they patterns in space (visual images or words) or in time (sound waves)—to random anonymity. While the original patterns (face, poem, symphony) seem different, they are all expressions of a common, underlying concept—information.

Obviously, information is encoded in the sequence of letters that embodied your favorite poem. This is what we commonly mean by information—messages we can read. The Vaughan Williams theme is also information, encoded not in a specific sequence of alphabetic letters, but in a specific sequence of musical notes. The music arises from the mechanism that expands the encrypted two-dimensional information into three-dimensional sound waves. That is why we can speak of "reading" music.

What unedited copying does in all cases is destroy information. What is left at the end is noise. Most of us simply associate noise with sound, but in physics noise has a universal meaning: It is defined as the total absence of information, irrespective of context. If you tune your radio to a frequency outside the bands occupied by radio stations, the crackling static you hear is entropy expressed in the familiar context of acoustic noise. The aimless "snow" of randomly moving spots you see on your television screen when you turn on the power but not the channel is also noise. Noise is the emblem of anarchy, the very fingerprint of entropy.

The entropy concept is a cornerstone of one of the most fundamental theorems of physics—the second law of thermodynamics. The second law encodes a fatalistic and implacable feature of the real world that dooms all physical processes, in the absence of energy from without, to move toward a state of increasing entropy. Where classical physicists used to describe the second law as the tendency for order to decay into disorder, modern scientists often prefer to define it as the tendency for information to decay into noise.

In its rigorous physical formulation, the second law applies most readily to processes at the micro level of atoms and molecules. However, analogous processes occur everywhere on our own scale of observation. Un-tended gardens run wild, pyramids decay, used cars rust and develop faults, human bodies grow old, minds become infirm, memories fail. Across the spectrum of human experience we notice that complex structures, if left to themselves, lose their orderly condition and decay into more disordered states. We see the imprint of entropy everywhere. The second law of thermodynamics builds into physical reality an inevitable and unavoidable tendency to decay, which, in the final analysis, seems to doom all complex patterns of organization to eventual disintegration. It is small wonder that scientists call the entropy concept "nature's law of sheer pessimism." Or, more simply, 'Sod's Law'.

Religion predated science by millennia in seeing entropy as the destroyer. As we have seen, the Hindu god Krishna called time "the waster of the peoples," and we now know that time is a manifestation of entropy. Even more evocative is Krishna's saying, "Now am I become Death, destroyer of worlds," for death in its turn is a product of time.

Entropy paints a doom-and-gloom picture of reality. It is the negative in the cosmic equation, the dark side of God.

The pessimistic nature of entropy has given rise to a curious ambivalence among scientists about the second law. On the one hand, their rational intelligence compels them to accept it as a valid description of real processes; indeed the second law is one of the few pillars of classical physics that has not been reworked by relativity and quantum mechanics. On the other hand, their forward-looking human nature compels them to look for an escape route—an avenue of hope.

At first sight one is easy to find. There is a phenomenon staring us in the face that seems intuitively to contradict the whole thrust of the second law: life itself. One need only think of the growth processes of life to see why it seems to violate the principle of entropy. A seed grows into a plant, its leaves symmetrically disposed around its stem, the petals of its flowers symmetrically aligned around its stamens. A caterpillar, which is little more than a tubelike eating machine, becomes encased in a cocoon or chrysalis, from which, in time, there will emerge a full-fledged butterfly, whose wings of iridescent blue or orange are among the many marvels in nature's showcase.

There is, of course, what many people regard as the supreme example of the denial of entropy: the development of a human baby from a microscopic speck of matter. Through the eyes of modern technology, we can watch the fertilized egg become a ball of cells, which then undergoes the subtle chemical patterning that summons forth limbs and eyes and brain, the whole tremendous explosion of growth taking place in such a way that the differentiating parts blossom into the integrated whole. It seems like a miracle as a new human life, unique and perfect, unfurls like a delicate sea flower in the waters of the amniotic bubble.

All these processes seem the opposite of decay; they are processes of unfolding, of creation, that seem to defy the downhill tendency built into the second law of thermodynamics. Indeed, life seems to reverse the direction of the second law, creating the very complexity entropy is targeted to destroy.

But does it? Unfortunately, those who point to growth processes as a violation of entropy overlook (unforgivably in the case of scientists who should know better and often do) the "hidden factor" that explains the apparent contradiction. Consider the case of a human embryo, growing in the womb. The plain fact is that the baby does not grow in isolation. It is plugged into a life-support system (the amniotic sac) that provides it with a continuous supply of food and oxygen from the mother's blood via the placenta. The significance of this is that each molecule of food represents a tiny bit of order (food chemicals are themselves manufactured by other living creatures). During pregnancy, billions of food molecules are "burned" to power the myriad growth processes that collectively make up the baby's development. If one adds up the entropy balance sheet, setting forth the degradation of order due to the burning of food particles on the debit side, and the increase in order due to the processes of development on the credit side, one finds that the overall account is in debit. The increase in disorder due to the burning of food over nine months of pregnancy massively outweighs the increase in order due to embryonic growth.

Life, then, cannot escape the second law of thermodynamics. Rather, its whole machinery has been built around the consequences of entropy. The very processes of thought you are using to read these lines involve entropy. The electrical charges in nerve cells arise because charged particles, called ions, are unevenly distributed on either side of the nerve cell's membrane, just as the dye molecules were cleanly separated from water in their initial state. Why don't they diffuse across the membrane until this concentration difference evens itself out? The answer is, they do, transiently, as the nervous impulse travels down the nerve cell's "wire." However, the living system uses energy to pump them back against the concentration gradient, to re-create the charge differential that allows nerves to fire.

Living systems have to use energy, constantly and unremittingly, to "push chemicals uphill," to prevent the concentration inequalities on which life depends from reaching the state of equilibrium toward which they constantly and unremittingly tend.

From many points of view, life can be defined as a dynamic organic system that is held far from equilibrium by a regular intake of energy from the environment. Reciprocally, death can be defined as the *attainment of equilibrium.* In the case of your brain, when the charge differentials on either side of your nerve cell membranes are allowed to even out, you are irreversibly "brain dead."

Life is a classic example of what physicists call an open system, a system prevented from succumbing to entropy by a regular input of energy from outside. The baby in its mother's womb is an open system because it receives a constant supply of food from its mother's blood. The mother's body is an open system because she regularly takes in food from her environment. All animals are open systems because they sustain their own life processes by eating other creatures (an animal is defined as "an organism that feeds off other organisms").

What keeps this whole ensemble going? If you trace back any food chain far enough, you always find an animal that feeds off a plant. Plants tap directly into the greatest source of power in the solar system, the sun. As a gigantic nuclear fusion reactor it delivers about 1,300,000 trillion calories of energy to the earth each year. Included in this stream of energy is the narrow band of electromagnetic radiation we call light.

By trapping sunlight and converting it into carbohydrate (sugar), plants maintain the organized structure of almost the entire biosphere in the face of the second law of thermodynamics (the only known life systems that do not [ultimately] depend on sunlight are the exotic creatures that get their energy from volcanic vents in the lightless deeps of some ocean beds, and a few unusual groups of microbes). Life on earth is a child of the sun.

What is true of life is just as true of evolution. Many people point to the "upward sweep" of evolution, from microbe to man, as irrefutable proof that there is a law of upward cosmic growth (evolution) just as there is a law of downward cosmic decay (entropy). It is true that the two "themes" stand in marked and symmetrical opposition to each other. But the total process remains fixed in the downhill mode that entropy requires. The process of biological evolution has, across four billion years, trapped only a tiny fraction of the radiant energy the sun pours forth each decade. Evolution is a solar-powered "complexity generator," which creates increasing levels of order, but only and always at the cost of energy wastage on a truly astronomical scale.

We are now in a position to approach what is, from the point of view of this book, the most fundamental question about the nature of life: Given the fatalistic "downhill" character of Sod's Law, is life by its very nature doomed to be a fleeting thing, the ephemeral creature of an hour? Are the sorrowing words of the Christian burial service an apt description of an unchangeable reality? "Man that is born of woman hath but a little time to live. He springeth up and is cut down like a flower."

To answer this question, we must remember that all living creatures, including ourselves, obey the second law of thermodynamics in the sense that they dissipate more order than they generate. However, so long as the sun continues to shine, any living thing can maintain its complex, far-from-equilibrium structure, using energy from without to balance the inevitable breakdown of its component parts by a corresponding synthesis of their replacements.

Figure 2.5 shows a hypothetical "life loop," a schematic representation of a basic principle of living things—that life preserves the status quo by continually re-creating the molecules that inadvertent wear and tear and deliberate scavenging destroy. Proteins, for example, are constantly being degraded into their component building blocks, the amino acids, but all cells contain an intricate molecular manufacturing machinery that incessantly strings amino acids together to rebuild proteins. A typical human being, for example, contains some 6,000 quadrillion molecules of the protein hemoglobin in his blood. Every second, 400 trillion of these molecules are destroyed, but their concentration in the blood is unaffected because

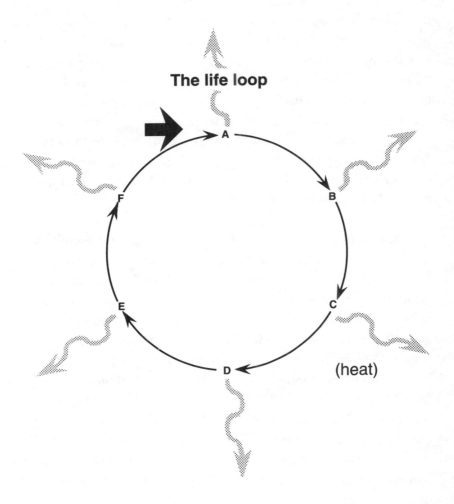

The life loop

FIGURE 2.5

How energy keeps the life loop going: a highly schematized version of a basic principle of life. Living things maintain their structure by re-creating key chemicals as they decay or are selectively broken down. There are many such breakdown/buildup cycles in the cell. The sequence A to F in this "life loop" represents a hypothetical composite of these interlocking turnover cycles. All these cycles are powered by an input of energy, solar energy in the case of plants, preformed organic chemicals (foodstuffs) in the case of animals. Each cycle loses some of this energy as heat every time a given compound is resynthesized. If this energy input is cut off, the life loop must inevitably decay. If the energy input continues, the loop can last indefinitely. It is theoretically immortal.

they are replaced as fast as they are removed. What is true of proteins is true of all other basic ingredients of the life machine. Figure 2.5 tells us that these various interlocking mechanisms maintain this cyclic turnover by sucking in energy from the environment and using it to rebuild crucial functional elements as they develop faults and are removed by the "house cleaning" mechanisms of the cell. Each subsystem obeys the second law, because the conversion of energy to structure is never 100 percent efficient; some energy is invariably lost as heat, so the total entropy of the system increases. However, the generalized life loop (which is simply the idealized composite of its component cycles) is stable.

Given that it is stable, how long can it last? A number of biologists have developed mathematical models to test the durability of loops like this in the framework of the second law. Early studies supported the pessimistic view, suggesting that the loop must always eventually decay and break down. Biochemist Leslie Orgel and others pointed out that errors in key molecules (those whose effects feed back into the integrity of the loop itself) would inevitably set up a kind of chain reaction, the original error producing a set of second-generation errors, many of which would in turn set up third-generation errors, like multiple ripples spreading out from a single disturbance in a pond. The unavoidable end result of such a runaway process would be a total collapse of the system, dubbed an "error catastrophe."

Recently, however, several mathematical theorists have shown that this conclusion is incorrect. To illustrate some of the essential elements of the new thinking, I have selected a model developed by English theoretical biologist Tom Kirkwood (in conjunction with geneticist Robin Holliday). The question Kirkwood addresses is how the average accuracy of any one generation of chemical products (proteins) in the cell is related to that of its predecessor. If the accuracy of the second generation is less than that of its forerunner, the system will deteriorate. If the accuracy of the second generation is greater than its forerunner, the system will improve. If both values are the same, the accuracy will remain constant.

By making a number of plausible assumptions and incorporating them into a mathematical model, Kirkwood arrived at the situation shown in Figure 2.6. It plots the average accuracy of the system in a given generation against the average accuracy of its predecessor. The bottom-left corner of

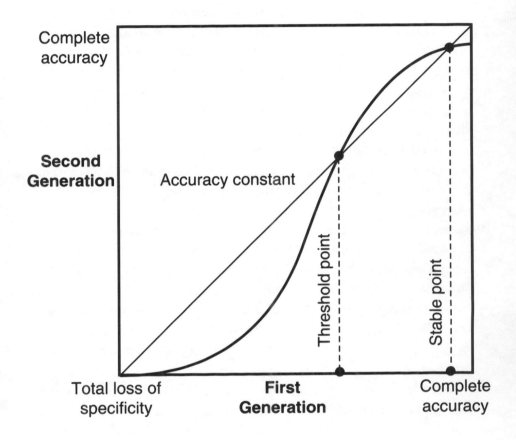

FIGURE 2.6

Can a living system last forever if its parts decay because of the accumulation of errors? This diagram shows how errors are transmitted from one generation to the next. The horizontal and vertical axes of the graph map out a path from total inaccuracy to total accuracy. The model discussed in the text derives an S-shaped curve to describe the behavior of a living system in all conditions between these extremes. Below a certain critical threshold the system always decays into randomness. At the point of stability the system will always revert to a sufficiently accurate condition to maintain itself ad infinitum even if it is disturbed. A stable system is potentially immortal. The elements that may contribute toward enhanced accuracy include improved "proofreading" mechanisms (see Chapter 3) and better "housekeeping" systems to clean up damaged cell parts. (From T.B.L. Kirkwood and R. Holliday, Accuracy in Molecular Processes.*)*

the graph defines the point of total randomness, i.e., a total breakdown in which no meaningful instructions are passed from one generation to the next. From this point-of-error catastrophe, we move to a point of complete accuracy, in which no mistakes at all are made. The diagonal line joining the bottom-left and top-right corners of the graph is the "accuracy constant," i.e., the point where the average accuracy of one generation equals that of its forerunner. You can prove this simply by measuring a horizontal line, at any point, from the vertical length needed to reach the horizontal graph line at right angles to your first line; the two lines will always correspond exactly; i.e., you will always draw a perfectly square box.

The model is based on a mathematical representation of two real variables in the cell's processing machinery. The mathematical symbolism need not concern us. What matters is the result (Figure 2.6). And the result is that, provided the accuracy coefficient remains above a critical threshold value, the system will always settle into a stable state, while below this threshold it will inevitably experience a progressive decrease in accuracy, leading to an error catastrophe.

The variables that define this balance are under the control of natural selection, so the position a system reaches in the accuracy "scale" can be fixed by evolution. What this tells us is that any system sufficiently far to the right of the danger point (the threshold) can maintain itself indefinitely. In short, evolution can create a self-perpetuating mechanism that is potentially immortal.

The importance of these findings is fundamental. They demolish the instinctive belief that entropy necessarily dooms living things to die by an inexorable process of decay. They tell us that there is no theoretical reason why a living system should not endure as long as a suitable power source is available to support it in its far-from-equilibrium state. That does not mean that a living thing can last *ad infinitum*, since the power that sustains life—the sun—will not last forever. On a deeper level, the whole concept of an "open system" collapses when one comes to consider the cosmos as a totality, since there is, by definition, nothing outside the universe. Put another way, whether the cosmos is open or closed, the universe itself is the ultimate thermodynamic system, and as such it cannot itself escape the second law. This is the "end of time" issue I have already touched on.

Nonetheless, what these models tell us is that the idea of immortality (in the sense of something able to endure on a cosmic timescale) is not a wishful human fiction; it is a pragmatic possibility, which does not violate any known law of physics.

If that is so, where is the catch? Because there is a catch. The "life loop" has an Achilles' heel. The chemicals that comprise it are fragile, perishable structures, easily destroyed by any one of a thousand forces that are common on the surface of the earth. For example, since life is water-based, the life loop is an exercise in aqueous chemistry. Consequently, a living system will be disrupted by any temperature fluctuation outside the narrow "life band" of 32 to 212 degrees Fahrenheit (0 to 100 degrees centigrade). The life loop is also extremely sensitive to changes in acidity or alkalinity, and most living creatures flourish best close to the midway point between the two extremes on the scale. And so it goes on. To put it another way, a loop like that shown in Figure 2.5 would have a maximum life expectancy of no more than a few hundred hours under the highly variable environmental conditions in which it would be most likely to find itself in the real world, irrespective of its own intrinsic stability.

I can give a better feel for this issue by feeding some numbers into the scenario. Envisage a living system that can survive in only one out of ten environmental slots in a randomized habitat that shuffles these slots once every day. Clearly, its daily chance of survival is 1 in 10, and its weekly chance of survival is a vanishingly small .10 to the power of 7, i.e., divided by 10,000,000. This seems to indicate that it cannot endure. Is there a way out? Yes, there is one and only one way—a single "road to tomorrow." The life machine's chances of survival will rise to virtually 100 percent if it can make several thousand copies of itself each day, since that ensures that each slot will always be occupied by one or more individuals.

The phenomenon of life has always been utterly dependent on mechanisms for copying the loop. *To endure through time, a living system must always be able to generate more copies of itself than the environment can remove.* Unless this margin of safety is met, the loop will perish. Thus the life machine has had to design itself around one absolute imperative—reproduction.

This brings us to nature's copier machines: genes.

3

THE GENE
MACHINE

Where is the dust that has not been alive?
—EDWARD YOUNG

In his book *Profiles of the Future,* science-fiction writer Arthur C. Clarke poses a delightful conundrum. After describing a hypothetical machine with the ability to copy anything (a universal Replicator), he makes a key point, which I have rephrased in terms of a question:

If it costs a trillion dollars to make the first (prototype) universal Replicator, how much will it cost to make the second?

The answer is, of course, almost nothing, because the first thing the Replicator will copy is itself.

If we swap cost for time, the same principle applies to the origin of life. While it may have taken several hundred million years to produce the *first* gene, it probably only took a few hours to create the *second.* That is because genes and their creations are examples of a unique category of entities called "von Neumann machines." The defining property of a von Neumann machine is that it can remake itself in its own likeness.

The ability to self-copy endows von Neumann machines with a remarkable capability not possessed by any other structure. I had a powerful personal illustration of this capability almost every week, when I was working on my Ph.D. degree at Auckland University. At that time, I regularly had to grow very large quantities of the virus I was studying. This virus, code-named r17, is one of the smallest self-replicating entities on earth.

To grow the virus, one has to first grow the germ it preys on, the gut microbe *E.coli*. I used to do this by heat-sterilizing twelve liters of broth containing all the nutrients needed to support the bacteria's growth. The sterilized tank was put in a bath kept at 99 degrees Fahrenheit (37 degrees centigrade), and a tiny smidgen of *E.coli* was added to the broth under sterile conditions to stop other germs from contaminating the culture. At that stage, the amber liquid in the inoculated tank looked clear; an hour later, it still looked clear. However, after another hour, a faint cloudiness became evident—the first hint of the population explosion that was taking place in front of me. That cloudiness increased rapidly from the time it became visible.

At this stage, the bacteria were still growing vigorously, and I added a small quantity of r17 virus. Each virus attacks a single vulnerable cell and injects its genes into it. The virus genes reprogram the cell to make more virus. After twenty minutes or so, each infected cell bursts open, liberating about twenty thousand progeny viruses; these infect other cells, producing still more virus. And so it goes.

The introduction of the virus sets off a kind of genetic chain reaction in the tank. The virus genes sweep through the population of bacteria, killing the germs and making more and more viruses. Soon the tank starts to foam as the wholesale destruction of the germ population results in billions of microbes bursting open. At that stage, one has to stand by the tank with a dollop of antifoam to damp down the frothy consequences of this genetic mass murder; failure to be on hand when the germ population is being explosively reworked into a virus population can result in tentacles of foam reaching out into the main area of the lab, like a washing machine overflowing—and a stern lecture from one's supervisor.

The end result is a tankful of cleared liquid (viruses are so much smaller than the germs they have replaced that they are virtually invisible, despite their numbers). This tank can contain as many as 24 quadrillion virus particles.

I have told this story at length because it is the story of life. Under ideal

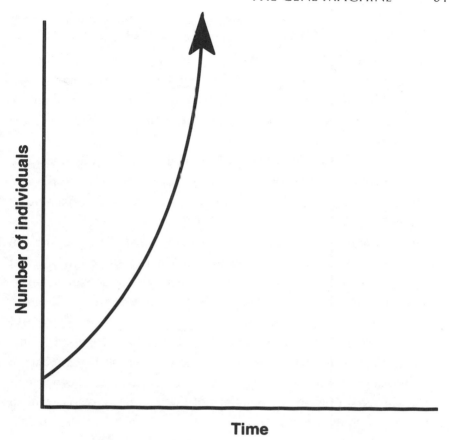

FIGURE 3.1

Runaway growth and the gene basis of foreverness. A single gene set under optimally favorable circumstances can create further copies of itself in a cumulative, runaway fashion called exponential growth. If one plots the number of genes in any freely self-replicating creature against time, one gets the exponential growth curve shown in the diagram. Note that the curve rises upward in an open-ended fashion; i.e., under favorable conditions the genes never stop multiplying of themselves. Any deviations from this open-ended growth pattern are imposed on them from without, by shortages of food, predation, and other factors.

conditions, genes replicate in enormous numbers. If one plots the path of their growth for cellular organisms, one gets a curve like the one shown in Figure 3.1. The curve is one any mathematician would recognize; it is called an exponential curve, and it is the hallmark of runaway, replicative growth. That runaway growth is a prerogative of von Neumann machines.

A characteristic feature of exponential growth is the suddenness with which the population explosion occurs. It is aptly summed up in a French children's riddle: A farmer's pond is gradually covered by a water lily that doubles in size each day. It will cover the pond in thirty days. The farmer, being lazy, decides not to cut the lily back until it has covered half the pond. When will that happen? On the twenty-ninth day. He has only one day to save his pond.

In the real world, explosive, self-copying processes are brought to a halt sooner or later: Food may run out, toxic wastes may pile up, physical limits may be reached. From the point of view of this book, what matters is that exponential growth is open-ended. The curve in Figure 3.1 is described as asymptotic in recognition of the fact that the trend line can never intersect either the horizontal or vertical axis of the graph. The fact that the arrow in the exponential graph points upward indefinitely—forever—is intimately related to the genetic open-endedness of life and to the psyche's longing for immortality.

The importance of exponential copying is seldom recognized in discussions on the basic nature of life. That is because most treatments of exponential growth focus shortsightedly on its importance in evolution.

Darwin recognized that populations of living things grow faster than the supply of food available to them in the space within which they live. The imbalance between an open-ended growth rate and limiting resources leads to competition for food and territory among rival forms of life. That competition leads to a struggle for existence, based on the survival of the fittest. This principle is embodied in Darwin's concept of natural selection.

However, obsessive emphasis on "survival of the fittest" obscures the fact that it is the simple existence of large numbers of living things (a result of exponential copying) that tilts the balance toward survival, not extinction. For example, it doesn't matter how fit or well adapted to its environment an ant is if it happens to find itself under a human boot. The ant species can afford to sacrifice millions of its members on the altar of chance, because there are always more where they came from.

Some people may object that I have engineered the impression of explosive population growth by using as my example a tiny entity that can make 20,000 copies of itself from a single input unit. What about our own species, which typically produces only one child from each birth? In fact, human beings exemplify runaway gene multiplication just as much as viruses. A healthy adult male can usually produce about 3–6 milliliters of semen each time he ejaculates. That amount of semen typically contains about 300–400 million sperm. That's 300–400 million cloned copies of his own genes.

If a man has intercourse three times a week, he climaxes, on average, 156 times a year. Using the above figures, one can easily work out that he produces about 500–900 milliliters of semen per annum. That is about 50–60 billion sperm. That means that, over the course of a normal life, a human male produces more genes than there are stars in a galaxy. On planet Earth, a single male can create enough genes to populate a universe every decade. From a reproductive point of view, the human male is little more than a gene machine, mass-producing his genes for export. There is a biological meaning as well as a moral point in the Jewish saying "When you kill a man, you destroy a nation."

One sees the same principle in operation everywhere. Watch a puffball explode on a spring day in the country. How many spores are liberated onto the wind? Thousands. Watch the golden rain of pollen from an acacia tree. How many grains are shed in the space of a few hours? Hundreds of thousands.

The chances of any individual life-form surviving the perils of the environment are astronomically small. However, the number of genes in populations is astronomically large. Each gene is a von Neumann machine, capable of re-creating millions of replicas from a single starter copy. This is nature's strategy—to offset enormously long odds with enormously large numbers.

Open-ended fecundity is necessary because living systems are fragile things, easily destroyed by accidents of time and place. That is only one side of the story, however. Life is not only at risk from accident from without, but also from error from within.

Take the example of the r17 virus again. Unlike the forms of life made of cells, this virus has a very inaccurate copier system. To reproduce its genes, it strings their building blocks together in a step-by-step fashion. Every one thousand or so steps, it makes a mistake—the wrong building block is put in or a step is left out. Since it takes over three thousand steps to make a complete copy of the genes in each virus, this high error rate means that most viruses in the population contain one or more errors in their genes.

Only a fraction of these mistakes are lethal. Viruses use the gene-to-protein processing system of the cells they grow in, and that system is impressively efficient. However, the incessant introduction of errors into the replicating population means that millions of replicas of the original input virus are automatically culled out of the life game by their inability to multiply farther. Thus the identity of the r17 virus is maintained only because the environment continually removes most of the mutants that are generated unceasingly and inevitably by the faulty copier process.

This is a reflection of Sod's Law in action. The information encoded in the virus genes is decaying; identity is being lost. The result is that any large population of viruses contains a significant number of dead genes. Likewise, the huge population of sperm in a male ejaculation contains a surprising number of defective sperm, i.e., damaged genes, so much so that experts in reproductive biology sometimes describe human semen as a "genetic junkyard."

In terms of size, a virus like r17 lies at the lower limit of life. Most bigger creatures have copiers that are much more accurate. The germ on which the virus grows, for example, makes (on average) only one mistake in every 100 million copier steps. That means that the vast majority of cells in the tank are fit, in the sense that they can reproduce farther. This improved accuracy is due to the evolution of a complex array of editing mechanisms. The germ cell actually makes primary mistakes at about the same rate as the virus, but, unlike the virus, it has a variety of secondary proofreading processes that allow most mistakes to be identified and corrected, just as a good typist is able to pick out and correct errors in a newly typed letter.

Proofreading is an almost universal feature of life—only some of the smallest viruses lack it. The reason is that most tiny viruses are the only surviving life-forms that retain today what was almost certainly the primordial design of genes. Such viruses have "single copy" genes—their genetic instructions are encoded in a single "sheet" of chemical "computer tape." This one-time system means that, if that tape is damaged, there is no backup memory to enable the mistake to be corrected.

The evolution of proofreading capabilities has been made possible by a principle that any communications engineer would spot at once. If you want to send a message through a noisy channel, i.e., a transmission system that makes mistakes, and you can't afford to upgrade the quality of the system, what can you do? The answer is to send the message more than once. In other words, use the principle of *redundancy*.

This brings us, finally, to the basic structure of genes, the one structure on earth that can lay claim to a kind of immortality. I ask the reader to step back with me to Shark Bay on the coast of Western Australia. I have already made the point that the tiny creatures that build the Shark Bay stromatolites are probably very similar to the cells that flourished in this region over three billion years ago.

Those Shark Bay creatures were built by their chemical copiers, their genes. Genes are fragile things, easily destroyed by extremes of heat or cold, or by sunlight, or by mechanical (shear) forces. Yet the genes I could extract from the Shark Bay microbes today would be indistinguishable in architecture from those of their remote forebears. Across this mind-bending span of time, a characteristic pattern has been held constant, even though the atoms that make up that pattern have been recycled many millions of times.

What we see today is not the original, but a copy of a copy of a copy. Yet, despite the randomizing influence of entropy, the structure of the copied gene has retained its unmistakable identity, unmarked by the attrition of the ages, unscarred by decay.

This is why the chemical substance that comprises genes is described as the *immortal* molecule. It is given the scientific name of deoxyribonucleic acid, or DNA. DNA has a characteristic and (by now) famous shape: a double helix. From the outside, it looks like a thread of two-ply wool, consisting of two intertwined chains (Figure 3.2). Internally, it has a ladderlike structure; the two chains coil around each other at regular intervals, each twist corresponding to ten rungs of the ladder. However, the rungs are not physically cross-linked. Rather, every rung is "broken" near the middle, and the cross connections that keep each half-rung in position are very weak chemical bonds.

The most important feature of the double helix is contained in its title: *double*. The fact that DNA consists of two chains means that the memory

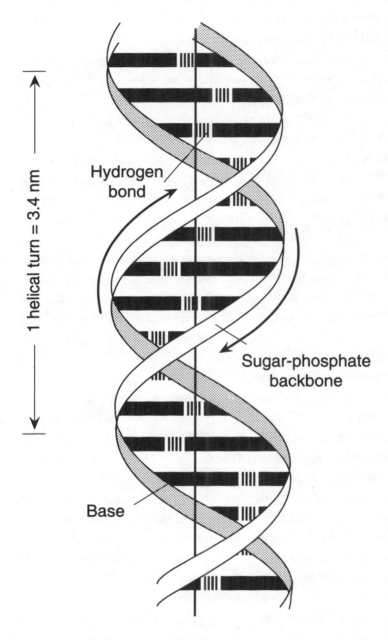

Hydrogen
bond

Sugar-phosphate
backbone

1 helical turn = 3.4 nm

Base

FIGURE 3.2

The basic structure of the gene: the characteristic double helical format of DNA. Its ability to accommodate any sequence of bases enables DNA to act as the information storehouse for virtually all the living things on this planet and carry the code of life.

of the genes is redundantly coded. It is this redundancy that makes proof-reading possible; if one chain is damaged, the lesion can be repaired by using the undamaged information on the partner chain as a restorative backup.

DNA's redundancy is, however, of an unusual type. The genetic message is not represented in two identical copies. Rather, one copy is the complement of the other. Consider this analogy. Suppose I wish to make an exact copy of my face. The easiest way to do it is to cover my face with some malleable substance and allow it to set firm. That creates a negative image or mold of my face. When this is filled with clay or plaster of paris, it will produce an exact replica of my face. The mold (negative image) and face replica (positive image) preserve the configuration of my face twice (redundantly) but in inverted ways. One image is the mirror image of the other, or, to be more precise, one image is complementary to the other. To copy my face, one uses the negative image template, and to copy the template one uses the positive image face replica.

This is the technique genes use to copy themselves. One side of the DNA ladder can be thought of as the negative image of its positive complement on the other side. Because the steps in the DNA ladder are so weakly held together, the two complementary chains are easily separated. One can then see that the half steps of the ladder consist of sequences of four unusual chemicals called bases, which are code-named A, G, T, and C.

Those bases are the four letters in the alphabet of life—literally. Just as human writers arrange the twenty-six letters of the English alphabet into sequences (sentences) that encode specific messages and have specific meanings, so nature has arranged sequences of the four bases on given strands of DNA's double helix into sequences that encode specific messages or "sentences" written in the four-letter language of DNA, each gene specifying the design of a particular product (usually a protein). In metaphorical language, we can think of a particular gene, like the one that specifies the structure of the hemoglobin in the red blood cells of higher animals, as a single page from the book of life.

The bases that spell out these genetic messages have a unique property, which is the very root of life on earth—they pair in specific ways, A with T, G with C. Even at this elementary chemical level, "pair bonding" retains its central importance in reproduction. The ability of the bases to pair in this specific way is why each side of the DNA spiral is complementary to the other.

Figure 3.3 shows a schematized pair of A-T and G-C bases. The bases in these pairs have been deliberately modeled on the cardboard cutouts used by a young American, J. D. Watson, in 1953 when he first realized the basic structure of DNA and, in one intuitive leap of understanding, solved the riddle of life. Readers who have read Watson's book or seen the television movie *Life Story* will remember that Watson was sitting at his desk in Cambridge, England, trying to get the four bases in DNA to "fit together" in a way that made sense chemically; to do that he was shuffling his cardboard cutouts into various combinations. The truly magic moment, a cardinal event in human history, when Watson solved the riddle, is described in his own words:

> When Jerry came in, I looked up, saw it was not Francis, and began shifting the bases in and out of various other pairing possibilities. Suddenly I became aware that an A-T pair held together by two hydrogen bonds was identical in shape to a G-C pair held together by at least two hydrogen bonds.

The significance of this is apparent instantly in Figure 3.3. If an A-T pair is superimposed on a G-C pair, they preserve their essential symmetry. The pairs retain that symmetry, they "look the same" if the order of bases is inverted; i.e., T-A looks the same as A-T and C-G the same as G-C.

Why is this remarkable? Because we are creating essentially the same paired couple from different units. Simple though it sounds, it brings us to the crux of the immortality issue. To take the last and crucial step, imagine you have a "life die"—a four-sided die, each side bearing a letter representing one of the four bases, A, T, C, and G. Throw the die sixteen times and record the result. Suppose you get:

GGTCGTAATGCTAGGT

Provided the pairing rules are obeyed, the partner sequence is automatically defined as

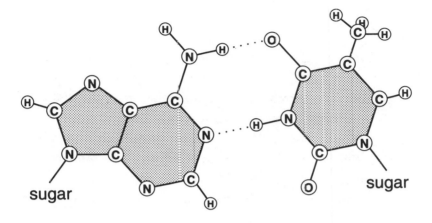

Adenine   **Thymine**

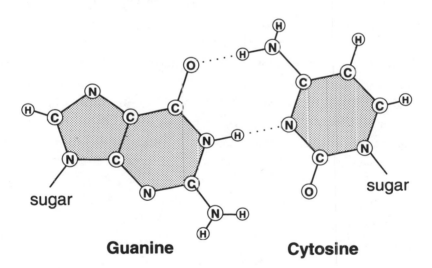

Guanine   **Cytosine**

FIGURE 3.3

Base pairing—the crux of the gene machine. Looked at quickly, it is easy to believe that these two-paired cross struts (base pairs) in the DNA ladder are identical. Closer inspection shows that there are subtle but all-important differences. If you cut these bases out and try to reassemble them into pairs that preserve maximum strength links between the partner units, you will find that no other combination works. Only these particular pairs are nearly identical and superimposable. (From J. D. Watson, The Double Helix.)

CCAGCATTACGATCCA

The point is that, subject to the same proviso (that the pairing rules are obeyed), a different set of throws would give us exactly the same helical format. DNA is a real example of an impossible paradox—a distinctive structure whose unique architecture can be sustained by an infinite number of different combinations.

Does this sound too easy? Why is this copier mechanism so different that it alone holds the key to life eternal? Suppose that something does go wrong. Suppose that when the sides of the ladder separate, the pairing rules fail (as they do occasionally) and because of some molecular slipup, A pairs with G, not T. Now the regularity of the helix is broken. A bit of noise has crept in, and the structure has begun to decay. In any other copying machine, that would be disastrous. However, when the partner strands of this distorted helix separate, the flawless symmetry of the molecule is automatically restored by the pairing rules. The lesion can be reproduced only if the same mistake occurs a second time at the same position, and the very laws of chance that make mistakes inevitable also dictate that identical errors are statistically very unlikely (just as it is unlikely that one will get two successive royal flushes in a game of poker).

Thus if we have a chance mistake, A pairing with G (not T), when the partner strands separate during replication, one strand will have the correct letter (A) and the other a "mistake" (G). Because the pairing rules are almost certain to be correctly obeyed during the next round of copying, the outcome is almost inevitably one offspring DNA with a (correct) A-T pair and one with an (incorrect) G-C pair. However, since the G-C pair has the same basic symmetry as the A-T pair, each new DNA will preserve the same three-dimensional helical format. A mistake has crept into the code, but the architecture of the code's carrier, DNA, remains unaltered. Thus, in DNA, alone among known copying machines, chance acts to preserve order, not to destroy it.

This is the crux of the immortality principle; double helical DNA combines two seemingly incompatible opposites—the symmetry of a crystal and the caprice of a roulette. A crystal is defined by a repetitive pattern of atoms in space. The double helix is an organic crystal in just this sense as its twin strands twist around each other repetitively with a spacing interval of exactly 3.4 nanometers. This crystalline structure (the epitome of order) can be built by chance (the epitome of disorder) from random throws of the life die, provided that the constraints imposed by the pairing rules are obeyed. Hence the paradox of life: *DNA has stayed the same (in structure) by endlessly becoming different (in sequence).*

The life-die game has a twofold message: It shows that the DNA double helix can accommodate any sequence of bases down its axis, which means it can carry any set of coded information; it also shows that changes in the sequence enter DNA at random, like throws in a game of dice.

This raises a crucial question. What makes one sequence meaningful while another is garbage? How does nature know which sequences are winners in life's lottery and which are rejects? To put it another way, why did DNA need to become different in sequence in order to endure down the ages? To answer this question, let us go back to the beginning. Many scientists believe that at the dawn of life, genes reproduced more or less without help from other substances. A typical scenario might envisage a pool of replicating genes bathed in a solution of their own energized building blocks. In such a situation, the sequence of bases in the gene would be irrelevant (it would correspond to random throws of the life die). Other things being equal, any one gene could replicate as well as any other.

Such a situation is inherently unstable. Other things are never equal. What is certain to happen is that one sequence (or, more probably, a population of similar sequences clustered around a weighted average) will reproduce faster, or "better," than others. Over time, this favored sequence will outbreed the others. Now the code, i.e., the sequence of bases carried in the genes, is nonrandom.

Take a specific example. Let us suppose that in the pool where the genes find themselves, the temperature fluctuates between 36 degrees Fahrenheit (2 degrees centigrade) at night and 86 degrees Fahrenheit (30 degrees centigrade) by day. Inevitably, this suits some gene sequences—let us call them type A sequences—better than others; for example, type F. The replicating population becomes nonrandom in the sense that type A sequences increase in frequency while type F sequences become less numerous. The end result is a set of genes with a statistically defined base sequence (type A) that is optimally "fitted" to its environment. Most variants from this "best fit" sequence fail to survive.

What makes one sequence fitter than another? The answer is that, early in evolution, genes "learned" to make "tools" for their own protection and replication. They did that by specifying the "design" of the tool in terms of the sequence of letters down the helix. That is, each "page" of genetic information or gene came to be "translated" into a particular product geared to carry out a particular task.

By the nature of things, some of these tools were better than others. Consider a tool that aided replication, in particular a universal copier tool that speeded up the replication of all the genes it came into contact with. In this situation, the whole gene population benefited from the presence of a single good toolmaker in its midst; even genes that made bad tools themselves had the rate of their reproduction improved by the good tool, thus disguising to a degree the failure of their own products.

The problem with this situation is that the good toolmaker gains little from the excellence of its own invention. That means that it pays the good toolmaker to keep its invention to itself. It can best do that by quite literally "fencing in" all the tools it makes. In other words, it must surrender its free-floating state and encase its genes and their toolmaking machinery in a "box" that prevents any inadvertent "lending" of its products to its neighbors.

The consequences of this "container" strategy are enormous and have in a fundamental sense shaped the evolution of life on earth. Before fencing, products were shared and adaptation was a collective enterprise. After fencing, products were jealously retained for the exclusive use of their own makers. Genes had become *selfish,* and life had irreversibly become a *competitive* process.

To use a seductively dangerous metaphor, when genes became property owners, life turned its back on a socialist (cooperative) mechanism for gene propagation and opted for a capitalist (competitive) one. It is not entirely accidental that the rules of evolution have such strong similarities to the rules of the marketplace.

Proof of the success of the fencing strategy is found in the fact that every living creature (apart from a few tiny viruslike entities) now keeps its genes inside their own box, technically called a *capsid* in the case of a virus and a *cell* in the case of everything else. Organisms, like human beings, contain billions of gene sets, each set encased in its own cell. All those gene sets are clones of each other, since they are derived from the same source—a single fertilized egg.

The selfish-gene concept has become a powerful force in modern biology since it allows us to view the struggle for existence from the point of view of the genes, and it is genes that underwrite the whole process.

The central axiom of the selfish-gene idea is that every creature on earth can be thought of as essentially a survival machine for the genes it contains. On our human level of observation, we see the struggle for life as a battle between organisms: lions versus gnu, ants versus beetles, caterpillars versus plants. On a deeper level, however, we are beginning to see that the real war is between the genes, which build these creatures to ensure the survival of the encoded self-image they contain. In this perspective, lions are simply survival machines for lion DNA; gnu, for gnu DNA, and so on.

Some scientists have criticized the term *selfish* as being a human attribute and therefore not a possible feature of genes. One can, I believe, overcome this objection by taking the word selfish in its literal semantic sense—*selfish*—concentrating on oneself to the exclusion of others. This me-versus-you quality is characteristic of genes. That is why dissimilar genes that have no coding kinship compete ruthlessly in the struggle for existence.

An image from my ABC television series encapsulated for me what gene "selfishness" means. The camera caught a predatory bird called a skua filching an egg from a penguin's nest while the parent penguins protested in outrage. What the snapshot showed was that the egg meant two different things to the two bird species: to the penguins, a commitment to the future; to the skuas, simply food.

The author John Wyndham has summed up the essentials of the selfish-gene concept in his science fiction. In *The Midwich Cuckoos,* a character comments:

I wonder if a sillier and more ignorant catachresis than "Mother Nature" was ever perpetrated? It is because Nature is ruthless, hideous and cruel beyond belief that it was necessary to invent civilisation. One thinks of wild animals as savage but the fiercest of them begins to look almost domesticated when one considers the viciousness required of a survivor in the sea; as for the insects, their lives are sustained only by intricate processes of fantastic horror.

Does this sound a bit strong? Watch a spider poison a fly in its web, or a female mantis eat her partner during intercourse, starting with his head. It puts evolution in perspective.

Wyndham makes the same point even more eloquently in *Web*:

> I perceive the old idea that "Mother Nature" knows best. . . . It is a concept that could only have arisen in a comfortable, well-fed society which has forgotten what it is to struggle for existence. Nature is not motherly, she is red in tooth and claw, she ravens for food—and she has no favourites.

Here is the genetic basis of life's immortality compulsion. Genes, key components of von Neumann machines, will maximize the number of copies of their own encoded self-image whenever they can, wherever they can, without limit, *ad infinitum*. This "urge to eternity" is jealously partitioned among the millions of species that inhabit the planet. Each species tries to perpetuate one genetic image, and one only—its own. It is the primary characteristic of genes that they look after number one.

The selfish-gene concept allows us to put death in its proper evolutionary perspective. Let me begin by asking the childlike question, Why do living things die? The answer is so surprising that most people, at first sight, tend to reject it. Many, perhaps most, living things on this planet, do not die—they are killed.

Because the end of life is, by definition, death, the distinction between dying and being killed may seem like a play on words. It is not. I cannot stress too strongly that the processes that cause creatures to wear out from within, i.e., to die in the sense that an old person dies in a hospital bed, differ completely from the processes that destroy them as a result of outside agencies and factors (accidents of time and place).

The bulk of life on earth is microscopic. Much of this microbial life is ageless in the sense that the individual cells of bacteria and their kin have the potential to maintain their structure indefinitely. They do not "die." When bacterial populations decrease in size, it is because their members are killed—by toxic compounds such as antibiotics, by extremes of heat or cold, by drying out, by exposure to UV, etc.

Such microscopic creatures reproduce by cloning; each daughter cell is a carbon copy of its parent. That means that the whole bacterial cell is as "immortal" as the genes that made it; the survival machine has the same durability as its own genes.

Many large single-celled creatures, like the amoeba, are also ageless. But as we ascend the scale of life, we find that organisms increasingly abandon cloning in favor of sexual reproduction. This is especially true of organisms whose bodies are made up of millions of cells knitted together into tissues and organs. Such sexually reproducing creatures have typically defined limits to life (life spans). The fact that each species has its own characteristic life span strongly suggests that the rate of aging is a genetically determined parameter, which has been fixed by natural selection (if aging was a simple consequence of entropy, we might expect all cells to age at the same rate).

Table 3.1 shows the maximum life expectancies of some familiar animals. There are no such limits to life in bacteria. The only genetically determined reproductive parameter in bacteria is "doubling time," i.e., the time taken for a given number of cells to double in number. Doubling time in microbes can be equated with generation time in higher creatures. Man, for example, has a generation time of about sixteen years (the time it takes for a child to reach physical reproductive maturity and beget a further generation). However, the generation time of the human species (sixteen or so years) is much less than its life expectancy (seventy-six years on average).

All this leads to two fascinating questions: How did nature engineer this fundamental difference between ageless and mortal cells? And why?

To understand what is thought to happen, one has to go back to Sod's Law. We have seen that the copying of DNA is seldom perfect. As genes are repeatedly copied, mistakes inevitably creep into the genetic message, and those mistakes often have damaging consequences for the chemistry of the cell in which they occur. The redundancy of the double helix allows

TABLE 3.1

Maximum Age Reached by Selected Species of Animal

Mayfly	1 day
Fruit fly	0.1 year
Bat	2 years
Mouse	3 years
Cat	21 years
Chimpanzee	37 years
Human being	156 years
Giant tortoise	177 years

With the exception of mayfly and man, all values given represent the maximum age reached by animals in captivity, away from the dangers that eliminate aging members of animal populations in the wild. The age of the "oldest human being that has ever lived" is disputed as it is difficult to authenticate the true age of very old people.

most of these mistakes to be edited out. However, the editing and proofreading processes consume a significant amount of the cell's energy budget—they are expensive. The cost factor is even higher when one comes to consider the upkeep of the complex and tightly integrated machinery needed to keep the cell's life processes running smoothly. Damaged proteins need to be tagged and destroyed before they do undue harm; energy reserves have to be invested in the mechanisms that check the efficiency of the cell's protein-making factories, and so on.

Microscopic creatures like bacteria can pay this energy bill without difficulty because they are economically organized, streamlined organisms with a relatively small number of genes. As creatures get bigger and more complex, the cost of damage control becomes prohibitively large. That is not because cells cannot find the resources to pay the bill (they can) but because the diversion of too many resources into proofreading processes makes the creature less competitive in other ways.

An analogy may help us understand the dilemma nature faced as the problem of damage control escalated. Consider two types of pen—a carefully crafted piece designed to last forever (an immortal pen) and a ballpoint designed to be replaced every few months (a throwaway pen). Which pen will win in the competitive world of a marketplace with an insatiable desire for pens but a limited amount of cash with which to purchase them? The ballpoint. Why? Because it is cheaper to make and can be mass-produced. The manufacturer trades quality for quantity.

These points are illustrated in Figure 3.4, which graphs fitness against investment in accuracy. The key point about this graph is the shape of the resulting curve. On the right side of the curve, we reach a point beyond which the system can survive indefinitely, but only on a lower fitness rating. The point of optimal fitness lies inside the area of finite life span.

Apply this principle to the body of a complex creature like man. Suppose it costs 100 arbitrary energy units to preserve human DNA in unaltered form. If this amount of energy were required to preserve each of the 60 trillion DNAs in the adult body, the human life machine would have to commit most of its resources to housekeeping, i.e., simply to maintaining itself. As such, it could not compete successfully against DNAs in rival life systems that invested most of their energy reserves in the development of specialized survival skills. There is not much point in having a high-accuracy deathless body if it has no defenses against low-accuracy short-lived predators.

According to theoretical biologist Tom Kirkwood and geneticist Robin Holliday, who put forward these ideas, evolution's answer to this dilemma has been to strike a compromise between accuracy of reproduction and efficiency of reproduction. That has been achieved by setting the gene complement of a complex creature in two distinct cellular environments: that found in *germ line*, or reproductive, cells (those that occur in the tissues that give rise to sperm and eggs) and that found in *somatic* cells (those that occur in the rest of the body). Genes in germ line cells are a tiny fraction of total body genes (often less than 1 percent); hence the cost of maintaining expensive error-correcting and editing processes in the ovaries and testes is minimal. Somatic cells make up the bulk of body mass, and here nature has devised an ingenious tactic to keep costs down. Somatic cells are programmed to maintain high levels of accuracy *only*

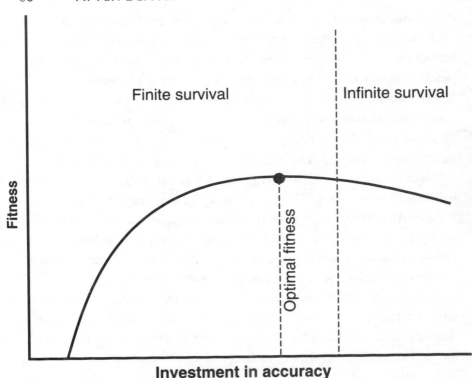

FIGURE 3.4

A schematic representation of a model that graphs a creature's fitness to survive against the amount of its reserves it invests in the maintenance of a fault-free structure. If this model is correct, it tells us something basic. A creature that is optimally fit (in the sense of having the best chance of passing on its genes) invests less of its reserves in "upkeep" than one that has the potential to last forever. Because the energy investment needed to make low-upkeep, disposable bodies is less than that required to make high-upkeep, deathless ones, such bodies can be made in greater numbers. Thus, during evolution, nature has evidently traded immortality for cost-effectiveness. (From T.B.L. Kirkwood and R. Holliday, Accuracy in Molecular Process.*)*

until the germ line genes have been given their chance to pass into the next generation. After that, nature no longer cares about them, and they are allowed to run down.

The effect is to create a class of cells with a programmed limit to life. Unlike the ageless cells of bacteria and the immortal cells that make up sperm and eggs, body cells have a genetic time fuse that dooms them to decay after a statistically predetermined interval, which may be intimately related to the creature's life span.

One can demonstrate the reality of this time fuse in man by teasing cells from soft body tissue and allowing them to grow in culture fluid in a glass dish. One sees that these body cells multiply for only a fixed number of divisions before they become visibly sick and die. This number has been found by experiment to be about fifty doublings. It is called the Hayflick limit, after its discoverer.

Thus, at some point in the remote past, evolution produced a novel solution to the problem of reproduction: a perishable survival machine "wired" to self-destruct in time: a throwaway body. With this came a new phenomenon: *programmed death*. Death that was, within statistical limits, predictable.

If we allow ourselves a little poetic license, we can say that at some (early) stage of evolution, death was invented as a cost-effective mechanism for optimizing the spread of genes. At that time, evolving organisms surrendered eternal youth for a cheaper mode of reproduction. Immortal genes in throwaway bodies became a successful formula that was to create most of the familiar creatures in the biological calendar—including man.

So, at last, we come to ourselves, and the crux of the issue. The survival machine built by human genes contains the most highly developed brain in biology. That brain, like the body, is perishable. Yet it is the vehicle for our sense of self.

The human brain was the first brain in evolution to sense the serial passage of time; the first brain to learn to predict events from experience. Inevitably, it was also the first brain to foresee its own end. Note the wording "its *own* end." The end, not of the species (which goes on), but of the individual (which does not). It is the individual's powerful sense of *identity*, of "I am," that fears extinction.

This explains our ambivalent attitude toward procreation. We nurture and love our children. We recognize them as our future, our genetic passports to tomorrow. However, our conscious minds retain the me-first individualism that is evolution's legacy. Our psychologies are indissolubly pegged to a compulsive need for personal survival, which is as open-ended as the unlimited copying the von Neumann machines make possible. The ego is the true heir of the selfish gene.

When the ego was born, death entered consciousness; the serpent came into Eden.

4

SELF-IMAGE

The universe resounds with the joyful cry, I AM.
— S C R I A B I N

One of my favorite poems when I was young was "Invictus," by W. E. Henley, which ends with the quatrain:

It matters not how strait the gate,
How charged with punishments the scroll,
I am the master of my fate,
I am the captain of my soul.

This quatrain shows vividly the way we regard the me-sense as the focus of our world. Everything takes its cue from this feeling of ego. We are the self-created centers of our own universes.

What do we mean by the word "ego"? What do we mean when we say "I am"? Sit still and focus your concentration on yourself. You are aware of your extremities—your arms and your legs. You know they are part of you, yet you are also aware that the entity that is observing these parts is located inside your head. Indubitably, the locale of the self is the brain.

Now empty your mind of images—listen to music, or relax in some other way, and deprive your mental processes of an immediate focus for concentration. You will experience a temporary loss of self, a moment of self-forgotten escape from which you may quite suddenly snap back into an awareness of the here and now.

If an undistracted mind cleansed of images is "self-unaware," then, by reverse logic, our sense of self must be linked to the presence of images in some active context. That sounds implausible until we realize that the images in question are verbal symbols. I will try to show that our sense of "I am" is indissolubly correlated with the human faculty of language in particular and our ability to create symbolic codes (speech, math, musical notation, etc.) in general. That is not to say that mental coding is the sole determinant of self, but rather that any description of self that ignores the way we represent the world in symbols will miss what many scientists believe is its central element.

How may language underpin the sense of self? Look at the structure of the human brain. The brain is bilaterally symmetrical; i.e., it is divided into two halves (hemispheres), each of which is a mirror image of the other. The two sides of the brain are connected by a thick bundle of nerve fibers, the corpus callosum, which allow the hemispheres to engage in cross talk. Despite their physical similarity, each half-brain is not a redundant copy of its partner (although there is an important sense in which each hemisphere does provide a backup for the other).

What matters to us is that the faculty of language is largely localized in the left side of the brain. Two areas are involved; Broca's area seems responsible for the grammatical construction of speech, while Wernicke's center seems necessary to a proper understanding of the meaning of language. Brain-imaging techniques reinforce and confirm this dominant role of the left hemisphere in speech.

Brain biologists like Roger Sperry and Michael Gazzaniga have helped to clarify the role of language in the creation of a sense of self by studying "split-brain" patients. In split-brain patients, the right and left sides of the brain are surgically separated by cutting the corpus callosum. This drastic operation was originally developed as a treatment for epilepsy, but its use, while it lasted, provided researchers with an inadvertent opportunity to monitor the way the two halves of the brain influence personality and consciousness. It is possible to ask questions of each side of the brain separately by flashing images to the right or left of a dot positioned in the center of a screen in front of the patient. Since the optic fibers cross from one side of the body to the other en route from eye to brain, an image picked up by the left eye connects to the right half of the brain and vice versa.

The results of such experiments with split-brain patients are fascinating. Consider the case of PS, who, soon after his split-brain operation, was asked to describe who he was and what he most wanted to do. Questions were first put to his right hemisphere by displaying them on a screen.

Q: Who are you?
A: PS.
Q: What do you want to be?
A: An automobile racer.

But when the same questions were put to his left hemisphere, the question-and-answer sequence became

Q: Who are you?
A: PS.
Q: What do you want to be?
A: A draftsman.

Experiments like these have convinced many researchers that each side of the brain has a separate personality—a separate self. We may literally be split personalities. Some brain biologists think that the human mind is a composite structure with multiple subsystems. What, then, gives us our vivid sense of being a single individual, a personality, a self?

Consider the case of PS again. In an often-quoted test, PS was presented with two pictures on a screen, separately shown to each hemisphere; the left hemisphere was shown a chicken's claw, the right hemisphere a snow scene. PS was then presented with a sequence of pictures including a chicken's head and a snow shovel (Figure 4.1). When asked to indicate which pictures in this sequence related to the image on the screen, PS picked the chicken-head picture with his right hand and the snow shovel picture with his left. But when asked to explain this choice, PS responded with the giveaway answer: "That's easy. The chicken claw goes with the chicken, and you need a shovel to clean out the chicken's shed."

This demonstrates that PS's left hemisphere used its faculty of language to construct a logical but incorrect explanation for what had happened. The dominant left-side brain solved the puzzle of its right-side partner's choice by creating a fictitious story to link the two unconnected selections.

Gazzaniga summarizes his view of the place of language in the creation of a unitary sense of self from what is essentially a split-personality situation in these words:

> There's some final system, which I happen to think is in the left hemisphere, that pulls all this information together into a theory. It has to generate a theory to explain all of these independent elements; and that theory becomes our particular theory of ourself and of the world.

This seems a surprising conclusion to people who are unfamiliar with brain research, so let us explore it further. How can we tell what goes on in the mind when we use language? An interesting set of experiments has been performed by brain researcher Benjamin Libet. He exploited a technique in which an electrode is fixed to a subject's scalp. The point of departure for the experiment was the well-attested observation that when someone does something voluntarily, i.e., by a conscious act of will, the electrical potential of the scalp shifts to the negative. This has been called the readiness potential.

Libet asked subjects to flex their wrists or fingers whenever they felt an urge or desire to do so. To measure the timing of that urge or desire, subjects were also asked to watch a revolving spot and report its clock position at precisely the time they experienced the urge to move. The results were consistent and significant. The readiness potential came *first* and the urge to move almost half a second (400 milliseconds) *later*.

This strongly suggests that any conscious act is preceded by some surge of activity in the brain; consciousness is an afterthought. If that is so, then speech—the conscious use of the vocal chords to articulate thought—must surely be a consequence of events that have already taken place in the mind. But what about unspoken thought? Does it not fit the same

FIGURE 4.1

Mike Gazzaniga's split-brain patient PS sees the picture of a chicken's foot with the left hemisphere and the snowy scene with the right. Each hand, controlled by the opposite hemisphere, points to an appropriate card. (From Colin Blakemore, The Mind Machine.*)*

see itself in the act of perception—to see itself as the seer. Only man can say, "I know that I know." That suggests to me that the introduction of full-scale self-awareness restructured human psychology in ways that contemporary science cannot as yet formulate in terms of either psychological or neurophysiological models. I will develop this idea into a more tightly focused theory shortly.

What I am saying is that the "me" self-image was not just another element in the brain's repertoire of linguistic symbols: It was (or became) an *organizing* agency that caused the brain to restructure its memory programs in terms of a new integrative nexus, for the first time centering them, by giving them a point of internal reference. To describe this self-centered entity, I will use John Hick's useful term, the *ego-self.*

As the brain improved its ability to encode the world in symbolic equivalents, it may have, at some critical point, flipped into a new stable state centered on its internal symbolic representation of itself, rather than on its prior wide-screen experiential processing window to the outside world.

Thus, while it cannot be rigorously proven, I believe I am justified in adopting, as a provisional working hypothesis, the view that the role of language and other symbolic codes is the pivotal feature in the creation and maintenance of our sense of self. We create self-consciousness by giving unrealized mental options a concrete symbolic structure.

So far I have used the term "language" loosely, without differentiating between spoken and written speech. To take matters farther, I believe we must understand that the difference is crucial. Spoken conversation is almost exclusively a mode of communication between individuals. However, reading is in an important sense a self-conversation between the individual and the text. The only observer of a sequence of written symbols is the mind, which scans them. The same point can be made even more forcibly of a mind that writes down its thoughts on clay or papyrus or paper, for the brain in this situation has an external representation of its own internal workings.

I strongly suspect that the need to construct self-symbols external to the individual has played a formative role in the evolution of the ego-self. It is one thing to have a mental model of oneself inside one's head; it is another to have an outward image of it that has an independent reality outside the brain. I am aware that this is an unusual position to take, so in the following section I present some evidence in its favor.

Look first at the significance of writing in the widest possible context. Evolution on earth has been made possible by the evolution of two codes, two mechanisms for storing and transmitting information from one generation to the next. The first is the language of the genes. Information remembered in genes can be transmitted more or less unaltered across the millennia, leapfrogging time by passing from body to body. The second code is human language itself. Information remembered in human language can also leapfrog the generations, passing from brain to brain just as genes pass from body to body.

However, spoken language has many limitations as a mode of memory. Information passed on by word of mouth can be notoriously unreliable, as the data tends to be reinterpreted and colored by each mind it passes through. That is why lawyers tend to be suspicious of purely anecdotal evidence. In addition, spoken tradition relies totally upon the ability of the brain to recall messages in their original format, and all of us know how easily the exact wording of a phrase can be altered by the passage of time, even if we still remember its general sense. Written codes do not suffer from these defects. I can understand the military strategy of Julius Caesar clearly and accurately, even though he has been dead for over two thousand years, because he wrote it down. Through writing, his mind can speak to mine across the centuries without suffering any loss of detail or focus.

This is not to say that spoken language is an inefficient instrument of information transmission when it is used in a ritualistic way. The oral traditions and myths of many hunter-gatherer peoples who lack written language have been preserved for hundreds of generations in amazingly accurate form. In these situations, however, the tradition is passed from elder to novice during solemn ceremonies, under conditions designed to maximize the impact of the words. It is often done by repeating the message, formatting it in rhyme and coloring the content with music, etc. Precisely because such orally transmitted myths are fixed in character and length, however, they do not allow for a rapid accumulation and integration of new data, as the more flexible instrument of the written word does. The distinctive features of written language are that, unlike spoken language, its ability to absorb fresh information is genuinely open-ended and its capacity to transform the message is virtually unlimited, because old and new data can be checked and compared.

In the hunter-gatherer phase of evolution, the sum total of tribal lore, including folk myths and rituals, could probably have been set down within the pages of a single large book. By contrast, the amount of knowledge available to modern man requires a vast library with hundreds of thousands of volumes; this is equivalent to progressing from the genetic memory capacity of a small virus (some 3,000 genetic letters) to the genetic memory capacity of a human being (some 300 million genetic letters).

Thus the critical breakthrough in the evolution of the human species was the invention of writing, not the invention of speech. *There is only one event, in the whole of prior evolution, comparable in importance to the origin of writing, and that is the origin of genes.* In this sense, we are but newly human.

If this concept of newness seems unfamiliar or implausible, look carefully at the time when writing evolved. The first known written symbols, inscribed on tablets of baked clay, were found in places like Kish in the Middle East. They were evidently written about 5,500 years ago. That places the approximate origin of writing among the Semitic peoples of the Tigris-Euphrates-Nile region (for whom we have the best records and the best uninterrupted chronology) at somewhere between 4,000 and 8,000 years ago.

This date is crucial because it also corresponds with the conclusive transition from the hunter-gatherer lifestyle to large-scale agriculture and organized city life (obviously the origins of writing and the origins of city life are interwoven, but for the purposes of this chapter it is not important which was the cause or which the effect). City life is congruent with civilization; the very word *civilization* comes from the Latin *civis* ("citizen"), from the same root as *civitas* ("city-state"), a place where citizens congregate. Men who live in cities, intermingling with their fellows, exchanging goods, living in permanent houses, etc., have a different perspective on life from those who follow the ancient nomadic lifestyle.

In particular, the age-old sense of shared experience common to all hunter-gatherer groups easily breaks down in a city environment. A hunter-gatherer is an organic part of his or her clan, bound indissolubly to the tribe by a communal "dreaming" and utterly dependent on it for survival. A city dweller can live off the labors of others. It is not accidental that city life, almost from its inception, saw the rise of power structures, elites, privilege, and the evolution of the institution of slavery. In the tribal commune, food was gathered/harvested for the good of all. In the city, the distribution of food (and of other goods and services) became biased in favor of the few. Men no longer shared; they hoarded. Just as selfish genes learned to build boxes to hold the goods they created, so urban man developed the concept of property to describe the material possessions that came to symbolize his power and position. The development of these differences in class structure and status helped the evolution of the ego. The very concept of ego, of self, is rooted in our perceptions of the ways we differ from others. When certain men began to feel more important than their fellows, the stage was set for the emergence of that sense of me-first individualism that so characterizes urban man in the competitive West.

City life also opened up a new dimension of human awareness—symbolic thought. The hinge role that language played in this process has been brilliantly analyzed and trenchantly described by historian L. L. Whyte:

> But with the advantages of urban life ancient man was able to exercise faculties that had previously had little opportunity; he developed new tools for action and new words for thought. . . . Speech, script and conceptual thought are now of rapidly growing importance in the organization of society. The concept or idea has become one of the main instruments of social coordination, and ideas begin to be linked in sequences which permit reasoned attention to be given to novel situations, and so lead to the long-delayed deliberate responses which result from sustained thought.

Continuing this argument, Whyte is able to link the evolution of this new, language-based mentality to the emergence of the ego-self:

> Instead of being aided primarily by instinctive responses to external stimuli and by mimicry of the forms of a stable social tradition, the individual was now increasingly dominated and controlled at mo-

ments of decision by the special forms of his own thought processes. This dominance of the individual's own mental process means, in unitary thought, that his attention was drawn to these processes. . . . Thus man became (ego)-self conscious. The individual became aware of his own thought.

Now a new and crucial element enters the picture. Whyte is at pains to impress us with the view that the growing sense of self that emerged in cities about 4,000–8,000 years ago depended critically upon the use of memory. This manifestly depends on the use of a sophisticated symbolic language. Since the physical brain faculty of memory had not enlarged or improved, the only memory capacity that had acquired new dimensions was the conceptual memory of the past that written language made possible.

As Ken Wilber says: "The ego-(self) is in part a memory-self, and that is what allows it to rise above the fluctuations of the body." That is crucially and centrally important because it brings *time* into the picture.

Our sense of self is inextricably linked to our sense of time. We can get some impression of this linkage by examining our own mental processes. When we awake on a fine Sunday, we may not consciously say, "What will *I* do today?" but our thoughts are undoubtedly organized around our personal expectations of what will happen to *us.* Note that the essence of this me-oriented thinking is the ability to project forward in time.

An animal almost certainly does not have that ability. It will do things in the course of a day, but it will not map out the possibilities in its mind before the event. The ability to structure behavior predictively (before it happens) is indissolubly linked with the point of central reference—the I—that provides the focusing lens for the imagination.

If the self is partly defined by its ability to project forward in time, it is equally defined by its ability to project backward in time, to access past experiences via the mechanism of memory. But how? Surgeons like Wilder Penfield, in the course of early attempts to treat certain kinds of severe brain disorder, tried a technique in which electrodes were inserted into specific parts of the brain's outer layer, the cerebral cortex. In some cases, the results were startling. Patients suddenly remembered scenes and events from their past. The electrical stimulation seemed to trigger not just a memory, but the actual event itself; patients seemed to relive the past with extraordinary vividness. Penfield describes the recall as a "hearing again and seeing again—a living-through-moments-of-past-time." And yet the patient is still aware that he/she is in the operating room. Brain surgeons have coined the term *double consciousness* to describe these parallel modes of awareness.

If the flow of current was cut off, the induced recollection was immediately lost, but it could often be recalled by stimulating the same area again. Significantly, however, the recall did not pick up where it had left off. Rather, it started again at the beginning, as though, in the words of science writer Dean Wooldridge, "it were stored on a film or tape which automatically rewinds each time it is interrupted."

This seems to suggest that the record of our past experiences is stored subconsciously in the brain in considerable detail. I wonder whether the need to sequester past memories from present experience is not in itself a clue to the way we are forced to perceive time by the demands of biological survival. If we were not intensely aware—conscious—of that narrow time-slice we call "now," we could not deal with emergencies in an effective, life-preserving way. The electrode experiments seem to suggest that the whole history of our prior experiences exists in the mind concurrently with this sense of present time, but that it is not normally permitted to intrude into the here and now. Perhaps the main reason we are conscious only of now time and not of past time is that simultaneous awareness of past and present would put the instrument of perception itself (the brain) at risk. As physicist John Wheeler said, time is what keeps everything from happening at once.

Direct evidence of the brain's ability to "keep time" has come from the discovery of a tiny collection of nerve cells called the suprachiasmatic nucleus in a deep brain structure called the hypothalamus. If microelectrodes are implanted in this area, they show that the nerve cells in the cluster fire in an amazingly regular pattern—almost, as brain biologist Colin Blakemore has said, "like the ticking of a clock."

Significantly, the rate at which cells in the suprachiasmatic nucleus fire is not constant; in the case of a rat, for example, the cells fire somewhat faster at night (when the rat is active) than during the day (when the rat is asleep). In other words, the nucleus is integrated into the alternating cycle of day and night. I believe this diurnal periodicity is fundamental to the way the vertebrate brain evolved, to our sense of time, and to our perception of death. Indeed, this issue is so important that I deal with it in detail in the next chapter.

Other clues to the biological basis of our perception of time come from patients who have suffered from rare forms of brain damage. Deep in the brain lie two ancient structures, the hippocampus and the amygdaloid nuclei. When these are damaged, the time sense is strangely affected. Perhaps the most dramatic example is the case of Clive Wearing. Clive was once a world expert on Renaissance music, but in 1985 he suffered a rare brain infection resulting from the virus that causes cold sores, herpes simplex. This virus selectively attacked and destroyed large numbers of nerve cells in Clive's brain, conspicuously in the hippocampal lobe. The result was that Clive lost his sense of past time completely; he now lives his life in an eternal present, forever believing that he has just woken up from a long period of unconsciousness. His diary reflects this nightmare condition:

9:04 A.M.	Now I am AWAKE.
10:00 A.M.	NOW I AM AWAKE.
10:28 A.M.	ACTUALLY I AM NOW FIRST TIME AWAKE (crossed out) for years.
10:54 A.M.	Now I am awake for the first time.

Every time Clive's wife, Deborah, enters the hospital room, he greets her as if it is their first meeting for a long time—even though it may be their third encounter for the day. Deborah sums up Clive's condition sadly but aptly: "Clive's world now consists of a moment, with no past to anchor it and no future to look ahead to."

Clive can still speak, which shows that his ability to use language remains unimpaired. What seems to have happened is that he has lost the ability to lay down or imprint new, long-term memories in such a way that these can be accessed by consciousness. The position of the hippocampus and the amygdala in the brain may provide some clue to their role(s) in this process. They are "halfway houses," which gather information from those areas of the brain's upper story, the cerebral cortex, that have to do with the processing of information from the senses. They also relay messages up to the cortex and down into the deeper brain structures that control emotions. As such, they seem admirably placed to activate the retrieval mechanisms that bring long-term memories out of storage and project them into consciousness.

Clive's problem is more than one of mere amnesia: He seems to have lost the ability to structure his thoughts in time. His case is important in the context of this book because it demonstrates that *our sense of the serial passing of time, which we take for granted as an axiomatic feature of the real world, is very much a construction of our own minds,* a feature of neuro-psychology, not physics.

Chapter 2 showed us that, from the standpoint of physics, there is no observable quantity called time, only space-time. How then does our human sense of time arise?

Think about language again. What language does is *replace the external world with a world of symbolic equivalents.* For example, a heavy physical object like a rock will remain fixed in position unless a great deal of effort is expended to shift it. However, the word "rock" can easily be manipulated, played with, set in new conjunctions; i.e., the symbol has a freedom that its object lacks. Moreover, the symbol has a subjective mental immortality. Our experience of any individual rock is usually transitory—a quick snapshot that is filed and buried. But the word "rock," once learned, becomes part of our inner world, joining the vocabulary of reusable symbols we use to construct things, not in the outer world of action, but in the inner world of thought. Man is the only creature who can be highly active while sitting still.

We take this mental activity for granted, so accustomed are we to it. Consider what must have happened when this process of creating symbols first began to gather real momentum in cities some 4,000–8,000 years ago. Then, new mental constructions (new thoughts, hence new words) were arising in the expanding urban environment at an ever-increasing rate, creating the conceptual world that was the new *modus operandi* of the mind. If the brain had simply absorbed these novel constructions en bloc, this process of conceptualization would have produced an indigestible glut of unrelated images, mental overload, chaos. To make sense of this new conceptual dimension, the human brain must have needed an *ordering principle,* something that would format and pattern the new input. That ordering principle, I submit, was *time.*

Remind yourself yet again that time has no independent reality in physics. When language started to become the preeminent force in psychology, the brain invented a sequencing device to arrange events and experience (encoded as verbal symbols) in space (the inner space of subjective awareness) into storage systems (memory) that could be accessed in a way that created coherence. Our sense of time is a mental map by which we order our memories. We flag the intervals in this map by points of fixed reference, like dates (1890, 1915, etc.), but our sense of sequential time is just a categorizing system, imposing a deep and hard-to-remove sense of before-during-after on memory entries that coexist simultaneously in the mind.

Something as profound as our sense of serial time could not, however, spring into existence as a mental construction without being married to some preexisting feature of brain physiology. That was, I believe, the serial firing of nerve cells in the suprachiasmatic nucleus together with the diurnal periodicity of the day/night cycle.

These features of the brain had not been selected with the purpose of creating a time sense. Evolution does not foresee in advance the demands that may later be made upon the biological material with which it works. The periodicity in the brain was an adaptive response to the periodicity of nature, but it was easily diverted to underpin the emerging sense of time. The brain learned to use the ticking of its internal clock to sequence its register of memories in a way that preserved its functional integrity, that prime prerequisite of survival; in so doing, it inadvertently created one of the most enduring and tenacious of all our illusions, the feeling of things flowing by from past to future.

Whence comes the feeling of "movement"? A reel of movie tape may offer a helpful analogy. In a reel, snapshots of experience—pictures—exist as a static sequence of frames ordered in serial sequence. All the frames coexist at once; that is the reality. The illusion of movement arises if the frames are moved past an observer in sequence, or if an observer is moved along the frames. This second situation may be closer to human reality than the first. As an animal moves through three-dimensional space, its awareness is focused on its immediate environment; it has, as far as we know, no ability to project back in time through memory, or forward in time through prediction. But human consciousness operates not just in the physical space of its surroundings, but in the mental space of its symbols. This ability to re-create, and extend, the world in symbols enables human consciousness to remember things past and forecast things future. To maintain the integrity of this new world of mentality, an ordering principle was vital. That principle was time.

This still does not present a satisfying explanation of the illusion of time "moving," so let me put it a different way. As our mind/bodies move through space-time—and this movement is real—they encounter new elements of the world, which the brain records as experience. Somehow, I believe, these new experiences are organized in a way that reflects the periodic structure of one (or some or all) of the brain's internal oscillators, like the sequential firing of the nerves in the suprachiasmatic nucleus. When that happens, the ordering mechanism, whatever it is in biophysical terms, counts them off in a serial—one, two, three, etc.—fashion. Thus real motion through space-time (movement along a "worldline") gets transfigured into the false feeling of motion through (or across) the sequence-templated states of the mind's recording system.

Another analogy may help. When we visualize time, we usually think of a timekeeper, like a watch. The moving hands of a watch seem a perfect representation of our sense of the passage of time. But the hands of a watch trace out a circle in space, not a movement through time. We identify the moving finger of the watch as the moving finger of time purely by convention, because we have learned to associate the watch with time so often that the link has acquired the status of law in our minds. Onto the physical movement of the watch's hand, which is real, we have grafted a sense of the psychological motion of time, which is illusionary.

If time is an ordering principle that sequences mental entries in space, then self is an ordering principle that organizes such entries around a point of internal reference. Thus time and self are different sides of the same coin. It is impossible to sequence mental (symbolic) entries without relating them to some common focus. Once the counting mechanism became the referent of the system, it became quite literally impossible for the brain to accept data in any way other than through this sense of self. So close is the connection between self and time that, for the remainder of this book, I will use the term "ego-self" to mean both our sense of persona and our sense of serial time.

Time and self have become so firmly rooted in human psychology that they form the very basis of the way we look at the world. Yet they are mental constructions, useful fictions, not features of the real world. These ideas will, I hope, become clearer as we proceed through the various chapters of this book.

This view of the twin origins of time and ego-self automatically answers an obvious criticism of its credibility. I can almost hear someone to whom this point of view is novel saying, "But initially only a tiny fraction of city dwellers could write; are you saying that only they had a strong sense of ego-self?" My answer is, "Of course." Five thousand years ago, only a minute fraction of the human species had settled in cities; the vast majority still hunted and gathered in the hallowed Stone Age mold. Yet it was the few who settled in cities who carried the fate of the species in their minds. That has always been the pattern in evolution—change never affects a whole population uniformly; in any population there are always a few "mutant" individuals who are "ahead of their time." It may take tens or hundreds of generations for the new property, if it is selectively useful, to become the norm for the species. Of the minority who settled in cities, an even smaller minority—the tiny elite of the rich and privileged, and their dependents—had access to the art of writing. Yet they wielded the power, and precisely because they could record their experiences, fragments of their stories have survived (in places), while those of the anonymous crowd have vanished without trace.

The time when a rich and flexible symbolic language developed in the context of a dynamic city life is fraught with significance. We often speak of the dawn of "recorded history" without realizing what a telltale phrase it is. The impression usually given is of a historical continuum that becomes "accessible" at the point where written records come into being. I believe the truth is otherwise. The origin of writing was not a historical convenience, a mere point on a continuous graph-line. It is, in my view, a *fracture in consciousness,* a fundamental fault-line marking the boundary between two modes of human awareness.

* * *

A fracture in consciousness is a bold statement. But it provides us with a way to test the controversial ideas I have summarized about ego-self and time. My postulate is that our modern sense of self/time not only corresponds with, but was caused by, the changes in human psychology that followed the abandonment of the hunter-gatherer lifestyle and the adoption of urban life. The most significant of those changes, by far, was the evolution of a new and extended mode of language.

This theory makes two testable predictions: that man's sense of self showed some fundamental change in quality at this fracture point, and that the same should apply to man's sense of time (even though we have seen that these two are inseparably linked, it will be convenient, here, to treat them as distinct).

What, then, do the records show? What was man's self-image during prehistory? It is possible to get an insight into the way humans thought before the origin of cities by examining the psychology of those peoples who still practice the hunter-gatherer lifestyle that was the common lot of the whole human species during the neolithic ages.

As a citizen of Australia, it is natural that my thoughts should turn first to our aboriginal peoples, who have lived on this ancient continent for forty thousand years or more. Aboriginal languages offer us a window into the remote past of our species.

It is difficult for a Western person to get inside the complex patterns of aboriginal tradition, but certain features of the aboriginal attitude toward self emerge from scholarly analyses of aboriginal culture carried out in a manner sympathetic to the different mentality involved. For the pre-European aborigine, the concept of self seems focused less on the person than on a complicated set of interlocking relationships that were indissolubly linked with the land. Those interwoven interrelationships, with their sense of deep identification with the land, are summed up in the beautiful and evocative Australian expression, the Dreaming. Likewise, the pattern of aboriginal life had been laid down, fixed and forever, in a mythical creation era dubbed the Dreamtime.

In the words of a student of aboriginal culture, Jennifer Isaacs:

According to Aboriginal belief, all life as it is known today, human, animal, bird and fish, is part of one unchanging, interconnected system, one vast network of relationships which can be traced back to the great Spirit Ancestors of the Dreamtime, Alcheringa or Tjukurpa.

Anthropologists Ronald and Catherine Berndt echo the same message:

All human and other beings are believed to share a common life-essence, derived from the major creative spirits—the original creators. . . . It seems that a binding "social" relationship was established and maintained in supra-kin terms, with each person, mainly through "gunmugugur" territorial group membership. Through this channel in particular man kept the same, sacred essence held by the major beings.

Aborigines saw themselves not simply in terms of bloodlines or families, but deeply and inseparably united with the wider context of the social group and, beyond that, the whole mythic structure of life.

Hence Aborigines were never isolated; they saw themselves as acting with others, and the bonds of kinship were extended outward embracing the nonhuman and nonempirical world.

This sense of belonging shows up clearly in aboriginal attitudes toward their totems. As Ronald Berndt has noted:

A mythic symbol [a totem], in the form of a creature or some associated manifestation, animates a foetus, bringing with it a life force emanating from the Dreaming. This symbol [totem] . . . serves as an agent, a manifestation of that bond. In doing so, it underlines the belief that he or she has the same spiritual quality as a particular mythic being and is closely identified with that being.

The evidence suggests that aboriginal consciousness was, in an important sense, unitary, communal, collective—the identity of the individual being merged into nature and subsumed by the group, often symbolized by its totem.

What is true of aborigines was true of other archaic cultures, widely separated in space and time. As Hick notes:

> The generality of [primitive] men and women saw themselves as parts of a collective social organism whose life continued on earth out of an indefinite past and into an indefinite future: as individuals perished and went down into the underworld others were born and the life of the tribe went on. What we call the soul was originally vaguely thought of as a larger life embodied in the successive members of the group. Durkheim expressed this by saying that "the soul is nothing other than the totemic principle incarnate in each individual" and at death this individualised life returned to the tribal collective.

It is important to be clear as to what this means. The human species evolved, according to recent estimates, between one and two million years ago. For most of that period, human societies were organized on a communal tribal basis in which the rights of the individual were subordinate to the overriding rights of the group. This clan-based hunter-gatherer lifestyle did not fade out until some eight thousand years ago (or later). Thus, for well over 99 percent of human evolution, men and women, tightly bonded and mutually interdependent in the natural unit of the group, had no strongly developed consciousness of individual identity, no sharp sense of a separate ego-self.

This evidence suggests strongly that, on one side of the fracture in consciousness that I referred to earlier lies a communal consciousness. The question then becomes, *When* did this communal consciousness fragment into the sense of separate ego? American psychologist Julian Jaynes has suggested that identity in its fully developed ego-self form did not appear until about the second millennium B.C. Jaynes bases this view on a study of early writing like *The Iliad* (written about three thousand years ago). He notes that *The Iliad* contains no clear references to concepts such as mind, thoughts, or feelings. In Homer's writings, human actions were a result not of human self-will, but of external forces directed by gods. This view is consistent with aboriginal tradition in which the actions of the individual drew their inspiration and authority from the mythological spirit ancestors of the Dreamtime.

If this view is essentially correct—and I believe it is—we must conclude that the self-conscious ego, the lodestone of identity and ambition, emerged at roughly the time when a vigorous urban life was springing up 4,000–8,000 years ago, at the dawn of recorded history. By a different route, we again arrive at the same conclusion: The beginnings of a sophisticated, symbol-rich, written language correlate with the origins of self-consciousness. To a significant degree, one made the other possible.

We now come to the second test. Does this fracture in consciousness about 4,000–8,000 years ago show up in the predicted form as a congruent shift in man's perception of time? Look again at aboriginal life. One of the first things that strikes us about aboriginal thinking is that it was not time-structured. It was a continuum in which the rigid boundaries between subject and object, past and future, which typify European attitudes, did not exist, because they had never developed. Australian anthropologist W. Stanner came close to capturing the spirit of this timeless community consciousness when he remarked of aboriginal totems: "A totem is an abstract symbol for the possible membership, over all space and time, of the sets of people symbolised by it—the dead, the living, the unborn."

This is only one element of a further, deeper difference. This Dreaming period of human consciousness was characterized by a concept of time so alien to modern Western man that he finds it hard to grasp. Dreaming time is, in a fundamental sense, *cyclic*. Each major event or activity is a repetition of a mythic prototype, created in and sanctified by the enduring pattern of the past. Nothing is lived; everything is relived.

The cyclicity of archaic time can be illustrated by myths based on the moon, which were common in prehistoric cultures. The moon was used to measure time (even today the Jewish calendar, or *luach*, is based on the lunar cycle, not the solar cycle, and our word "month" comes from "moon"). Archaic man watched the moon wax and wane, then disappear for three nights only to reappear and repeat the cycle. (On the third day, it "rises again from the dead.") In this lunar cycle, he divined a basic rhythm of renewal, which was powerfully reinforced by the other great environmental cycles. These cyclic "clocks of nature" gave him a stable conception of reality, which was essentially infinite in its duration—everything that is, has been and shall be again. Mircea Eliade, an expert in the history of religions, summed up the significance of this elegantly when he said: "The primitive, by conferring a cyclic direction upon time, annuls its irreversibility."

The great circular Stone Age "clocks," like Stonehenge, almost certainly served to formalize and symbolize this sense of cyclic repetition. By aligning the megaliths with the varying positions of the sun and moon, the circle of stones mapped out the stable structure of cyclic time, enabling priests to identity dates for religious rites year after year, age after age.

The changes that occurred in human consciousness about 4,000–8,000 years ago had a profound influence on this immemorial sense of cyclic time. As mankind abandoned the hunter-gatherer lifestyle and began to congregate into settled groups, social specializations emerged. The leaders of the community needed to keep records—tallies of harvests, head counts of fighting men, computations of taxes, etc. Along with the beginnings of written language came the first means of keeping permanent count. Even today, the symbol for three in languages as divergent as Chinese and Latin is three lines in parallel: upright (Latin) representing three fingers, or lengthwise (Chinese) representing three sticks. They are true language fossils.

A special caste arose—the scribes, or people who wrote things down. It cannot be coincidence that it was those scribes who became the priests. The priests were intimately concerned with the measurement of time because they owed their position and their power to the practical necessity to keep written records.

This is what distinguishes the priests of Sumeria and Egypt from the Stone Age priests who encoded the secrets of the skies in their megalithic clocks. Both groups kept records of astronomical patterns. However, the Druidic priests of Stonehenge maintained the continuity of their tradition by word of mouth, whereas the priests of Egypt maintained theirs by inscribing symbols on stone or papyrus. The difference is crucial. By perusing their written records, the priests of Egypt were able to see that each year, while similar in outline to its precedessor, differed to a greater or lesser degree in detail. Furthermore, writing enabled the dates of disasters like floods or portents like comets to be pinpointed in time. It is impossible to record dissimilar, nonrepetitive events like these without gaining a sense of *linear time.*

During the unlettered Dreaming ages, the past had been vague, indefinite, unsequenced, and unsequenceable. When a North American Indian wished to refer to an event outside his immediate past experience, he simply said "many moons ago." Priests possessing a written record had a different time sense. From their records, a dim "map" of the past slowly emerged; an impression of fickle novelty, a dawning sense of the irreversibility of time.

Thus it was the priests of Egypt and Sumeria who developed the first great calendar civilizations. In so doing, in a quite fundamental sense, they created "history"—they were the first men and women to see time on a larger scale than the individual lifetime, the first human beings to gain that sense of past perspective that we take for granted.

It is probably not a coincidence that these Semitic peoples developed the religions of revelation, in which God intervenes directly in history. Moses received the Ten Commandments at a fixed point in time. Christ died on the cross at a fixed point in time, which caused Christians to divide history into two segments, B.C. and A.D. The sense of linear time engendered by the religions of revelation—Judaism, Christianity, and Islam—was a result of their singular, goal-oriented character—history was directed toward a consummatory finality, the coming of the Messiah, the Battle of Armageddon; time was heading in a straight line toward a climax.

The passing of the old order was marked out in another way. During the Dreaming ages, the gods of humanity had been overwhelmingly female. An examination of the myths that have come down to us from the period of cyclic time show a focus on the cult of the Earth Mother or Earth Goddess in her various and manifold forms. With the arrival of linear time, the gods of our Western heritage suddenly took on a male character—Zeus for the Greeks, Yahweh for the Hebrews. The Almighty became, not the familiar and fertile Mother Figure, but the distant and judgmental "Our Father, who art in Heaven."

Memories of this dichotomy remain with us today, encoded in the very words we use. The words "material" and "matter" come from the same root as the Latin *mater* or "mother" and still have a lingering sense of the earth about them. The word "rational" comes from the Latin *ratio* and is conspicuously applied to the logical processes of science, which, until recently, have been a largely male preserve. Even now there is a tendency to describe female behavior as "irrational" or intuitive.

So yet again we come back to that fracture in consciousness that occurred about five thousand years ago—and the deeper meaning of the myth of the expulsion from Eden. What the legend of the Fall truly commemorates is the trauma of that forgotten moment when man first stepped out of the Dreaming and into time.

The evidence, then, converges toward a time about 4,000–8,000 years ago as marking out a change of state in human evolution, a transfiguration of psychology, whose consequences reverberate down to the present day. At this Rubicon in time, the quality of consciousness was irreversibly altered by several developments so interwoven and interdependent that it is impossible to tease them apart. Man learned to externalize the inner workings of his mind, in symbols, on impressionable materials like clay, thereby fashioning a mirror to his own consciousness. From this came, I believe, a sense of ego-self, an ability to build a representational model of his own mental processes and so perceive himself in the act of perception. The pivotal role of language shows through clearly here, for it is language that defines "structure," creating thought by giving it form.

Thought was the new vehicle of evolution. As the hunter-gatherer lifestyle was replaced by city life, new possibilities, new concepts, were born at an accelerating rate. The newly emerging ego did not operate in the old world of direct perception; increasingly it operated in the new world of symbols, a world in which more and more verbal images came to represent ideas (like "work," "truth," "guilt," "God") that had no concrete existence outside the mind. The outer life of physical action was replaced by an inner life of conceptualization, and that inner life acquired a reality, a momentum, of its own. In this process, the modern psyche was born, able to project backward in time through memory, and forward in time through prediction, simultaneously liberated and trapped by the power of its own symbols, focused always on the convenient fiction it had invented to impose order on the world, the sense of "I."

This transfiguration carried a heavy price tag. As the communal Dreaming of Eden faded, as the sense of shared necessity gave way to the sense of competitive individuality, the ego-self felt itself alone and vulnerable. For the first time, it saw and recognized a new and terrible image: the specter of death.

Implicit in my argument so far is yet another consequence of the "fracture in consciousness," the Fall. It is impossible profoundly to change the human attitude to self and time without causing an equally profound change in the human attitude to death.

Evidence of human attitudes to death during the Stone Age period can be found in the surviving traditions of contemporary peoples who, until recently, still practiced the hunter-gatherer lifestyle. What is striking about these beliefs is that archaic man had no conception of death as the inevitable lot of all flesh. It was not that he did not see death—he observed death in himself and other creatures far more than modern man. It was that the Stone Age mind seemed unable to grasp the fact that a person who died could simply cease to exist. The faces of dead people remained real in the dreams of their relatives, and they remained alive in memory; that seemed axiomatically to imply some continuity of ongoing life somewhere else; i.e., it implied an afterlife.

This inability to grasp the fact of human mortality harks back to a topic I raised at the end of Chapter 3. There we saw that most living creatures do not die in the sense of growing old and wearing out. The same was true of neolithic man. During the hunter-gatherer period, the human species was still part of the natural order. The average life expectancy was, according to some estimates, no more than eighteen years. That means that human populations were kept in a state of perpetual youth by the same culling mechanisms that remove weak or unfit members of animal species in the wild. Death when it came was likely to be due to some violent cause, not to the full working out of the aging process (which may have been extremely rare). In these circumstances, death was often attributed to magical causes, to the work of evil or malevolent spirits.

This attitude is clearly illustrated by the aborigines. Aboriginal life is inseparable from the life of the land and from the complex, stable set of relationships among men, animals, and inanimate things incorporated in the term "the Dreaming." Since the forces of nature are part of the Dreaming, they cannot be held responsible for the death of an individual; death therefore has to be caused by some antagonism toward the dead man on the part of a living person or a ghost.

One quality of the Dreaming that is particularly relevant in the present context has been aptly summed up by the Berndts:

> It is rather that the land is him/her in spiritual terms. It cannot be removed from him/her—not even by death, since this concept is relevant to both past and present generations and the spiritual part of man/land is considered as being eternal, returning on death for *recycling*, to the mythic beings concerned.

This passage is revealing, as it shows us a key element of the Dreaming— the relationship between man's attitude to death and cyclic time. In a real and literal sense, primitive man could not fear death as a phenomenon because, in his experience of things, *nothing died.*

Time was cyclic, and so was life. Life was the great cycle. Grass sprouted in spring, grew green in summer, withered in autumn, died in winter, but always returned again next spring. This was the observed pattern, the never-challenged truth of the world. This was the ancient and reassuring promise of renewal. Was man the exception? Of course not. Immersed in nature, primitive man felt himself pulse with the seasons; his myths reflected their cyclicity, his lifestyle was based on their rhythms.

However, the fracture in consciousness that broke the protecting walls of Eden brought death into this instinctual world. When cyclic time was replaced by linear time, the newly born ego had, for the first time, to face the inescapable truth of its own mortality. I repeat the last words of the preceding chapter: "When the ego was born, death entered consciousness; the serpent came into Eden." Death was the first fruit of that tree of knowledge whereof the first (ego-conscious) man ate.

We are fortunate to have a memory of this "phase transition" in the Assyrian folk legend called *The Epic of Gilgamesh,* written, significantly, over four thousand years ago. The best-known version of this ancient myth is preserved on twelve clay tablets from the library of Ashurnasirpal at Nineveh. The details of the story do not matter. What matters is Gilgamesh's confrontation with the fact of his own mortality:

Enkidu, I weep for you like a wailing woman. You were the axe by my side, the sword in my belt, the shield before me. *I will also die and worms will feast on my flesh. I now fear death and have lost all my courage.*

This short fragment speaks to us across the centuries with a poignantly contemporary sadness. It opens a window into the human psyche in the Middle East at a critical time in its evolution. Note how Gilgamesh is forced to face his own death by observing the death of someone close to him. Note, too, how he relates this to himself: "I will also die . . . I now fear death." This is the ego-self speaking, not the collective consciousness of the tribe.

In Gilgamesh's dilemma, we see the pre-Western psyche tremble on the edge of the precipice. The same sense of deep loss, of a Fall, is what gives the myth of the expulsion from Eden its potency and its power.

How did Western psychology survive the psychic crisis embodied in this Fall from innocence, the triple shock that resulted from this sudden inbreaking awareness of self, time, and death? The answer is, I believe, relatively simple. So far, I have referred only fleetingly to the supporting roles played by human beliefs—myths—in the maintenance of the psychological integrity of the feedback loop described in Chapter 1 (see Figures 1.1 to 1.3). We now reach a point where it is no longer possible to ignore the pivotal function of what I will loosely call religion. To advance matters farther, I must now bring my argument full-circle, by returning to this key point.

During the Dreaming, the human race evolved a fascinating variety of religions, of myths, which explained man's origins, his fate, his future, and which gave meaning to his life and patterned his behavior. In our secular culture, we have forgotten the power of myth; we tend to lose sight of the fact that each major age of history has drawn its coherence, its identity, from some deep story that both informs its culture and underpins its social structure.

Thus to see why the psyche survived its Fall, we need to examine the powerful role(s) played by myth. And when we do so, we find something unexpected, something strange. The advent of linear time (with its associated elements of self and death) modified but did not—could not—destroy a central feature of the Dreaming, a feature that is universal in the human species because its deep roots in our minds reach far, far back in time, beyond our human origins: the concept of regenerative renewal—rebirth.

5

THE FACE IN
THE MIRROR

In 1923, Lebanese poet-philosopher Kahlil Gibran wrote a book called *The Prophet,* which has become enormously popular in the West because of the evocative power of its words and images. In the concluding paragraph, the Prophet speaks the following words:

> Forget not that I shall come back to you.
> A little while, and my longing shall gather dust and foam for another body.
> A little while, a moment of rest upon the wind, and another woman shall bear me.

Here is a twentieth-century restatement of one of the oldest—perhaps *the* oldest—human beliefs, the concept of rebirth. Although I do not believe in any form of personal reincarnation (as this chapter will make clear), the concept raises a paradox that we will encounter again in this book: that to understand the end, one must understand the beginning; to know death, we must first know birth.

Birth plays a fundamental role in what we think and what we are. Yet few people realize how fundamental that role is. If you ask yourself, "What is my earliest memory?" the answer is likely to be something you may be able to trace to the first or second year of life. I have a sharply defined memory of my mother's face bending over what I assume was my cot, but I can't precisely place that memory in time. The point I am making is that if memory goes back close to the moment of birth, why should we reject the idea that our brains record some imprint of life in the womb itself?

During the fifth and sixth months of development, a fetus begins to sleep and wake just like a newborn child. By the eighth month of embryonic life, a human baby is a developed individual—if it is born prematurely, it can usually survive. Facial expressions occur—squinting, frowning, and the mechanism of the sucking reflex is established. Most important, although considerable development takes place after birth, the brain is basically established in its adult format shortly before birth. Electrical activity (brain waves) can be recorded in the cerebral cortex of the fetus, from about the seventh month onward.

Complementing the biological evidence is the important work of transpersonal psychologist Stan Grof, which suggests that patients can "relive" the birth experience under the influence of LSD. Thus I believe that one can say with some confidence that subliminal memory extends back, beyond birth, to the unborn state.

Consider what that means. Intrauterine memories, the base on which all later recollections will be imprinted, are unique in experience. The fetus is encased in a warm universe of water, its needs completely satisfied by its mother's body, which provides nutrients and oxygen as required. This universe is globally dark and unconditionally safe. It is the primal state of the human mind, its genesis "dreaming."

From this perspective, examine the "deep structure" of the genesis myths of the human species. In the genesis myth of the Old Testament, for example, the universe was originally *formless*, and "darkness was upon the face of the deep. And the Spirit of God moved upon the face of the waters." These images are highly suggestive of the fetal state. Is it possible that the genesis myths of our kind are merely personal genesis writ large, the dim origin of self magnified into a cosmic theme?

This hypothesis makes a testable prediction because it carries the consequence that fetal images like primordial darkness, formlessness, ancestral water, should be encoded not just in the Judeo-Christian tradition but universally, since all human beings undergo a common rite of passage into the world.

What do the data say? The ancient Egyptians thought of the world as a bank of earth surrounded by the Great Circular Ocean. This watery mass had its origin in a vast primordial Abyss of Waters, personified by the god Nu (Nun), the source of all. The Papyrus of Nes-Menu (312 B.C.) contains a genesis myth that may date back to the third millennium B.C. In this myth, Nu says:

> I am the creator of what hath come into being, that is to say, I formed myself out of the primeval matter, and I made myself out of the substance which existed in primeval time.

Egyptologist J. M. Plumley states that the "basic principle of Egyptian cosmology may therefore be said to be the primeval waters, which existed before the beginning." The same motif appears in the Sumerian Enuma Elish (second to third millennium B.C.):

> And the primeval Apsu, who begat them
> And chaos, Tiamet, the mother of them both.
> Their *waters* were mingled together. [Italics added]

Egyptian, Sumerian, and Jewish traditions spring from a common cultural root, so the appearance of a common thread in their creation mythology is not surprising. The argument becomes much more convincing when the net is more widely cast. In the Sanskrit Rig Veda, the Hymn of Creation says:

> There was no air, no sky that is beyond it.
> What was concealed? Wherein? In whose protection?
> And was there deep unfathomable *water*?
> Without distinctive marks, this was all *water*.[Italics added]

In the Americas, the creation myth of the Lenape Indians (the Walam Olum) states that at first "water was everywhere." Turning to the Polynesian branch of the human family, one notes that the Maoris of New Zealand believed in a supreme god, Io. The description of the creation of the universe by Io is significant:

Io dwelt within the breathing space of immensity.
The universe was in *darkness*, with *water* everywhere.
There was no glimmer of dawn, no clearness, no light.

The Australian aborigines exemplify a culture that developed in virtual isolation from other strands of the human race (their colonization of Australia may date back well over forty thousand years). Yet even here the same telltale motif appears. In the creation myth of the Karraru tribe of South Australia, we find:

Once the earth was completely *dark* and silent.
Nothing moved upon its barren surface.

In other words, in this isolated tradition, the emphasis on primordial water is absent, but the emphasis on primordial darkness remains.

Turning from intrauterine life to birth itself, the process of birth provides the most dramatic and traumatic crisis that the mind will ever encounter. Birth is intensely painful—the bruising on a baby's head as it is forced by the muscular contractions of the mother's uterus to pass through a channel much too small for it is evidence of that. In considering birth, we are immediately confronted with yet another layer of meaning in the myth of the Fall, for the story of human expulsion from some arcadian state (Garden of Eden) is deeply related, I believe, to the shock of this apocalyptic mechanism that brings each human individual out of a safe world into an uncertain one. The myth of the Fall thus has a twofold significance: As we have seen, it also symbolizes man's expulsion from the Dreamtime into history.

At the risk of exaggerating my point, I invite the reader to consider the extent of this transition. Initially, all the developing brain has ever known is warmth, darkness, and, above all, security; encased in a self-contained universe, it is weightless, like an astronaut in a space capsule equipped with a guaranteed life-support system. Then, in the space of a few hours or less, this safe enclosed world is transformed and reworked in a way and on a scale that will never be repeated during the whole life process. There is intense pain, and noises, unknown and unknowable, break in from all sides. The force of gravity pulls the infant down as its body struggles to adjust for the first time to its own weight. The lungs labor to take their first breath of an alien element, air, after the security of the primal element, water, in which life itself was "born" three and a half billion years ago, and in which it has existed for all but the last few hundred million years.

Truly, the child has been expelled from Eden. It is small wonder that some of our most fundamental myths have a permanently retrospective character—a kind of psychological crick in the neck, as they look forever backward at this Paradise Lost.

Above all, the birth process lives out the creation dictum "Let there be light," as the eyes of the newborn perceive for the first time the brightness of the sun's radiance. The power of light to activate the creation process is a near-universal motif of most creation myths. For example, in the folklore of the Karraru aborigines, the Dreamtime myth quoted earlier continues:

> Inside a deep cave below the Nullarbor Plain slept a beautiful woman, *the Sun*. The Great Father Spirit gently woke her and told her to emerge from the cave and *stir the universe into life*.

Similarly, in the Maori creation myth mentioned previously, Io begins the creative process by saying:

> Darkness became a light-possessing darkness
> and at once *light appeared*.

I am not saying that cultural myths like those of the creation and the expulsion of Adam and Eve from the Garden of Eden arose from actual physical memories of life in the womb and the crisis of birth. My hypothesis is that these early brain imprints provide a mental "mold" that predisposes myths to evolve particular configurations of symbolic imagery that strike deeply responsive chords in psychology.

A personal experience may give some insight into the nature of this responsiveness. I remember, when I was a boy, walking along a deserted beach north of Auckland, New Zealand. It was a wild day. The wind was up, and the waves came curling shoreward, row after row, bottle-green and lipped with foam, to break on the rocky headland where I stood. It was a scene that should have unsettled me with its image of repetitive destruction, wave-forms being ceaselessly created offshore only to die in white ruin on the black fangs of coastal rock. Instead, it gave me a sense of inner peace I remember to this day. Why? Could it be that the repeated surge of the surf reverberated down the recesses of my mind, reactivating some memory deeply embedded in my first moments of unremembered time when, as a baby in my mother's womb, I listened to the repeated thunder of her heart, secure in the dark sealike safety of that Edenic paradise?

In his fascinating essay "The Amniotic Universe," American astronomer and author Carl Sagan suggests that the popularity of baptism springs from its use of "holy water" to bring about a "rebirth" of the spirit. Another echo of our common origin in the womb.

Religions have a strong mystical element that seeks to reunite the individual with some cosmic spirit, some universal source of power and safety, some vision of divinity. Could this be, as Sagan suggests, the expression of some atavistic urge to reverse the process of separation by which we come into the world? Are the basic forms of our religious yearnings encoded in our minds as archetypes, allowing a rich diversity of detail to emerge in response to differing environmental conditions, but only within the universal boundary conditions set by our common brain-biology heritage? I believe the answer is yes. We all carry imprints of our personal beginnings, a not-quite-forgotten sense of primordial waters and, at the root of our being, the echo of an ancient darkness.

Granted that the experience of birth provides the initial setting for the development of our psychology, does postbirth experience modify this in a predictable way? Of course it does. The transition from dark (in the womb) to light (in the open) is reinforced every twenty-four hours by the alternating cycle of night and day. Each night we return to darkness, and normally we return to a fetal state of consciousness; i.e., we sleep (although we are dimly aware of our own mental processes through dreams). Each morning the light returns and our brains activate to the waking state of consciousness; we are reborn.

It is important to be clear about the biological basis of this fundamental periodicity in our psychologies. Our brains have a day/night switch located in the tiny, pineal gland that sits atop the brain's stem. The absence of light activates the switch, while its presence flips it off. Thus during the night the switch is on and the pineal secretes a hormone called melatonin, which reaches its maximum concentration during the hours of darkness. Melatonin affects mood in an as yet ill-defined way. (Have you noticed how irritable or depressed you tend to feel on gray days?) During the day, the switch is off, and melatonin levels fall.

The inhibition of melatonin production during daytime is somehow brought about by the suprachiasmatic nucleus we encountered in the preceding chapter. As we have seen, nerve cells in this center fire in an amazingly regular sequence, like a clock ticking. This innate timing device seems to be set by the external day/night cycle through a wisp of nerve fibers that provide a connection between the optic nerves and the suprachiasmatic center. Morning light falling on the eyes may thus calibrate the mind's internal clock so that it beats in synchrony with the diurnal pulse of nature.

Melatonin has a profound and ancient association with the light/dark rhythms of nature. In sparrows, injections of melatonin induce the nighttime activity of roosting. In other species, artificial shading of the pineal can prevent seasonal enlargement of the ovaries, i.e., reproductive changes that correlate with long periods of extended light or dark. Thus the pineal gland, the so-called third eye, regulated in some way by the suprachiasmatic nucleus, seems to function as a biological timekeeper.

A more significant insight can be gained by monitoring brain activity through a device called an electroencephalogram (EEG). EEG data show fundamental differences in patterns of brain activity between sleeping and waking, i.e., between night and day. At night, when we sleep, the EEG records a regular, rhythmic sequence of brain waves of relatively low frequency. These are called delta waves. Delta waves occur much of the time in infants, who spend long periods asleep. During deep sleep, the brain generates a higher frequency pattern, which is associated with a rapid twitching of the eyes (hence the term *REM*, or *rapid eye movement, sleep*). Significantly, ultrasound imaging techniques show that such REM activity occurs constantly in unborn babies. Is that because the fetal brain is initially attuned only to its primal darkness, its original dreaming state, and slowly learns to adjust to the activating effects of sunlight?

When we are fully awake, brain waves take a different and more complex form. Simplistically, when we are awake but relaxed, the EEC records a slow, regular pattern called an alpha wave. When we become excited or alert, the pattern changes again into a more complicated sequence of small, rapidly fluctuating waves called a beta wave pattern.

The brain, then, reveals through its electrical activity, several quite different states, which are strongly correlated with night and day. The basis of our consciousness is cyclic and repetitive. After ten years of life, a child has experienced about 3,650 day/night cycles. Its psychology has been totally and irreversibly structured in terms of this periodicity; it accepts unconsciously, instinctively, that light follows dark.

This periodic and reiterative structure of consciousness is encoded in our very speech. The Latin prefix *re* usually has the sense of "again." Can it be coincidence that the words we use to describe our fundamental myths and activities are not things we do, but things we do again?

> *re*production
> *re*presentation
> *re*cognition
> *re*surrection
> *re*demption
> *re*incarnation
> *re*birth

Even the word *re*ligion may fit this pattern: one of its possible meanings is "bind (join) again." In the Christian tradition, we are told that Christ "rose again from the dead," despite the fact that the resurrection of his body was supposedly a unique affair.

Taken together, these facts tell us something quite fundamental—that there is a natural and inevitable association between the concept of an afterlife and the enduring legacy of cyclic time. Far from being an inno-vation or an invention, the religious idea of rebirth, of life (light) after death (dark), is an expression of one of the oldest aspects of life on earth. Most "higher" creatures exhibit daily circadian rhythms (from Latin *circa* meaning "about," and *dies* meaning "day"). It is possible to isolate mu-tants of the common fruit fly in which the clock governing these innate cycles no longer runs in twenty-four-hour intervals. The gene governing that clock has now been identified and shown to be virtually the same in chickens, mice, and humans. As the definitive text *The Molecular Biology of the Gene* notes significantly: "The inescapable conclusion is that we human beings, proud possessors of sophisticated intelligence, will find that our behavior is governed to some extent by elementary biochemical reactions."

Thus resurrection and reincarnation have been successful in gaining adherents because they correspond to the way our brains work. In an important sense, the rebirth of the self is a memory, not a prediction— by the time we die, our mind clocks will have recorded, on average, about 27,000 successive "rebirths." This kind of calculation becomes more com-pelling if we extend it to cover not just the course of a human life, but the course of life on earth. The mind clock carries a memory of approx-imately 1.4 trillion day/night cycles—the number of times the earth has turned on its axis since life began. No single feature of life's environment has impressed itself more strongly on the basic character of biological systems than this repetitive process, which has synchronized outer and inner time. Indeed, as I indicated in the previous chapter, our very sense of time is, I believe, partly a product of this profound imprinting.

Environmental cycles of day and month and year have become inter-nalized in the workings of the human brain. The environmental clocks have become neural clocks. It is hardly surprising, then, that primitive man, in his quest to find order in the world around him, has reversed this process, externalizing these cycles, basing his religions on the rhythms of the earth because they resonated so comfortingly with the rhythms of his mind.

At the risk of overkill, let me repeat that the human experience was (and is) dark (night) always followed by light (day). Long periods of dark-ness (winter months) are always followed by long periods of light (summer months). The chemical and electrical patterns of our brains reflect and reinforce this oscillatory character of nature. Hence, inevitably, death has become identified with sleep, to be followed (as our most basic experience "proves"), by awakening.

I could cite thousands of examples from the traditions of many cultures, but a few familiar quotes show how profoundly this link between death and sleep influences us:

> I gaze on him and say: he is not dead
> But *sleeps*, and soon he will arise and take
> Me by the hand, I know he will *awake*
> And smile on me as he did yesterday.
>
> —Jerome Bell

> To sleep, perchance to dream, aye there's the rub;
> For in that *sleep of death* what dreams may come,
> When we have shuffled off this mortal coil . . .
>
> —William Shakespeare, *Hamlet*

> Resurrection to come is the first fruits of those *who have fallen asleep*.
>
> —1 Corinthians 15:20

Are these ideas mere speculation, or can they, in any meaningful way, be tested? I believe a test is possible. If the deep structure of these religious beliefs reflects innate patterns, which are universally encoded in the human brain, then, according to my thesis, myths embodying these basic motifs should have appeared independently over and over again during the course of human evolution, in cultures that developed in isolation. (Isolated, independent development means that a myth originating in one culture is unlikely to cross-contaminate others.)

The death-and-resurrection motif is a case in point. Myths built around the idea of rebirth permeate religious traditions in cultures as far apart in space and time as the aborigines of Australia, the Hindus of India, the peoples of ancient Egypt, and the Jews of Palestine. From a global perspective, perhaps the two most successful rebirth myths are those of Osiris in Egypt and Jesus in Israel.

Osiris was the son of Nut, the sky goddess, and Geb, the earth god. He married his sister Isis and reigned over earth in a paradisic time of peace and justice. Osiris was killed by his jealous brother Set. He was eventually found by Isis, but Set rediscovered the body, dismembered it, and scattered it throughout Egypt. Isis successfully reassembled the fragments, with the exception of the penis. At that point, the sun god Re sent Anubis, the jackal-headed god, to supervise the putting together of Osiris's body, which was wrapped in its own skin. Hence images of Osiris show him clothed in a shroud that covers his legs and his hands crossed on his chest. Isis and another sister, Nephthys, brought Osiris back to life by waving their arms to fan breath back into the mummy. Thus Osiris was born again, but as lord of the dead.

When an ancient Egyptian died, he or she *became* Osiris. When members of Howard Carter's famous expedition broke into the tomb of Tutankhamen, they found gold plaques, carrying speeches of welcome from the gods to the young king as he entered the underworld. These clearly show the identification of the dead king with the god of the dead. Thus Nut, the Divine Mother, says: "Thy members are firm, thou smellest the air and goest out as a God, going out as Atum, *O Osiris Tutankhamen.*"[Italics added]

In the living Egyptian religion, people saw the resurrection of Osiris as a pledge that they would live forever, provided their survivors did for them what the gods had done for the body of Osiris. Thus the ceremonies performed over the dead human body were exact copies of those performed by Anubis and other gods over the dead body of Osiris.

The intimate relationship between the basic day/night brain cycle and the saga of death and rebirth in ancient Egypt is powerfully shown in the union of Osiris, Lord of the Dead, with Re, the sun god. One can see the link clearly in the reconstructed burial ritual of Tutankhamen. After the young king's body had been mummified and encased in its golden shell, ceremony focused on resurrection—the rebirth of the dead god.

Rather than recount this ceremony, which was exceedingly complex, I will quote passages from the elegant description by Egyptologist Christiane Desroches-Noblecourt, which clearly show how deeply the day/night cycle shaped the Egyptian concept of rebirth after death. Thus:

At the end of his arduous search for survival, the dead Osiris would appear *in the aspect of the rising sun, Re.*

The graves of the masters of Thebes repeated the dramatic story *of the sun's gestation and its rebirth* at the fifth hour.

Emulating the sun, the king was to draw from the world of the dead renewed strength *for his morning rebirth.*

There remained the last act of the drama: *rebirth.* The room the excavators called the annex was entirely dedicated to this, and its door, *which faces East,* suggests that it was deliberately orientated in this direction to favour the pharaoh's rising.

After his transformations Osiris the King was to spring from the horizon as *Re, star of day.*

What could be clearer?

Experts on religion may object that the pharaohs were god-kings, hence the mode of their burial is not representative of the common faith of ancient Egypt. That may be true as regards the grandeur of the burial ceremonies, but the indestructible link between Egyptian belief in an afterlife and the image of the sun goes back to the roots of Egyptian life. Listen to this hymn to the sun god Re by an unknown Egyptian.

> O all you gods of the Soul-mansion who judge sky and earth in the balance, who give food and provisions; O Tatenen, Unique One, creator of mankind; O Southern, Northern, Western and Eastern Enneads, give praise to Re, Lord of the Sky, the Sovereign who made the Gods. Worship him in his goodly shape when he appears in the Day-bark.

Echoes of this ancient belief persist into the modern age. During the First World War, soldiers spoke of their dead comrades as having "gone West," i.e., followed the setting sun. Similarly, some of our most popular hymns retain day/night symbolism:

And with the dawn those angel faces smile
That I have loved long since and lost awhile.

—Cardinal Newman, "Lead Kindly Light"

Is this, one wonders, one reason why they are so well-beloved?

The antiquity of the idea of rebirth and its deep association with the day/night cycle is shown in the idea of reincarnation. Whereas the religions of the Middle East show rebirth as a once-only affair, the older faiths of India show it in its repetitive form, which corresponds more closely to the underlying biological reality. In Indian tradition, the soul is repeatedly reborn: Each death is followed by new life, just as each night is followed by new day, each winter by new spring.

Thus in the *Bhagavad Gita* of the Aryan Indians, the lord Shri Krishna says:

At the *dawning* of that day all objects in manifestation stream forth from the Unmanifest, and, when *evening* falls, they are dissolved into It again.

The same multitude of beings, which have lived on earth so often, all are dissolved as the *night* of the universe approaches, to issue forth anew when *morning* breaks. Thus it is ordained.

Perhaps the most telling trace of the age-old association between God and the sun survives in language. Our word "divine" stems from the Latin word for God, *deus*. But this in turn evolved from the Latin word *dies*, meaning "day" (daylight). English and Latin are both branches of the Indo-European root language in which *dei* meant to shine or be luminous. Thus the symbolism of sun worship has remained encoded in speech long after men have ceased to deify the sun in practice (of course the word "deify" comes from the same, ancient source). Likewise, the holy day of the Christian week is still referred to as *Sun*day. The head of Jesus on church frescoes and stained-glass windows is often shown surrounded by a luminous halo, showing how a symbol of the sun has become identified with the central figure of Christian belief. And the date of Christmas,

December 25, coincides closely with the winter solstice in the Northern Hemisphere.

It is small wonder that the Swiss psychologist Carl Jung described rebirth as "an affirmation that must be counted on among the primordial affirmations of mankind."

The birth experience suggests at least some of the archetypal forms in which religions stabilize, for the most part, mirror biological processes built into some of the oldest parts of our minds. To see how far we can travel down this road of discovery, consider another myth that has exercised an enormous influence over human psychology for centuries—the concepts of heaven and hell, as portrayed in Christian teaching and elsewhere.

Brain biologist Paul MacLean has put forward the attractive idea that the human brain is a composite structure, composed of three interlocking but distinct elements—three partly separate brains, each with its own software, its own input and output channels. The oldest is the reptilian brain. Next, layered above it, is the paleocortex, or limbic system; while layered above that is the neocortex (Figure 5.1).

In the context of this chapter, our attention focuses quickly on the limbic system. My emphasis so far has been on the cyclic nature of human behavior and the way this reflects brain chemistry. It goes much, much deeper. The limbic system (together with associated brain elements like the hypothalamus) is the engine of the so-called instincts, which MacLean has wryly described as the four Fs—feeding, fighting, fleeing, and fucking. This behavior is conspicuously cyclic and repetitive. In the rat, for example, food intake runs in a three-hour cycle, and recurring estrous (sexual) behavior has a four-day clock. The menstrual cycle of the human female has essentially the same periodicity as the phases of the moon, suggesting that these ancient parts of the brain have an internal clock that follows a monthly cycle like the moon, just as they have an internal clock that follows a daily cycle like the sun.

Instinctive behavior is governed by mechanisms of positive and negative reinforcement located in discrete sites in the limbic and hypothalamic systems of the brain. The experiments that demonstrate this are remarkable examples of the blending of physiology and behavior. A commonly used device is a Skinner box, i.e., a box in which a lab animal such as a

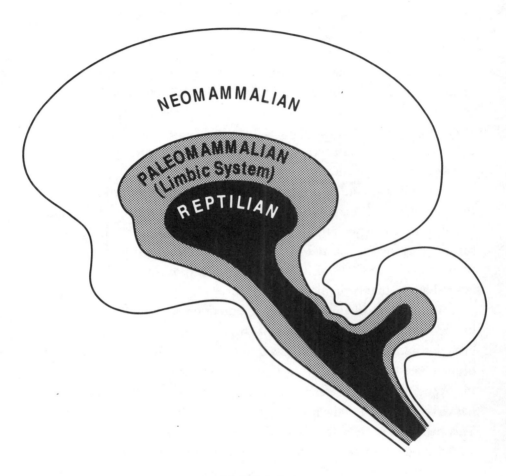

FIGURE 5.1

The prehuman part of our brains still listens to the beat of nature. According to brain biologist Paul MacLean, the human brain consists of three largely separate components, layered around each other like the skins of an onion. The outermost layer is our "thinking cap," the part that boasts the cerebral cortex, the seat of language, imagination, and reasoning skills. Under this lies the limbic system, which may be loosely thought of as the seat of emotions. These two layers enfold the ancient reptilian core common to all (higher) animals. These deep brain structures predate the human species by hundreds of millions of years: It is here that the brain still dances to the great cycles of nature, the alternating rhythm of day and night, the phases of the moon, the passage of the seasons.

rat pushes a lever to obtain a reward such as food or drink. Electrodes are implanted into the animal's brain so that when the creature presses the lever, it delivers a stimulus directly to that part of the brain in which the electrode is positioned.

Experiments with this technique have shown that there are antagonistic sites in the hypothalamic and limbic regions of the brain for the basic instincts of the four Fs. Stimulation of the positive center for eating activity will cause an animal to eat copiously, beyond the demands of its real needs, while stimulation of the negative center will cause the creature to starve to death in the presence of its normal food. Scientists have labeled these positive and negative reinforcement centers the reward and punishment centers. Animals with electrodes implanted in the reward center quickly learn to self-stimulate their brains in order to enjoy the reward sensation. In some cases, animals have stimulated themselves for twenty-four hours without rest, and the rate of self-stimulation has reached a figure of eight thousand impulses per hour. Conversely, animals with electrodes implanted in the punishment center work with equal dedication to switch off the inflow of current.

Deeply embedded in the mind, then, are dual programs that are exactly reciprocal in the sense that one arouses while the other diminishes the desire to consummate the drive in question, be it eating, fighting, or mating. These linked opposites are reflected in a wide range of contrasting human attributes: pleasure and pain (the primary feelings) and reward and punishment (the derived values).

Carried to an extreme, the primary feelings of pleasure and pain become intensive emotive hyperstates: ecstasy and agony. I believe these linked opposites find direct, unambiguous expression in two of our most fundamental myths, the opposing hereafters of heaven (bliss-reward) and hell (agony-punishment); they are also strongly linked to the contrasting opposites of good and evil. The concepts of heaven and hell do not have the universality that the idea of rebirth enjoys, but they are sufficiently pervasive to suggest a biological basis along the lines I have mapped out. The ancient Aryan Indians talked of the gods Indra and Soma hurling sinners down to hell, and Vedic scripture contains dark references to a black underground for "wrongdoers." The heaven/hell duality was also mirrored in and reinforced by the other great contrasting principles of human experience—day and night (again), male and female, hot and cold. Most religions contain some symbolism based on the duality of linked opposites—yin/yang (widespread in oriental religions), light/dark (Zoroastrianism), heaven/hell (Christianity).

Indeed, the farther one goes into this issue, the more one sees that much of human psychology has been molded around the innateness of linked opposites. That is evident in the either/or way we think, especially in the West. We see evidence of this all around us. A decision is either right or wrong; a business associate, either a good guy or a shark; an electron, either a wave or a particle; a person accused of a crime, either guilty or innocent. Yet these either/or judgments distort reality. Many years ago, I heard a radio play called (I think) *The Pinadus Affair*. It concerned a court judgment in which an individual called Pinadus was sentenced to death for murder. The moral of the play lay in its beautifully crafted climax, which showed how every character in the plot, from the judge who passed the sentence to a childhood friend of the accused who first planted the seed of violence in his mind, was in some degree guilty. No one was an island, and no act (hence no consequence of that act) could be judged in isolation, separate from the web of interactions that makes each one of us a confederate of the other. If Pinadus was guilty, so was every person who had shaped his life.

The deep structure of myth thus models the deep structure of the brain itself. This correlation gives a neuronal basis to the remarkable insights of Carl Jung. Jung suggested that all human beings inherit a collective unconscious by which the individual is linked not only to his own past but to the past of the species. Various expressions of that collective unconscious correspond to what Jung called archetypes. Australian psychologist Peter O'Connor describes archetypes as "the predisposition to act, the mould if you like, into which we pour specific images from life's experiences."

Jungian archetypes encode basic mythological motifs—the Magna Mater (Great Mother), the miraculous child, the hero/savior, etc. I can find no justification for the particular, explicit forms of these archetypes in my examination of brain biology, but I believe that Jung's concept of archetypal motifs is an elegant representation of what I have been trying to say in this chapter, that myths map the mind.

The Christian religion has always affirmed that man is made in the image of God. What this chapter suggests is that the converse is true—God is made in the image of man, intimately and inseparably so. In myths, the mind sees, dimly, hauntingly, and through a glass darkly, its own reflected image. Myth is the face in the mirror—mind looking at itself.

This treatment of mind and myth unites the message of this chapter with the theme of the book. What is striking about the Fall (the fracture in consciousness) is not that the deep mythic structure of the Dreaming died, but that so much of it remained for so long.

The core idea of rebirth remains enshrined in Christianity in the doctrine of the Resurrection. In the Christian vision, the rising of Christ from the dead on the third day (as in the ancient lunar cycle) became the archetype of all human deliverance from death. Jews look to the rebirth of Israel when the Messiah comes. In this, they hark back to the collective consciousness of the tribe ("Thy people, Israel") rather than the ego-self of the individual. Moreover, the traditional cycle of the Christian and Jewish religious years (Christmas, Lent, Easter, Epiphany, etc. in Christianity; Passover, Tabernacles, Rosh Hashanah, etc. in Judaism) preserves the basic structure of cyclic time, causing the faithful to reenact repeatedly and thus relive the events that form the foundation of their mythic heritage.

The legacy of Eden lingers, too, in secular life. The faces of our timekeepers—our clocks and watches—are circular. We still speak of work as the daily round. When a couple marry, they still give each other, as a token of the foreverness of their union, rings, the ancient, enduring symbol of eternity. It is only over the last few centuries that these last tenacious remnants of Eden have finally begun to falter and fade. In this important sense, the Fall, which occurred about 4,000–8,000 years ago, has not proceeded to finality until the present century.

Science in particular has virtually eradicated any sense of cyclic time by revealing the progressive character of evolution. Perhaps more to the point, science has revealed the timescale of evolution. John McPhee has coined the wonderfully evocative phrase "deep time" to describe the mind-bending vista of the billions of years that preceded the emergence of man. The destructive psychological power of the discovery of deep time shows up when one makes the inevitable comparison between deep time and human time: Deep time reduces the span of a single human life to utter insignificance. Modern astronomy has a similarly shattering effect, dethroning man from his divinely ordained place at the center of creation and relegating him to an unexceptional planet circling a middle-aged sun in an ordinary galaxy, one among the billions that glow in the cosmic dark. Biology has carried out a similar hatchet job on the mythic belief that man is made in the image of God, showing instead that man's relationship with chimpanzees is so close that they share 98 percent of their genes.

These developments have created another "fracture in consciousness" in human evolution. One can, I believe, with perfect accuracy, speak of a Second Fall to describe the massive and unparalleled loss of identity that science has brought about in the human psyche, the rapid breaking down of ancient, familiar patterns born of the innate rhythms of the brain itself.

The details of this breakdown have been amply documented elsewhere. It is the result that matters. And the result can be summarized in one word—*crisis*. The decay of the deep mythic basis to life has made the ego-self precariously aware of its own mortality at precisely the moment that its reassuring, earth-centered, brain-based points of reference have been erased by science. Without the shield of faith to protect it from the specter of the Reaper, the ego-self is vulnerable to fears and anxieties that destabilize its very essence. At this point, the feedback loop is finally unsealed; the "ancient covenant," to use the apt words of French biologist Jacques Monod, is broken.

At a time of unparalleled triumph in science, in man's understanding of and control over the physical world, there is a failure at the very core of the Western psyche. Where is this failure most evident? Where else but in our newly emergent terror of death.

6

THE DARKNESS
WITHIN

Eyes I dare not meet in dreams
In death's dream kingdom
— T . S . E L I O T

We are now at the halfway mark in our journey, a good place to pause, to look back over ground covered before moving on through new territory toward whatever destination may lie ahead. Let us quickly review the route we have followed to date. The first chapter set the scene and laid out the agenda. The second looked at the physical nature of time and the relationship between time's arrow and the aging process, which is the basis of our mortality. The third looked at the way life beats time by copying itself, which led us to consider the evolution of death—the emergence of built-in obsolescence and programmed death—as a feature of life. That led us, in the fourth and fifth chapters, to look at ourselves, at the tenacious but elusive sense of "I" that so dreads the death it has but recently learned to recognize through the first and the second Falls.

To use a risky metaphor, the first half of this book, in particular the two preceding chapters, has brought us to the entrance of the sepulcher. It is now time to go inside, into the dark catacomb where our most terrible fear lives. There, stripped of the protecting talisman of mythic reassurance, we must look at the one thing we do not want to face: the Specter of

Death, the death that is the inevitable and foreordained doom of each and every one of us. Our own personal end of time, our individual death of forever.

I have already made the point that the fear of death is not a psychological constant; it varies according to time of life and period of history. To put it somewhat more technically, the fear of death tends to be age-specific and culture-specific.

To get us into the theme of this chapter, it will be useful to map the way the human attitude to death has been changed by the simple fact of an increasing life span. No one can be sure what the life expectancy of prehistoric man was, but we can be confident that it was short. However, we must not fall into the trap of romanticizing the Dreaming ages as some writers have done. Eden was not a garden; it was a jungle, and the inhabitants of Eden lived by the laws of the jungle. During the Dreamtime, life was ruled to a large extent by simple physical imperatives such as food and shelter. As we have seen, in this instinctual phase of human evolution, the average length of life was probably no more than eighteen years; it typically ended at what we would today reckon as the beginnings of young adulthood. It goes without saying that a culture in which old age was rare would have a hugely different perspective on life from one where old age was common, quite apart from attitudinal differences due to accidents of time and place.

The dramatic improvements in the technology of survival that have occurred over the last century represent man's greatest assault on time, doubling the number of years that he can expect to live. Statistics reveal the lagged trend. It has been estimated that the average life span in ancient Rome was still only about 20 years, while in Europe during the Middle Ages it was about 33. In 1841 the average life expectation in England was 40 for a man and 42 for a woman. In 1910 it was 52 years for men and 55 for women. It is only during the last few decades that the bulk of the population has begun to reach the biblical limit of three-score years and ten.

The advances in hygiene and medicine that have so improved life expectancy have led to today's situation where each individual can predict not the exact date of death but the period of peak probability with some confidence. Figure 6.1 graphs the likelihood of dying against time. The

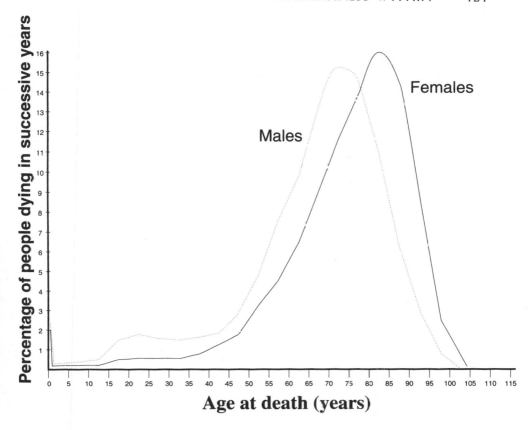

FIGURE 6.1

The probability of dying at various times of life, plotted on a percentage basis. This graph shows that, in a developed society, most people die in the decade beyond the traditional "threescore and ten." Note that females live, on average, significantly longer than males.

graph shows that one's chances of dying remain on a low and fairly constant baseline of between 0.3 and 1.5 percent until the age of 44. Between the years 50 and 54, the probability of dying starts to climb (up to 4 percent). The weighting thereafter rises steeply, reaching 11.3 percent between the years 65 and 69 and peaking at 14.3 percent in the 75–79 age bracket. On an aggregate basis, over 60 percent of all deaths occur in the 65–90 period.

This conventional graph is misleading because it seems to imply that the risk of death decreases once the period of peak vulnerability has been

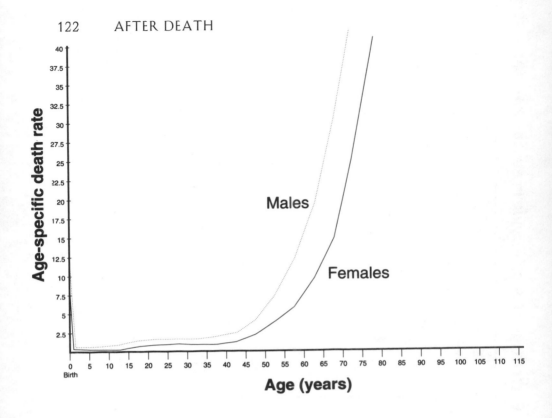

FIGURE 6.2

The same statistics as in Figure 6.1, plotted a different way. This graph shows that, after birth (a dangerous period), the average human has little chance of dying in the years between 5 and 50. From 50 onward, the likelihood increases, slowly at first and then with increasing momentum. On a probability basis, the average person has very little chance of still being alive at age 95.

passed. In fact, what happens is that fewer people survive to contribute to the later points on the chart. A better representation is shown in Figure 6.2, which graphs the age-specific death rate against age. Data like these indicate that a man aged 30, for example, can expect to live a further 43.51 years, whereas a man aged 60 can expect to live only a further 17.23 years.

The facts of human mortality can also be illustrated by examining patterns of age-associated deaths due to degenerative diseases like cancer. As Figure 6.3 shows, there is an approximately linear increase in the likelihood of dying from cancer if these statistics are plotted on a logarithmic (log) scale. The log scale is based on the exponential math we encoun-

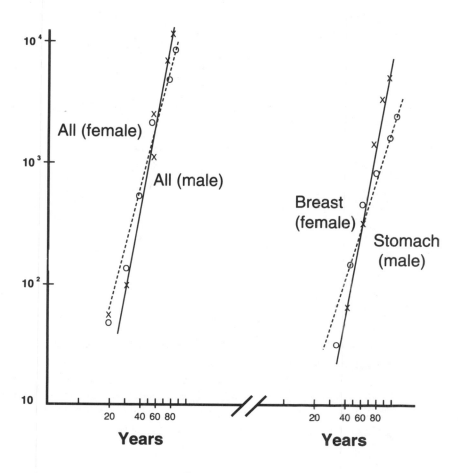

FIGURE 6.3

The incidence of some diseases increases with age. Cancer is one. To obtain sensible data, one takes the number of deaths due to, say, breast cancer in women in a ten-year interval (say, 21–30). One then looks at the data year by year, taking the number of women diagnosed as having breast cancer during a given year and dividing it by the number of women in this ten-year interval who were alive at the beginning of the year in question. The result is multiplied by 100,000. This process yields the age-specific incidence of cancer. The data are plotted on a "log" scale, which has the effect of transforming the curves in Figures 6.1 and 6.2 into straight lines. In a log representation, each major interval represents a tenfold increase over the one beneath it. What the data tell us is that the incidence of (many) cancers rises steadily from the first (21–30) interval onward. These cancers reflect mortality in general. (From Macfarlane Burnet, The Endurance of Life.*)*

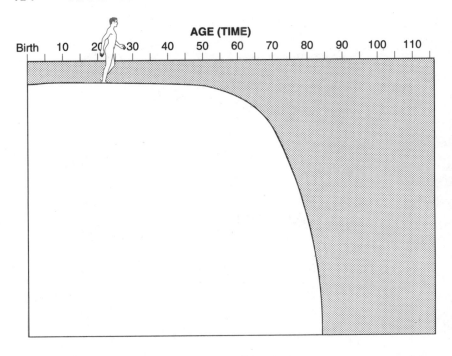

FIGURE 6.4

Everyman's journey toward death. This figure puts the rather dry data of the preceding three figures into a personal human perspective. Here we see an average human being, Everyman, walking life's road. From the first 45 years of life, he walks securely, his risk of dying minimal and relatively unchanging from day to day. From the age of 50 onward, his footsteps become less secure until by age 60, he is on the increasingly hazardous, ever-escalating, downward slope toward the abyss.

tered in Chapter 3. An easy way to visualise what is happening in Figure 6.3 is to imagine the possibility of dying as "multiplying in a runaway fashion" with time.

I dislike these conventional representations because they have no human dimension. Therefore I have redesigned the data into the representation shown in Figure 6.4. There we see an individual, Everyman, journeying down life's road. For the first 45 years, he walks a level plain, confident that when he sleeps, he will awaken, that the death of consciousness that comes with night will indeed be followed by rebirth with sunrise. From about 50 onward he reaches the edge of the pit. From here on, his feet are increasingly prone to slip into the bottomless well of nonbeing. This graph is not intended to frighten. Rather, I have sought to combine the statistics of science with a symbolic image that aptly describes the paradox and the pathos of the human condition in the West at this time.

In the light of this, we can now put ourselves in the picture by setting out a nine-phase life cycle for modern man based on the changes that occur in our attitudes to time over the course of life. The divisions of this cycle are based on my own experience, on anecdotal evidence, and on sociological studies. Not all experts will agree with me, and many will point out that teenagers, for example, can be intensely aware of death because it is the first time they see death with eyes that have lost the protective security of childhood. I accept this. All I am claiming here is that the nine-phase cycle broadly reflects sequential changes in the attitude to death of a large cross-section of individuals in Western society today.

PHASE 1: 0–9 MONTHS—THE GENESIS DREAMING

This is the period in the womb. In the West, we have developed the curious habit of dating the beginning of life from the moment of birth. Our "birthdays" celebrate (relive in the old sense of cyclic time) the moment we were severed from our mother's body by cutting the umbilical cord. In Japan, the beginning of life is measured from the estimated moment of conception. That is the more realistic method.

As we saw in the previous chapter, the genesis myths of mankind seem to have their origins in this time of watery darkness. Some authorities believe the intrauterine experience contributes not only to our memory of the Creation but to our premonition of destruction. Birth is a supreme crisis—the level of adrenaline in the blood of a baby being born is greater than that of a man having a heart attack. It is a time of massive readjustment, of pain and trauma—a passage from the known and the safe to the unknown and the insecure. The sense of impending catastrophe that haunts us in later life, of being a helpless victim of dark forces beyond our control, may be a throwback to the shock-intensive way we come into the world. This feeling of pervading, imminent doom may be the first element of what later becomes our terror of death.

In the womb we dream, without marking time, for subjective time has not begun.

PHASE 2: 9 MONTHS–3 YEARS—GROWING WITHOUT TIME

This is the period of early childhood. From our point of view, the most important aspect of this period is the learning of language. By the age of 3, while language skills are advancing fast, a sharply differentiated ego is still some years off.

A phase 2 child has no understanding of death. Phase 2 is the prehuman phase of consciousness; subjective time has not yet begun.

PHASE 3: 3–12 YEARS—AN INFINITY OF TIME

From the age of 3 to 10, the child's mastery of language reaches a sufficient level to allow it to speak and read. That is crucial because language is the child's entrance ticket to the stored experience of its species—the true key to the human kingdom.

For a large part of this phase, the child's depiction of the world has not yet advanced to an understanding of causality. As pioneering child psychologist Jean Piaget has shown, children at age 6 believe everything has an aim. "Organic life is, for the child, a sort of story, well regulated according to the wishes and intentions of its inventor" (God or parents). Thus accidental and unpredictable occurrences like death pose special problems for children in this age bracket, because death seems the most "fortuitous and mysterious" of phenomena. To quote Piaget again: "If the child is, at this stage, puzzled by the problem of death, it is precisely because in his conception of things death is inexplicable."

Piaget's views gain some support from work done by volunteer groups among young people who have contracted terminal illnesses like cancer. An experienced volunteer once said to me, "The kids cope with the thought of death much better than their parents. One can get the paradoxical situation in which a dying child will actually seek to comfort its parents, rather than the other way round, as in "It'll be OK, Mum."

For these and other reasons, its seems unlikely that a phase 3 child sees death for the finality it is. Psychologically, the child is still, in an important sense, immortal. If a child in this phase has any fear of death, it is likely to spring from the deep imprinting of the birth process, of the sense of being a helpless victim of dark and destructive forces that are poised to annihilate it.

PHASE 4: AGE 12–25—FOOTPRINTS IN TIME

Phase 4 encompasses the rite of passage into puberty, still celebrated in cultures like Judaism with special ceremonies (bar mitzvah). During the teens and early twenties, the overwhelming focus of life is on reproduction (even where individuals have no intention of begetting children). During this phase, a strong ego-self develops, but the emphasis on sexual activity, symbolizing as it does a biological commitment to the future, negates any morbid fear of death. The engine of life beats strongly, and age is far away.

Nonetheless, it is particularly difficult to generalize about this age group. I can remember that I personally became intensely conscious of my mortality in my teens. Other people have said the same thing. Much depends on individual experience. If one encounters death early in phase 4, it is likely to make an enormous impact because the psyche is at a particularly vulnerable stage of its growth: neither boy nor man, neither girl nor woman.

PHASE 5: AGE 25–40—MARCHING IN TIME

Phase 5 individuals are in the prime of life, overwhelmingly preoccupied with childrearing, career ambitions, and the acquisition of wealth and status. They are "too busy" to worry about their own mortality and, in the main, their bodies send them few signals to foreshadow the aging process to come.

PHASE 6: AGE 40–50—THE DENIAL OF TIME AND THE SHADOW OF APPROACHING NIGHT

Phase 6 encompasses the greatest crisis of the contemporary human life cycle in the West—the period when aging begins to affect function for the first time, when reproductive capacity usually ends (in women), and when the awareness of death becomes a major psychological preoccupation.

Carl Jung summed up the significance of phase 6 eloquently when he said: "For in the secret hour of life's mid-day the parabola is reversed, *death is born*. The second half of life does not signify ascent, unfolding, increase, exuberance, but death, since death is its goal."[Italics added]

Phase 6 marks the separation of man's biological and mental potentials.

Mental abilities remain sharp and decision-making processes may indeed improve as the weight of a lifetime's accumulated experience optimizes the ability to pick winners among options offered. However, with the menopause, the female fertility clock is switched off. The emotional aftermath of this in women is well known, often taking the form of a semi-clinical condition called postmenopausal depression. Men may also experience an age-related midlife crisis. The key point is that the waning of reproductive fitness cuts the lifeline that links the individual to his/her genetic future. Henceforth, the individual is in evolution's discard tray, unshielded from the fear of death by the inability to beget compensating life.

The phase 6 crisis is enhanced by the fact that it often coincides with the highest probability of kin death; i.e., it is during the 40–50 period that the individual is most likely to experience the loss of his/her parents. Even in today's mobile society, the legal responsibility for disposing of the newly deceased rests with their next of kin. Thus phase 6 people are forced to confront, usually for the first time, the fact of death in those individuals with whom they have the strongest emotional ties. The selfish-gene perspective is important here: Individuals share as many genes with their parents (50 percent) as they do with their children (50 percent). When their parents die, so, in literal truth, does a part of themselves.

Phase 6 marks the climacteric of life. Increasingly, as the phase 6 years tick by, the vision of an ever-contracting future impacts fearfully on the present despite the fact that phase 6 individuals are still typically fit. Indeed, it is precisely during this interval that men and women often develop obsessive preoccupations with health—jogging, joining fitness clubs, going on diets, undergoing elective surgery, beginning the battle with time, which henceforth and increasingly is seen as the enemy.

A noticeable feature of phase 6 is the speeding up of inner time. Phrases like "My God, where's the day gone" or "The year's just flown by" or "It can't be June *already*" bespeak an accelerating internal timekeeper. What causes this? The answer, I believe, is that the human brain measures time by the frequency of novel additions to its memory banks, of things that leave a strongly etched memory trace because they do not correspond to any previous experience—things that "stand out." Thus when we are very young, most of the experiences we encounter during the course of a week are new or have some element of newness. This abundance of novel elements fills the daily memory register with entries and hence causes our sense of retrospective time to stretch; i.e., the day seems longer because it contains so many stored memory traces. As we get older, more and more of life is relegated to the status of habit. We get into our car in the morning without, in an important sense, seeing it: We carry an internal model of the car and its various features in our minds, which minimizes the amount of conscious attention we have to devote to finding our seats and operating the vehicle. Indeed, the process of driving, once learned, becomes totally habitual and is displaced from the upper story of the brain (the cerebral cortex) into an adjacent brain part (the cerebellum).

Repetitive actions and sights do not register in consciousness, because the information they carry to the brain is already familiar and the mental route it follows has been smoothed (facilitated) by the hundreds of prior replicas that have gone before. The upshot of this is that phase 6 individuals, living and working within familiar, habitual boundary conditions, are largely unaware of perhaps 80 percent or more of what goes on around them. Consequently, time contracts and seems to run more quickly.

PHASE 7: AGE 50–69—THE ACCEPTANCE OF TIME

By phase 7, individuals have usually had long enough to devise strategies to cope with the knowledge of their mortality. While awareness of death remains high, the fear of dying often recedes somewhat because the shock has passed. Aging is now too obvious to be denied, and compensatory tactics have been put in place.

As we will see later, this can be the greatest period of true growth in the human life cycle, depending on whether or not the midlife confrontation with death has been faced or fled from.

PHASE 8: AGE 69–75—THE BLURRING OF TIME

By phase 8, age has begun to affect significantly most bodily and mental functions. Fittingly, this has the effect of dampening the awareness of death. The fear of dying blurs and becomes somewhat unfocused. A new dreaming begins—the dreaming of old age.

PHASE 9: AGE 75–120—THE END OF TIME

This is what computers register as "terminal status." It is the death experience. In Australia, the average life expectancy for males is now about 72.9 years and for females about 79.2 years.

People in this final category are, in Agatha Christie's memorable words, "sitting in the anteroom, awaiting the summons."

This brief outline clearly identifies phase 6 as the period of peak risk, the time when modern man is most likely to understand—and fear—the fact of his own mortality. This is not to say that individuals in other phases do not appreciate the reality of death, but simply to stress the self-evident fact that the fear of death experienced by a twenty-year-old is of necessity somewhat different from that experienced by a fifty-year-old.

With this caveat in mind, let us approach the problem death poses to the ego-self by asking a very simple, almost naive, question: "Why am I afraid of death?"

The answer exists on various levels. To continue to use the metaphor of the Fall, fear of death is part of our original sin. By that I do not mean that the fear of death is a feature of our cultural inheritance. Rather, I suggest that the fear of death is part of our genetically unforgotten animal legacy—the survival kit of instinct we inherit from our vertebrate ancestors. Thus, when we are threatened in any serious way, nature wheels into action a battery of survival strategies (chiefly the fight-or-flight reaction we saw in Chapter 1) that animals have learned over evolutionary time, all of which are aimed unswervingly at a single objective—the avoidance of death.

Language adds another dimension to this instinctual reaction. The ego-self was born when it learned to use language to remember the past and predict the future. As the words of *Gilgamesh* show, this ability created a deep-rooted mental crisis, for among the map of projections the ego-self learned to make under the heading of "the future," one stood out in stark and terrifying isolation—the projective ability to foresee one's own end.

The ego-self's terror of death is, however, different in kind from the instinctive fear of dying. It is unique to man, whereas instincts are universal among animals. It is a function of the conceptual world, and it can be neutralized in the conceptual world by using the symbolic weapons of myth to slay the symbolic image of the Reaper in the very place where it arises.

These explanations of our fear of death are, I believe, perfectly valid at their own level of reality, but they do not address the taproot issue: They do not tell us why, at the deepest level, we have the dread of death that permeates the modern mind. To find the answer, I believe we must turn to the motif of the selfish gene. Let us go back to the pivotal point of Chapter 3, the paradox of selfishness.

Self-ishness, me-ness, I-ness. What these words tell us is that the self is *different* from everything else, that the rest of its fellow creatures are similar, but they are other. To be a separate self is to be just that—*separate*, alone, isolated, vulnerable.

An analogy may help. Imagine a potter molding a vase from clay on his turning wheel. At the beginning of the process, he has a shapeless lump of clay. What he does during the creative act is fashion a recognizable image by giving it form. When it has form, it has identity, it has self, and when it has self, it can be destroyed. The anonymous lump that began the process cannot be harmed because it has no permanent feature to give it an identity tag. The perfected image at the end is vulnerable, separate, self-ish—and mortal.

Transpersonal psychologist and author Ken Wilber has summed the issue up splendidly: "There is nothing the separate self can do to actually get rid of death terror, since the separate self is that death terror—they come into existence together and they only disappear together." This is the most basic statement that can be made about our fear of death. Awareness of self and awareness of mortality go hand in hand. The meaning of the Fall is that the triple shock, due to the inbreaking awareness of ego-self, time, and death, took the human psyche in the West into a new and vulnerable state. It still rests there today, precariously poised, with the death fear an ongoing element in the cultural pathology of our time.

But this raises anew an issue that will not go away. If our fear of death is as basic as this, why can most of us affirm so stubbornly that we do not fear death? This apparent contradiction forces us to look at the problem from the complementary point of view. Having asked, "Why am I afraid of death?" let me now put the reciprocal question, "Why am I not afraid of death?" As with the first question, this query, which seems so easy to answer, quickly gets us into deep water. Very deep water.

The first reason we can "disown" a fear of death springs from the fact that, to the brain, death is, in a limited but important sense, an incongruous impossibility. That is another way of stating a position taken by many experts—that death does not exist for us because our minds are not able to recognize their own mortality. As Freud said: "In his unconscious, every one of us is convinced of his own immortality." We saw one reason for this in Chapters 1 and 5. In the deeply imprinted programming of the day/night cycle, the brain learns to expect that the little death of sleep and darkness will always be followed by the little rebirth of waking and light.

Another factor is so obvious that it is almost always overlooked. Allegra Taylor, a hospice volunteer who has worked extensively with the terminally ill, quotes an anonymous letter from a dying student nurse to her fellow nurses that includes the following poignant passage: "Death may get to be a routine to you, but it is new to me. You may not see me as unique, but I've never died before. To me, once is pretty unique."

Author-psychoanalyst Judith Viorst quotes a similar statement from her dying friend Carol: "I've never died before . . . so I don't know how to do it."

The message of these two statements was crystallized by the philosopher Ludwig Wittgenstein, who said: "Death is not an event in life. Death is not lived through." Likewise, Edwin Shneidman:

> Dying takes its only legitimate operational meaning from the fact that it immediately precedes death. . . . In my own life I have twice believed that I was dying. . . . Both times I was wrong. . . . But the logical point remains: the one time I shall have been right, there will be no "I" to experience the validating criterion. That is precisely what Bridgman meant when he said "I am always alive."

I believe this inability of the brain to foreknow its own end in an experiential sense goes far toward explaining why most of us can brush off comments about death by saying, "I'm not frightened of dying."

There is a second reason why we can disclaim any undue fear of death. We can ignore death because it is, to a significant degree, invisible, private. This privacy evidently has deep, prehuman roots. Biology commentator Lewis Thomas makes the pointed observation: "Whoever sees dead birds in anything like the huge numbers stipulated by the certainty of the death of all birds? A dead bird is an incongruity. . . . Birds do their dying off somewhere, behind things, under things, never on the wing." He further notes: "Animals seem to have an instinct for performing death alone, hidden."

I believe that, in this case, we can interpret the word "instinct" literally. In the world of nature, an animal that is in any way abnormal—wounded, sick, maimed, misshapen—is marked out by that very fact for rapid elimination. If the rule were absolute, I don't doubt that death would be much more visible than it is. However, animals that are only slightly wounded or sick can recover if they can find a safe place to hide from danger. In the context of hiding, safe means secret, away from prying eyes. Thus there must have been, throughout the evolution of higher land animals, a strong selective pressure to develop a hide-away-when-below-par syndrome. I believe it is quite logical to postulate that that syndrome is now "hardwired" into the nervous systems of land vertebrates.

In this sense we humans, nonconformists in so many ways, are strict conformists to nature's rule. We seem to have the same instinct. As Thomas says: "There are 3 [now over 5] billion of us on the earth, and all 3 billion must be dead, on a schedule, within this lifetime. The vast mortality, involving something over 50 million of us each year, takes place in relative secrecy."

The fact that most of us almost never encounter one of the most common phenomena in life tells us that there is, literally and metaphorically, a cover-up about death. When someone dies, the first thing we do is hide the cadaver in a shroud or winding sheet so it is no longer visible. Already, within hours of death, the person has ceased to be an identifiable individual and become an anonymous object. The person (him or her) becomes the corpse (it). This symbolic hiding continues with enclosure in a more permanent concealing device—a coffin. The final separation of living and dead comes with the disposal of the corpse; whether it is entombed in a cave or buried underground or burned in fire is irrelevant as long as it is removed so that the living do not have to face the phenomenon that revolts them most—corruption.

This is why we avoid images of death. Animals turn on their own kind if they are, in any way, abnormal. Death is conspicuously abnormal to the healthy-species prototype, so we revert to our instinct either to destroy our dead fellows (burn them) or to secrete them away (bury or entomb them).

Further, we can claim to disregard death because, while we may all experience the fear of death, we do not permit it to remain in our conscious minds. In a self-protective reflex, we automatically push it down into the subconscious. As psychologist Gregory Zilboorg explains:

> If this fear [of death] were as constantly conscious, we should not be able to function normally. It must be properly repressed to keep us living with any modicum of comfort. . . . We may take it for granted that the fear of death is always present in our mental functioning. . . . No one is free of the fear of death.

This is, I believe, the very crux of the matter. The adult brain has, throughout the greater part of human evolution, been quickly confronted with irrefutable evidence of human mortality. That evidence presents the brain with what to it, as to any computer that has attained the sophistication of a von Neumann machine, is a logical paradox, i.e.: "I am immortal in terms of my experience of what happens to myself but doomed in terms of my experience of what happens to others." The brain cannot resolve this paradox in terms of its own software, so, I submit, it does the only thing possible—it sidetracks evidence of the paradox into storage compartments so that its ability to operate in a normal workaday mode is not affected. Thus the brain sidesteps the problem of death by exploiting the well-known psychological tactic of displacement; i.e., it pretends that death is something that always happens to someone else, never to itself. Only in this way can it preserve in its deep psychic structure that sense of unending immortality that makes goal-oriented, forward-looking life meaningful and possible.

Simplistically, a von Neumann-type computer, which is programmed to last but which is repeatedly fed data proving that it must disintegrate, has a contradiction built into the very core of its operations. Hence the inevitable fudging of the issue to itself: "I'm not worried about my termination," i.e., I will not let it enter my normal operational mode because it renders meaningless the basis of my programming. This analogy lets us see the supporting role of religion in its proper light. Faith allows the mind machine to operate in an open-ended fashion, because it resolves the paradox by removing the contradiction; if the I of the ego-self is not extinguished at death, there is no need for a solution because there is no threat.

The computer analogy gives us the clue we need to cross the threshold into the modern age. I have said that the mind machine displaces into cold storage logical paradoxes that it cannot resolve in terms of its programming. I could just as accurately have used the term *represses*. *Repression* is a word well known to modern psychiatrists. It refers to the phenomenon that arises when an individual suppresses a powerful fear so effectively that it destabilizes the balanced working of the mind—it makes it possible for the mind to become sick.

Nathan Scott, in his book *The Modern Vision of Death,* applies this concept specifically to the fear of death when he says: "Yet, if the fact of death is in some sense an intuitive certainty belonging to the essential structure of human consciousness, it needs also to be remarked that this is a certainty, however, which, normally, is very deeply repressed." This notion of repression carries us directly into the heart of the modern crisis. It answers the question, When the feedback loop is finally unsealed, what happens? The answer, shorn of surface complexities, is relatively clear-cut. Without the protecting armor of myth to neutralize the fear of death, the modern mind has no answer to the foreknowledge of its own mortality. It adopts instead a short-term, blinkered coping tactic. Simply put, it *denies* death by *burying* the angst that death arouses.

You will often hear doctors say, "He just buries his fear." It is a telltale metaphor for I believe it aptly reveals the character of the mechanisms that entomb anxieties in the subconscious. I believe that contemporary Western society is collectively sick in just this sense, because the very thought of death has become "taboo." We do not just bury our dead, we

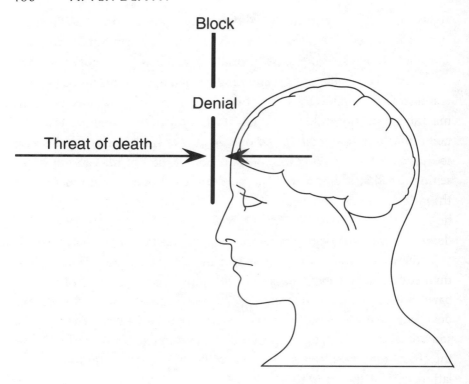

FIGURE 6.5

The modern denial, "I'm not worried by death." Most fit people deny they are bothered by the thought of death. Many experts believe that this is because the mind represses the very concept that it is mortal. Subconsciously, death is always something that happens to someone else. The modern denial of death springs in part from the deep-rooted sense of me-first individualism, of ego, that is such a conspicuous feature of competitive Western society. Western man has not developed strategies to deal with death. By and large, he simply ignores the problem, keeping his mind distracted with the multiple preoccupations of a technological culture.

try to bury death itself. In other words, contemporary society in the West has tried to solve the death paradox by pretending it does not exist (Figure 6.5).

Ken Wilber says, and I agree, that Western psychiatry has never grasped the true nature of the denial-of-death syndrome that afflicts modern man. Science inevitably confuses it with neurotic fear. The point is that the fear of death is emphatically *not* neurotic, as it springs from an accurate perception of reality, not a false one.

Modern psychiatry has built an impressive and doctrinaire structure of analysis and treatment around the works of Sigmund Freud. That structure makes sex the source of most of the guilt and anxiety that disturb the balanced workings of the human mind. I believe this emphasis on sex is not only misplaced but quite fundamentally wrong. The fear modern man suppresses most powerfully, the Pandora's box from which spring our most damaging anxieties and pathologies, is not sexual; it is related to death and dying. Like most strongly repressed terrors, the fear of death seldom expresses itself in its true colors. People seldom see death as the thing they fear. But the fantasy world of dreams, for example, indicates how universal the death motif is and shows us the diverse masks that death can wear in our subconscious.

The strategies used to hide death highlight the historical complexity of this issue. Cover-ups and burials of the newly dead are ancient, dating back to the dawn of the species. The uniqueness of the modern denial of death lies in the fact that contemporary man in the West has carried the separation process much farther by removing terminally ill patients from the social context before they die and enforcedly confining them in isolation camps, in old-age homes and hospitals. The statistics speak for themselves. Before 1700, most people died at home or among family. In 1908, 26 percent of the population died in public institutions in Australia. During the last decade, however, the hospitalization of the dying has increased to the extent that about 80 percent of the population expire hidden from public gaze, usually in hospital beds.

This trend points up the institutionalization of death that is such a conspicuous feature of the modern scene. From the moment a person becomes very sick, either suddenly or as a result of a critical turn during the course of a degenerative illness, professionals take over. Ambulance staff remove the patient to a hospital and trained nursing staff take on the task of terminal care. Visits by relatives and friends are confined to rigidly fixed time-slots and take place under supervised conditions. Once death has occurred, funeral arrangements are made by undertakers, who also arrange the burial or cremation. To this institutionalization of death comes a further change of attitude based on our embrace of, and belief in, technology. A nurse once made the point to me that many doctors "see death as a failure." So many sophisticated machines are available to prolong life, or life functions, that their failure to carry out the tasks for which they were invented is seen as some sort of breakdown of the system, an inadequacy of design.

Further evidence of our blinkered attitude to death shows up in the way we refer to it. Kenneth Kramer, an expert in comparative religion, notes that modern American idiom contains sixty-six euphemisms that allow individuals to avoid words like "death" or "dying": e.g., "passed away," "kicked the bucket," "checked out," "went to heaven," "breathed his last," etc.

The net result of all this denial has been to remove death from life. In a modern hospital environment, this final rite of passage is transformed into a bureaucratic routine. Despite the dedicated and loving care of staff on all levels, the ward for the terminally ill, by its very nature, tends to become a processing plant with a high rate of turnover. The process of dying thus easily becomes depersonalized, mechanized like the life-support machines to which the dying patient is so often attached.

Paradoxically, this denial of death also applies to the person who is dying. It is significant, for example, that behavior-modifying drugs have become an integral part of the contemporary dying process. Opiate-type pills, including morphine and heroin, are given to relieve pain. While few would quarrel with the goal of minimizing suffering, it is also true that these drugs affect brain chemistry in such a way as to "soften" reality. It can be fairly said that most people who die in hospitals are physiologically prevented from experiencing death in any meaningful sense.

In a final denial of reality, the terminally ill patient is often refused knowledge of his true condition. In the (ostensible) interest of the patient's "peace of mind," professional staff often see it as their duty to reassure the patient that death is not imminent—when it is.

To carry our investigation farther, we must look not just at death but at the process by which we reach it—dying. The man in the street seldom even thinks of dying, because he almost never comes into contact with dying people. Professionals who specialize in the care of terminally ill patients are vividly aware of the emotional consequences of that first glimpse into the abyss.

According to Elisabeth Kübler-Ross, who has worked extensively with terminally ill people, when individuals are told they are going to die, they pass through the following sequence of psychological states:

Denial. Almost invariably, the first reaction to the news that one is going to die is a shock-induced, point-blank refusal to face reality: "Oh my God, no—it can't be!" In this initial response, the patient reveals to the world the quintessential dilemma of an immortal ego trapped in a perishable body.

Anger. Denial soon passes into a strongly focused resentment; the "not me" becomes "why me?" This anger tends to be directed at both family and support staff who represent the closest examples of the prize of life and vitality the patient is in the process of losing.

Bargaining. When he realizes that he will soon die, the patient usually offers some token (often to God) in exchange for a deferral of death, a lengthened period of life: "Make me well and I will never . . . again."

Depression. Almost inevitably, as the reality sinks in, the patient goes through a phase of profound despair and wretchedness. At that point, his separation from the living really begins, for the quality of consciousness in the predeath period has no parallel in a fit individual.

Acceptance. Finally, the patient ceases to fight and accepts his lot.

I would like to add another reaction, in light of what I said earlier about feedback loops. Consider a specific group of people who are suddenly confronted with the foreknowledge of death—like people who are told they are HIV (AIDS virus) positive. After the denial phase ("Oh, my God, no"), such people typically engage in a frantic search for good news. They develop an obsessive interest in fad drugs, bogus claims, nonconventional medicine, etc. Moreover, they tend to accept uncritically any opening that offers them hope, especially the announcement of a "miracle cure." Putting this into biological terms, one can say that when reality ceases to offer an escape route to the threatened mind, the survival compulsion transfers itself to illusions. In this perspective, belief in a miracle cure has exactly the same evolutionary status as belief in resurrection through the belief in Christ. By revitalizing the promise of survival, the death-threatened human mind is able to readjust to its changed circumstances and proceed more or less as before. Whether the mental life-raft is a just-around-the-corner, genetically engineered vaccine or the imminent coming of the Lord is irrelevant. The biological result is the same: The status quo is rebuilt and the feedback loop is resealed—transiently.

Despite the evidence I have tried to bring together, I suspect that some people will still dispute the magnitude of the contemporary crisis that the denial of death creates at the core of our culture. This leads me to look at the issue from a different standpoint. Perhaps the clearest way to illustrate the social fallout of the fear of death is to examine some of its pathological consequences. To do this, I have chosen a case history that may, at first sight, appear strange because it concerns not an individual but a nation. I refer to the Nazi phenomenon that reigned in Europe from 1933 to 1945.

What has this got to do with the fear of death? How can the sin of one country, Germany, be representative of the "original sin" of the entire human race? My answer is that Nazism exemplifies par excellence a return to the collective phase of evolution. It was preeminently a *mass* movement in which the individual's sense of personal identity was submerged by and melded into the all-pervading, tribal identity of the *Volk* ("nation"), powerfully symbolized by the ubiquitous totem of the swastika.

Anyone who has ever watched photographer Leni Riefenstahl's propaganda epic *The Triumph of the Will* will appreciate the atavistic nature of Nazism. In one revealing segment, a group of young soldiers lowers lines of swastika-emblazoned flags to the ground, in tribute to Germany's war dead. Then comes the strident cry, "They are not dead—they live, in Germany." With that the flags are raised from the ground, skyward. The heroic dead are resurrected into the ongoing life of the *Volk*.

The seductive appeal of Nazism was precisely that it offered the ego-self an (illusionary) escape from its vulnerable aloneness, through reunion with the *Volk*. In the contagious mass hysteria of a Nuremberg rally, the ego-self ceased to be. It dissolved back into a prepersonal oneness, and the neolithic Dreaming returned in a perverted form, on a massive scale (Figure 6.6).

This is the psychological meaning of Nazism. It was a special form of sickness, a regression into a more primitive pattern of social behavior, in an important sense, a failure of consciousness itself. The paradox it has

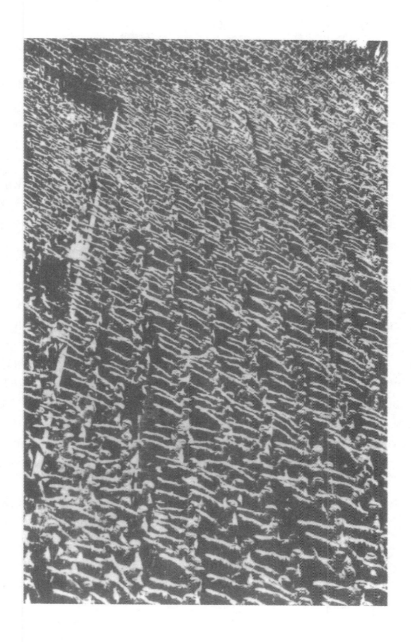

FIGURE 6.6

always posed—How could civilized people act in this way?—is, I believe, easily answered by looking at the Faustian bargain it offered. Below the words and images of its political propaganda, what Nazism was saying to the subconscious was "Give yourself, i.e., your sense of individuality, to the *Volk* and the *Volk* will give you the ancient immortality of the tribe."

The success of Nazism is eloquent testimony to the terror the ego-self experiences when it tries to stand alone, apart from the conformist safety of the group. While historians see Nazism as unique to Germany, I believe the Hitler phenomenon reveals to us an abyss into which the human mind, at this stage of its evolution, is always prone to fall. Nazism drew a key element of its strength not from its doctrines, which were grotesque, but from the way it tapped the terror of our time, the anguish that the subliminal foreknowledge of inevitable nonbeing inspires in human beings.

Finally, the reality of the death psychosis is apparent from the ease with which it can be brought to the surface. The covering veil is easy to tear. When I was in my late teens, I put myself through the university by working double shifts during the Christmas holidays. One of my regular jobs was to act as an orderly in an Auckland hospital. In reality, that meant doing the jobs no one else wanted to do. One of my most frequent chores was to pick up the bodies from the ward set aside for the terminally ill.

Normally the nursing staff was able to arrange matters so that the collection of cadavers was conveniently over by visiting time. On one occasion, however, they mistimed events, and I found myself going down in an elevator, with my gurney, with a group of people who had just finished a visit with a sick relative. Their eyes were drawn irresistibly to the gurney I was holding and to its hidden contents, moving from it to me with a kind of horrified fascination. When we reached the ground floor, they left in what I can only describe as unseemly haste, as if they had been in the presence of an obscenity.

French author André Malraux breaks through the barriers that mask our terror in a simple but pitiful verse that speaks straight to the heart of humanity:

There is ... no death. ...
There is only ... me ... me ...
Who is going to die.

To conclude this chapter, I would like to weave the various strands of my argument together. Consider again the biological perspective. The evolutionary trajectory that led from ancient fish to modern man has been characterized by a dramatic increase in brain size and complexity and by an improvement in the data-gathering power of the senses. In particular, the eyes in primates have rotated to the front of the head, giving stereoscopic depth of vision. The quality of the input channels has been upgraded, while the information storing and processing capability of their computer terminal has expanded enormously.

This means that the brain's ability to model reality has improved sharply during the last 400 million years of evolution. The nervous system of animals is like a mirror that natural selection has polished down the ages so that it reflects with greater and greater accuracy the structure of the world around it.

However, death is a part of the real world. It is a fact of life. The increase in brainpower that led to the emergence of man did not, at first, present death as a disruptive challenge to the improved correlative "fit" that nature had forged between the internal and external realities. As we have seen, during the Dreaming ages man's subliminal fear of death was largely annulled by the regenerative promise of cyclic time. Now that Eden has faded into myth, we face something unprecedented in the story of life on earth. The contemporary foreknowledge of death as the end of life has broken a fundamental rule of nature—that survival capacity is enhanced by improved awareness of the environment. Now, for the first time in evolution, enhanced awareness of reality is *life-denying*, not *life-promoting*.

Thus, in our time, humanity has reached the testing crossroad, where truth and illusion separate. I believe this is the greatest challenge that life on earth has faced, for unlike the threats posed by nuclear war or the greenhouse effect, it comes from within the psychology of the dominant species.

To appreciate the dimensions of this existential crisis, I recap my argument to this point. Purposeful human life is impossible if the future is denied, because purpose, by its very nature, is future-oriented. Death denies the future, and so death denies life. Man has coped with this problem in differing ways throughout the course of his evolution. In the prepersonal phase of evolution, the problem did not exist because archaic man, like the animals from which he sprang, was unaware of time. As humanity struggled toward self-consciousness, a temporal sense was born, but during the Dreaming ages and far into historical time, man's natural resonance with the cyclic patterns of nature, embodied in the ingrained belief in reincarnation or resurrection, quietened and tranquillized his fear of death. While the memory of Eden lasted, man was safe.

The memory of Eden has dimmed only recently; it is only during the last century or so that Western science has stripped the last protective veils of faith from our eyes. It is the second time human psychology in the West has "fallen" from a state of welcome ignorance to one of unwanted knowledge. The realization that death is the inescapable end of life becomes particularly acute in the midlife phase of the modern life cycle. Far from facing death, the contemporary mind denies the existence of the problem, displacing activity into side issues and self-gratification. At the core of the psyche there is now an emptiness, a gap at the center, disguising the bottled genie that is the cause of so much of the modern angst.

Nonetheless, the problem of death cannot be suppressed forever. In dreams, in anxieties, the serpent reappears, exposing the threadbare armor of the rational mind in the face of primal terror.

Evolution on earth is therefore at a crossroads, finely balanced between hope and despair. In the longer perspective of psychology, the serpent within is a greater threat to our continued survival than the dangers posed by our runaway technology, because foreknowledge of death eats away at the foundations of the life machine itself, sapping the psychic basis of our will to live.

I believe, passionately, that this is a darkness-before-dawn time, that every mode of evolution that struggles up to this level of consciousness must face this challenge—and be judged by it. It is, in the language of metaphor, a test of worthiness to inherit the future.

Arthur C. Clarke captured the spirit of this challenge in his short story "The Sentinel," which was the basis for the magnificant movie epic *2001: A Space Odyssey*. "The Sentinel" describes the discovery of a black monolith on the far side of the moon. The artifact is clearly of extraterrestrial origin, a beacon left by an alien race to watch over the evolving life on the planet below. However, its location puzzles its human finders—why was it put on the moon (earth's satellite), not on earth itself?

Clarke's answer is worth listening to:

Perhaps you understand now why that crystal pyramid was set upon the Moon instead of on the Earth. Its builders were not concerned with races still struggling up from savagery. They would be interested in our civilization only if we proved our fitness to survive—by crossing space and so escaping from the Earth, our cradle. That is a challenge that all intelligent races must meet, sooner or later. It is a double challenge, for it depends in turn upon the conquest of atomic energy and the last choice between life and death.

I believe that it is no accident that we have awakened to a knowledge of our own mortality at precisely the moment we have stepped into space. The science that sent the *Voyager* spacecraft out of the solar system is the same agent that forced man out of Eden's protecting sanctuary. Just as we shrink from the immensity of space, whose frontier we have just crossed, so we recoil from death, whose presence we have just acknowledged.

In my parents' day, the saying "reach for the moon" was a synonym for the impossible. In our generation, men have not only reached for the moon, they have stood on its surface. As the myth of Eden foreshadowed, the eating of this "forbidden" knowledge has stripped us of our innocence. Now when we look at the sky, we have a sense of scale—we know what it is we are looking at. We understand that the faint light that reaches our eyes from distant stars may have started on its journey through time before ancient vertebrates left the seas of earth to walk for the first time upon land. Poised on the frontier of immensity, at the edge of a vastness that lies beyond our power to comprehend, we feel vulnerable and lonely and just a little afraid.

Suddenly, on the farthest horizons of our perspective, we see a darkness that threatens to engulf the sum of all things, the universe in which we live and from which we came. At the precise moment we become fully aware of our own mortality, we are forced to confront the mortality of the cosmos itself. And with it, a hitherto unthinkable concept: *the end of time, the death of forever, not in the little sense of the end of me, but in the total sense of the end of All.*

7

AN END TO
ETERNITY

Between the idea
And the reality
Between the motion
And the act
Falls the Shadow
— T. S. ELIOT

Until now, we have encountered few concepts that challenge common sense with the possible exception of the selfish-gene idea and the Janus-like quality of DNA that requires it to be at one and the same time the unchanging guardian of life's immortality and the generator of its diversity. Now, however, we reach the threshold of the truly mysterious, for we must look to the far reaches of physics, to the paradox-ridden realms of the very small and the very large. There await us bejeweled creatures, strange beyond dreaming, that are born of the highest faculties of the human mind. In this mirror, we will see almost nothing we recognize.

Does this mean that we are abandoning reality for illusion? Not at all: We are doing just the reverse. In reaching this far into the realm of the invisible, away from the homey metaphors of everyday life, we are approaching reality. We must not complain if we find it strange. Indeed, it is this very strangeness that tells us that we are on the right track. When science was young, common sense was our guide. The model of the world we built up from new discoveries was based on familiar objects—clocks, pistons, billiard balls. As science has progressed through its great conceptual revolutions—relativity, quantum mechanics, supersymmetry—its discoveries have become more exotic, more remote from everyday experience. Easily recognizable images based on familiar things have given way to abstract theorems that tell of particles moving backward in time, of a universe structured in eleven dimensions, and so on. During this process, the status of common sense has been inverted: No longer our guide in the search for truth, it has become our adversary.

British astronomer Fred Hoyle wrote a science-fiction novel called *The Black Cloud.* In this tale, a huge gaseous cloud envelops the sun to gain energy. The cloud is home to a powerful intelligence, which reacts to the discovery of thinking humans with the same astonishment that they react to the discovery of thinking gas. In a clever climax, Hoyle sets up a scene in which the cloud, before departing from the solar system, agrees to relay its store of advanced information into a human mind. The astronomers in contact with the cloud debate as to who shall be the lucky recipient. They choose the most intelligent member of their group. Then follows the denouement. The awesome data that floods the scientist's brain unbalances his mind, and he dies. Before he dies, he makes the following statement: "The height of irony is that I should experience this singular disaster, while someone like X (the gardener) would have been quite all right."

The point is that an uneducated mind might simply have absorbed the data and so not been unsettled by it. However, the scientist, with his store of preformed assumptions and his trained faculties of critical analysis, instinctively judged the new by the standards of the old and hence found his mental processes becoming increasingly scrambled until they threw the balance of his mind totally out of kilter.

The moral is clear. In the new landscape of science, the familiar mental house we build from experience has become a formidable obstacle to our understanding of nature. Our whole perception of reality has been fundamentally shaped by the experiences life has undergone on the surface of this planet. That was an important part of the messages of Chapters 3 and 5. The models we build to explain the world are, inevitably, intuitively, profoundly, of this world. They make most sense when the images they create resonate with and correspond to the innermost structure of our thoughts. We find meaning in things we recognize (*recognoscere* means "to know again"), accepting most easily a future contoured around the past.

There are only two ways to escape this bondage. I will defer discussion of the first until Chapters 8 and 9. The second way is mathematics. Mathematics is like a fishing line we can cast into the future by virtue of its logical coherence and predicative power. When we analyze the cargo of information it brings back into the present, we find ourselves struggling to understand concepts for which there are no words, no images, no layers of reinforced experience. What we see in these mathematical cryptograms are signals from the future, which our brains, at this verbal, ego-self stage of their evolution, cannot hope to comprehend.

This loss of familiar guidelines becomes especially acute if we want to stretch our perception of time from the daily round of the day/night cycle to the far horizons, to the end of time. The only way to understand the remote future is to understand the remote past; just as we had to go back to birth to understand death. Therefore, in this wider context, to discover the end we must find the beginning.

The remote beginning is the Creation, the genesis event, which I touched on briefly in Chapter 1. The starting point for all descriptions of the genesis is the experimental observation that the universe is expanding. To use the well-worn but still-apt analogy, the galaxies are moving apart like dots painted on an expanding balloon. That has the important consequence of making the universe look the same from all points of reference; i.e., an observer on any dot will always see all other dots (galaxies) moving away from him in the same way.

This flight of the galaxies is the central feature of attempts to model the future of the universe, because the fate of the cosmos depends on the answer to the question, Will its expansion ever stop? The answer depends in turn on the total amount of matter that the cosmos contains.

Most scientists interpret this problem in terms of Einstein's general theory of relativity. One of Einstein's insights was to recognize that gravity is not a force but a curvature of space-time. Matter warps (curves) the structure of space-time, and the greater the amount of matter, the stronger the resulting space-time curvature. A second crucial insight of Einstein's was that light actually has mass (according to the famous equation

$E = mc^2$). By putting these two insights together, we can approach the question of the ultimate fate of the universe.

Obviously the total amount of matter in the cosmos will affect the space-time geometry of the cosmos as a whole. What it does, in effect, is give the cosmos a shape. Thus, if we design a thought experiment in which we shine two powerful laser beams into space along exactly parallel paths, the degree to which they remain parallel or are deflected from linearity will tell us something fundamental about the density of the matter they encounter along the way. (Remember, the density will be affected by the rate of expansion of the universe.)

As it turns out, only three things can happen: The beams can continue to run in tandem forever, they can converge until they intersect, or they can diverge indefinitely. Those three outcomes dictate three different shapes for space-time. If the beams run in tandem forever, space-time is flat and has the familiar properties described by Euclid. In flat space, the sum of the angles of a triangle is exactly 180 degrees (Figure 7.1a). That is the outcome if the galaxies are expanding at the rate that just—and only just—stops them from congealing because of their mutual gravitational attraction. If the rays intersect, space-time is positively curved, just as lines of longitude on earth converge toward the poles (Figure 7.1b). In spherical space, the sum of the angles of a triangle is always greater than 180 degrees. That is the outcome if the amount of matter in the galaxies and elsewhere is enough to cause the expansion of the universe to stop and reverse itself. Conversely, if the rays continue to diverge, space-time is negatively curved or hyperbolic (Figure 7.1c); i.e., it has a curious saddle shape. The geometrical properties of hyperbolic space are such that the angles of a triangle are always less than 180 degrees. That is the outcome if the amount of matter in the cosmos is not enough to stop the universe from expanding forever. Such a universe is described as open.

Which of these three outcomes corresponds to reality? The maddening answer is that we don't know. What we are reasonably confident about is that the value for the sum total of all the matter in the universe seems to lie very close to the dividing line that separates a closed (spherical) from an open (flat) cosmos. If the universe is closed, it is only just closed. If it is open, it is only just open. This difference between a closed and an open space-time structure spells out two different fates for the universe.

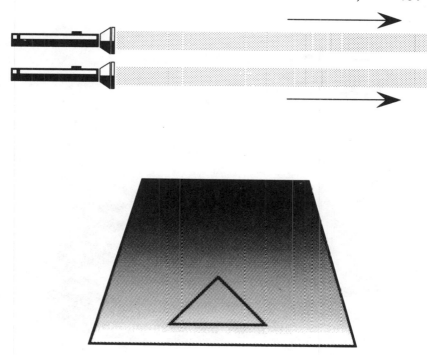

FIGURE 7.1a

The fate of the cosmos depends on the amount of matter it contains. In flat space-time (Fig. 7.1a) the sum of the angles of a triangle is exactly equal to 180 degrees. In curved space-time (Figure 7.1b) the sum of the angles of a triangle is greater than 180 degrees. In hyperbolic space-time (Fig. 7.1c) the sum of angles of a triangle is less than 180 degrees. (From W. J. Kaufmann III, Black Holes and Warped Spacetime.)

ALTERNATIVE 1: DYING IN FIRE

Suppose there is enough mass in the cosmos to give space-time a spherical shape. In this situation, the expansion of the galaxies will one day reverse itself, and the cosmos will shrink back toward a point of zero radius and infinite density. We know more or less what this will mean: a terminal black hole.

During recent years, scientists have become fascinated by black holes. A black hole can be loosely described as a region of space in which matter contracting under the influence of gravity becomes so dense that space-time is warped into a sort of bottomless pit (Figure 7.2) from which not

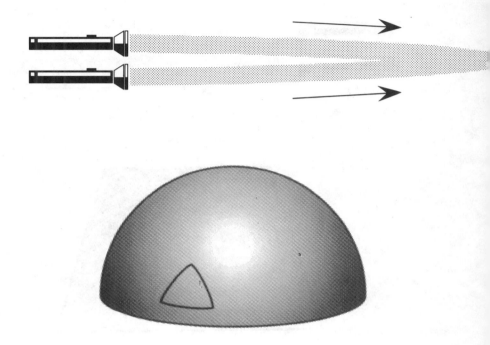

FIGURE 7.1b

even light can escape. The threshold at which light can no longer escape from a hole therefore constitutes an absolute information barrier, called an event horizon. Once inside the event horizon of a black hole, communication with the outside world is forbidden by the laws of physics, since no signal sent from inside the hole can ever break through the gravity trap.

This abandon-hope-all-ye-who-enter-here quality of the event horizon has made black holes the darlings of science-fiction buffs. Movies involving black holes give their viewers an adrenaline surge because of the horror the thought of being trapped in an ever-increasing gravity maelstrom, beyond all reach of rescue, arouses in the physiology of the onlooker. However, here nature may be playing an ironical trick on the viewer. If the structure of space-time is spherical, the onlooker is, in fact, in the very situation his heroes are fighting in fiction. If the cosmos is spherical, i.e., if space-time is closed back upon itself, *we are already living inside a black hole.* All of us.

In a curved space-time scenario, the end of the cosmos (the big crunch)

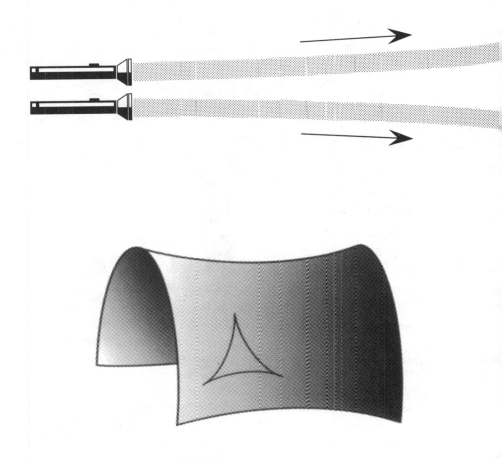

FIGURE 7.1c

may be similar to its beginning (the big bang). Therefore we return to the point that to foresee the end (which lies in the future) we must look at the beginning (which lies in the past).

Modern science has begun to come to grips with this problem only recently. It has done so by building a bridge between two of the corner-stones of contemporary physics, relativity theory (which encompasses the modern description of gravity) on the one hand, and quantum mechanics (which encompasses the modern description of the behavior of subatomic particles) on the other.

As we saw in Chapter 2, quantum mechanics is par excellence the field of science where common sense breaks down completely. In particular, the link between cause and effect blurs. In our everyday world of ordinary

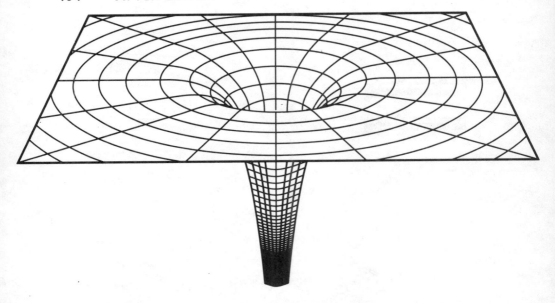

FIGURE 7.2

If matter warps the structure of surrounding space-time (Figure 2.1), it follows that the greater the amount of matter, the more dramatic the warp it generates. Beyond a certain critical mass, matter warps space-time so profoundly that even a beam of light can never escape. This figure shows a schematic representation of such a black hole. Scientists can describe the properties of the hole only because it is smoothly connected to the flat structure of surrounding space-time. If the amount of matter in the cosmos is so great that we are all living inside a black hole, how do we describe our situation? (From W. J. Kaufmann III, Black Holes and Warped Spacetime.*)*

experience, we take it for granted that a ball will not move unless some force (like a kick) is imparted to it. In the microworld of the quantum, an electron on one side of a barrier can simply reappear on the other without physically moving—an effect called quantum tunneling.

Quantum mechanics also demolishes another commonsense concept—the idea of nothing. The quantum view of nothing is crucial to our understanding of the genesis of the universe, which requires us to believe that nothing is where everything came from.

What do we mean by "nothing"? To the average human being, nothing is just that—no thing, emptiness, void. But a little thought shows that matters are more complex than this. We talk of empty air even though we know that air consists of particles whose combined force can, in the case of hurricanes, flatten a house. If pressed, however, most of us would equate nothing with a vacuum.

Here we run headlong into a quantum paradox. In modern physics, a vacuum is not empty—it contains space-time. Space-time is far from featureless. The smallest dimension at which the word "structure" has meaning in contemporary physics is called the Planck length, i.e., about 0.1^{35} of a meter). At this minute scale, the random fluctuations so characteristic of the quantum world are believed to give space-time a highly complex "topology"—a "foamy" texture. The nature of this space-time foam is bizarre in the extreme. Some scientists believe that space-time consists of a complex matrix of cross-connecting "wormholes." Others liken the space-time vacuum to a mishmash of Planck-sized black holes jammed together. None of these images conveys any hint of the real nature of a vacuum because the situation is so absolutely removed from conditions on our human scale of dimensions.

Perhaps the most startling aspect of the vacuum state is that it is filled with an evanescent flux of ghostly particles called virtual particles. Many nonphysicists think of virtual particles as somehow not real, and hence ascribe the seething movement in the vacuum state to some kind of mathematical sleight of hand. However, while the virtual particles that dance endlessly in the vacuum state may be evanescent, they have measurable effects on the activity of more familiar particles. Consider a hydrogen atom. It consists of a central proton and a single orbiting electron. Instead of following a smooth path around the nucleus, the electron can be seen to jiggle slightly (the Lamb shift). That jiggling results from the unceasing but brief appearance of tiny electric fields, due to the creation and disappearance of virtual particles in the vacuum through which the electron moves.

The realization that a vacuum contains an infinity of virtual particles embedded in a foamy space-time matrix makes the next feature of the vacuum state slightly—but only slightly—easier to comprehend. The vacuum contains energy in quantities that send the human imagination reeling. For example, American mathematician Richard Feynman has suggested that every cubic centimeter of vacuum contains enough energy to boil all the oceans on earth. Arthur C. Clarke puts it even more forcibly: "It's at least an interesting thought that the vacuum inside an ordinary light bulb contains enough energy to destroy the galaxy . . . and perhaps, with a little extra effort, the cosmos."

It is important to remember that the vacuum is the dominant structure in physical reality—the particles of the so-called real world are only minor blips in this ocean of incessant virtual action with its paradoxical background of space-time foam. Across the breadth of the cosmos, the familiar building blocks of matter are outnumbered by the infinity of come-and-go ghost particles that boil in the vacuum state.

The almost unthinkable amount of energy locked up in the quantum vacuum may turn out to be the key that unlocks the penultimate secrets of the universe's genesis. If a bulb of vacuum contains enough energy to destroy a universe, surely something equally small must contain enough energy to create one, under the right circumstances. The question then becomes, What are the right circumstances?

Physicists believe they may be approaching the answer to this question through a dawning realization that a vacuum can exist in different energy states. Just as an atom can jump from a (stable) ground state to an (unstable) excited state by absorbing energy, so a vacuum may be able to excite itself into a temporary false vacuum condition, which can have an energy density of almost unbelievable proportions. And just as an atom can fall back from its excited state to the ground state by giving up energy, so a false vacuum can decay by releasing the energy it enfolds.

To see what this means, let us suppose that the universe found itself in an excited vacuum state just after the creation. According to physical theorists, this false vacuum condition would result in an enormous repulsive force that would catapult the seed of the newborn cosmos into a massive outward expansion. The flight of the galaxies we see today may represent the aftershock of this primordial inflation. However, just as an excited atom loses energy when it returns to a stable state, so the false vacuum must sooner or later surrender its outward-racing momentum. When that happens, the titanic energy of the false vacuum is suddenly dumped into the structure of the expanding cosmos as radiation, creating a fireball of unimaginable power and heating the universe up to about 10^{27} °K This is the hot big bang.

The concept that the cosmos existed briefly in an unstable quantum vacuum state, while answering one question, merely uncovers another.

We must now face the final, decisive issue. Where did the energy of the vacuum come from in the first place? Can we start from nothing at all? Absolutely nothing?

Here we reach the very limits of human knowledge and imagination. Only one field of science holds the possibility of an answer; once again, it is quantum mechanics. At first sight this seems strange. Quantum mechanics deals with the microworld of subatomic particles—the realm of the very small. Yet, the question we are asking relates to the universe— the realm of the very large. This contradiction vanishes when we realize that, in its initial seed-state, the cosmos occupied a space much smaller than an atom. In this speck of infinitesimal smallness, quantum effects were not just important, they dominated and directed the course of events.

In this quantum world, the unimaginable somehow happened, courtesy of quantum effects, which, as we have seen, go a long way toward uncoupling cause and effect. To explain the genesis, all we are required to do is make that uncoupling complete. Then the Creation becomes a spontaneous event, *without prior cause.* Like a dream that suddenly flowers into reality, space-time itself erupts into existence. But not the familiar space-time of today. According to an attractive theory, the seed of the primordial universe is structured in ten dimensions of space. Three of those dimensions explode outward into the false vacuum condition, while the other seven implode into a near-invisible "hyperball." However, they do not vanish but continue to influence the fate of the cosmos as forces of nature. We have already seen how gravity, which we commonly think of as a force in the three-dimensional world of everyday space, becomes a crinkling of geometry in the four-dimensional world of space-time. In similar fashion, the dimensions that compacted early in the evolution of the cosmos remain visible as electromagnetism and strong and weak nuclear forces, the other three forces that shape the world.

English physicist and author Paul Davies has superbly expressed what is thought to happen: "Thus a microscopic quantum blob of ten-dimensional space suffers a spasm which inflates three dimensions to form a universe, and traps the remaining seven in a permanent microcosmos from which they are manifested only indirectly, as forces of nature."

If this glimpse gives us some faint feeling for the beginning of time, what does it tell us about its end? If we are living inside a black hole, then our only protection is the primordial momentum that the galaxies still carry as a legacy of the false vacuum inflation that preceded the hot Big Bang. When this outward stretching of space-time stops, the cosmos will pass from an expansionary to a contractionary phase. The cosmic background temperature will start to rise until the night sky becomes as hot as our present daytime sky. As the contraction accelerates, structure on various levels will begin to melt and stars and planets will disintegrate into a soup of radiation and subatomic particles. The nuclei of atoms will dissolve into their constituent protons and neutrons.

As the cosmos shrinks beyond atomic dimensions, the matter it contains will become dense beyond imagination and the radius of space-time will contract toward zero. At its ultimate limit, this process leads to a space-time *singularity* in which the curvative of space-time becomes infinite, enfolding in its vanished embrace a universe of imploded matter. Like an image fading in the mind of God, reality itself dies, and the sum of all things ceases to be.

Some faint hint of what this means can be garnered from an examination of Figure 7.2, which shows that an ordinary black hole is smoothly connected to the "flat" space-time structure of the surrounding universe. It is this matrix of surrounding space-time that enables science to measure properties of black holes, such as mass. However, if the cosmos is closed, everything is "inside" a black hole. Thus, as the cosmos implodes, there is absolutely no frame of reference to serve as a guide.

Here, then, is the Shiva of cosmology, the destroyer of worlds. Nothing can survive transit through a singularity. The space-time fabric with its embedded memories of past events (in which billions of human lives lie encrystallized) is annihilated. The fine structure of matter, everything that gives form to physics, is unremittingly ground out of existence. By this, I do not mean simply that it is destroyed in a physical sense, overwhelmed by the colossal tides of gravity: Rather, infinitely warped space-time sunders us completely from anything that might have gone before, just as it does from anything that might come after. The present incarnation of the cosmos can never remember its parents (if there were any) or transmit a legacy to its children (if it has any).

Mathematics, the tool that has carried the human mind back to within a micromillisecond of the genesis, cannot complete its backward journey to zero. All our imaginative powers fail us at the genesis point itself. It is not just that science cannot explain what happens at this time of mystery because it lacks the right tools. Rather, the laws of physics themselves break down at a singularity.

ALTERNATIVE 2: ENDING IN ICE

What if scenario number two is correct and the universe continues to expand? Here, the vision is one of a gradual thinning out of matter as space-time stretches farther. That stretching may continue forever, since the expansion goes on *ad infinitum.* However, this expanding cosmos is destined to live out the inexorable dictum of the second law of thermo-dynamics—that order must eventually decay until all physical processes reach a state of final equilibrium (heat death).

The road to this final state is, on the open-universe scenario, a strange one indeed. First, stars die as they use up their nuclear fuel. Across the cosmos the lights in the sky go out. As cosmologist Edward Harrison has so powerfully said:

> The stars begin to fade like guttering candles and are snuffed out one by one. Out in the depths of space the great celestial cities, the galaxies, cluttered with the memorabilia of ages, are gradually dying. Tens of billions of years pass in the growing darkness. Occasional flickers of light pierce the fall of cosmic night, and spurts of activity delay the sentence of a universe condemned to become a galactic graveyard.

At this stage, the cosmos, dark and cold, is littered with the corpses of stars and other leftovers of its past glory. These pieces of cosmic debris do not simply drift about. From time to time, inevitably, they collide with each other, or are sucked into black holes. The latter fate is the more significant for it results in a massive enlargement of many black holes that are believed to lurk at the centers of many (most?) galaxies. These gigantic gravity maws swallow increasing amounts of cosmic flotsam and jetsam.

Many physicists believe that the key building blocks of the atomic nu-cleus, in particular the proton, are unstable in the very long term and will decay over enormous periods of time. If this view is correct, all the protons in the cosmic debris will eventually disintegrate into smaller particles of opposite charge, electrons and positrons. These annihilate each other and any odd electrons that may be around. Perhaps the ultimate destiny of matter itself is to largely self-destruct.

How this process proceeds depends on how fast the cosmos expands. If the expansion is rapid enough, many electrons and positrons will be dragged apart by the stretching space-time fabric before they can interact. These surviving ruins of material reality cool down faster than the radiation produced by the self-annihilating particle pairs. That results in a tiny but definite temperature differential between the two, which never vanishes completely. On this model, the universe almost runs down to its lowest state but never quite makes it to absolute zero.

If a full-scale intermingling of electrons and positrons is permitted to occur, courtesy of a slower rate of expansion, events take a more bizarre turn. Physicists predict that, under conditions likely to prevail in this near-terminal phase of the slowly expanding cosmos, negatively charged electrons can enter into a partnership with positively charged positrons to form monstrous atoms called positronium atoms. These are unbelievably large—thousands of billions of light-years across. Over mind-bending eons of time, these fantastic atoms decay by giving off low-energy photons, finally allowing their orbiting electron/positron pairs to self-destruct.

Apart from decaying positronium atoms, the only other large-scale structures in the near-dead cosmos are the massive black holes. As long as their temperature remains above that of the surrounding space, black holes continue to grow by heat absorption. Once this critical threshold is passed, however, the process more or less reverses, and the hole tends to lose heat. As the heat loss accelerates, the hole shrinks and eventually evaporates into nothing, according to many physicists.

What might the end result on the open-universe model be? In physicist-author Barry Parker's words:

> This means that even massive black holes will eventually disappear as a result of Hawking radiation but it will take an exceedingly long time. Stellar-mass black holes will live for about 10^{25} years, super-massive or galactic black holes about 10^{100} years. Most of the particles that come off will be photons and therefore in its final stages the

universe will consist of mostly photons, with a few electrons, positrons and neutrinos. It will, indeed, be a dark, dreary, desolate place.

Or, in the words of Paul Davies:

These studies suggest a dismal fate for the universe we now know, so full of splendor and activity. Though the immensity of the times involved are beyond human imagination . . . there seems little doubt that all the currently-observed structures are destined to pass away eventually, leaving only cold, dark, expanding, near-empty space, populated at an ever-decreasing density by a few isolated neutrinos and photons, and very little else. It is a scenario that many scientists find profoundly depressing.

What happens to time in the open universe? The dye-droplet example in Chapter 2 highlighted the fact that time's arrow is defined by the direction of increasing entropy. Once the universe has reached a state of final equilibrium, entropy can no longer increase, so there can no longer be any definite time asymmetry, any meaningful sense of past-to-future. The fact that a rapidly expanding universe may never quite reach total equilibrium may seem to offer a flicker of hope, but it is little more than that. In such a rapidly expanding cosmos, the temperature gap that remains between cooling matter and cooling radiation is vanishingly small. It is extremely difficult to see how such a marginal source of usable energy could be constructively used by any hypothetical intelligent beings that might still be around. Thus, although American physicist Freeman Dyson, in a much-quoted paper, has suggested that life in an open universe might survive forever, one has to look at the quality of that life in a universe where the clock of time has virtually stopped. Eternal life in a near-dead cosmos seems more like an everlasting hibernation, a minimum-energy comatose sleep, than the dynamic evolutionary adventure we see around us today when time's clock is still ticking strongly. It has yet to be shown how Dyson's last survivors could figure out a way to survive the possible decay of their own protons.

This picture of the end of time differs from what happens at a singularity. At a singularity, the clock of time is destroyed. At heat death, the clock stops, or comes very close to it. These differences are at the same time profound and irrelevant. From our human perspective, all that matters is that time's arrow, as we know it, ceases to exist.

Science has found it harder to accept the Big Crunch scenario than the heat death scenario. I suspect the reasons for this have more to do with human psychology than with the search for truth. Science intensely dislikes the idea that the laws of physics break down at a singularity. That seems to place the question of our ultimate beginning and ultimate ending forever beyond the reach of human sight.

It is not surprising that some scientists have tried to find ways around this problem, to bring the cosmos in its totality back within the framework of physical law and order. Perhaps the most successful attempt has been that of Stephen Hawking. Hawking has put forward a model of endearing simplicity. He likens the spherical structure of space-time to the surface of the earth (Figure 7.3). The north pole is the Big Bang (the beginning) and the south pole is the Big Crunch (the end). This representation allows the universe to start and stop at "points," but those points are not singularities. The two poles lie on a continuous surface, not an edge. The laws of science apply at these points just as they do at the North and South poles of the earth. Thus the beginning and the end of time are brought back into the fold.

This works, however, only by using a (seemingly) unusual strategy. In order to bring space-time back into the realm of physics, Hawking is forced to abandon real numbers and use imaginary ones. Real numbers give a positive quantity when multiplied by themselves; imaginary numbers give negative values when multiplied by themselves. The special virtue of imaginary numbers in this context is that they cause the distinction between space and time to disappear. That makes it possible to use Euclidean geometry to build models of the cosmos, because, in this representation, time has no privileged status.

Hawking defends the use of imaginary numbers on the grounds that it is "merely a mathematical device (or trick) to calculate answers about real space-time." However, the universe we live in exists in real time. Hawking's model predicts that in real time, "it [the universe] would collapse again into what looks like a singularity in real time. Thus, in a sense, we

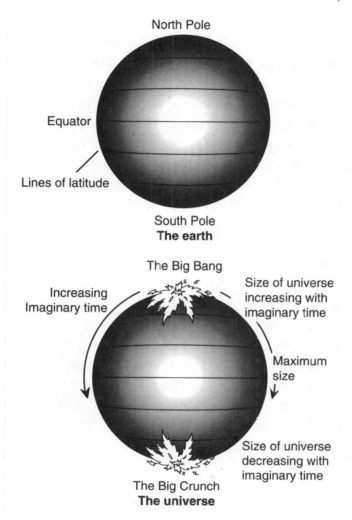

FIGURE 7.3

Hawking's universe in imaginary time. Science says that the cosmos began with a genesis event, commonly dubbed the Big Bang. If the closed-universe scenario is correct, the cosmos will end with a Big Crunch. This seems to suggest a beginning and an end to Creation. However, Stephen Hawking has proposed a model for the cosmos that eliminates the necessity for start and stop points in the story of time. He likens the closed spherical structure of space-time (see Figure 7.1b) to the surface of the earth. In this representation, the North Pole corresponds to the Big Bang and the South Pole to the Big Crunch. These points are not "edges" and they do not require prior causes. To obtain this model, however, Hawking has had to abandon real time and use imaginary time. (From S. W. Hawking, A Brief History of Time.*)*

are still all doomed, even if we keep away from black holes."

This brings us back from physics to psychology. The point I have been laboring is that all these projective models reveal the universe as a living creature. It was born, it evolves, it will die. Just as you and I started life as a microscopic speck and developed into a full-fledged adult only to return to a state of nonbeing, so the cosmos began as a singularity, evolves as an awesome, complex, and wonderful whole, but inevitably heads toward a death in which all that went before will vanish.

The sense of finality we feel when confronted with the death of the human self pales when confronted with the death of forever. The end of the cosmos is absolute and irredeemable. Even if an endless series of new universes do (as some have suggested) reemerge from the singularities in which the old ones die, no communication between parent and offspring is possible, since any transmitted data has to pass through the implacably unforgiving "gate" of the singularity, and in this final shutter, all prior structure is utterly destroyed.

At the present stage of human evolution, this foreknowledge is the property of a tiny elite, those who have studied and understood the implications of the new cosmology. It has not affected the thinking of the average person, who is of necessity still preocuppied with the tasks of the "daily round." However, those who have looked into this pit weep on behalf of humanity. Speaking of the heat death scenario, Bertrand Russell said:

> that all the labours of the ages, all the devotion, all the inspiration, all the noonday brightness of human genius, are destined to extinction in the vast death of the solar system, and the whole temple of Man's achievements must inevitably be buried beneath the debris of a universe in ruins—all these things, if not quite beyond dispute, are yet so nearly certain that no philosophy which rejects them can hope to stand. Only within the scaffolding of these truths, only on the firm foundation of unyielding despair, can the soul's habitation henceforth be safely built.

This note of despair runs through the writings of other scientists. The human anguish that the fate of the cosmos engenders is, for me, summed up by American cosmologist Steven Weinberg who says near the end of his book *The First Three Minutes*:

> As I write this I happen to be in an airplane at 30,000 feet, flying over Wyoming en route home from San Francisco to Boston. Below, the earth looks very soft and comfortable—fluffy clouds here and there, snow turning pink as the sun sets, roads stretching straight across the country from one town to another. It is very hard to realize that this all is just a tiny part of an overwhelmingly hostile universe. It is even harder to realize that this present universe has evolved from an unspeakably unfamiliar early condition, and faces a future extinction of endless cold or intolerable heat. *The more the universe seems comprehensible, the more it also seems pointless.*

Here is the existential crisis taken out of the human self and written on a cosmic scale. In our generation, for the first time, thinking man is faced with a twofold denial of the future. He will die, and so will the universe that created him. Personal death shadows our consciousness through life. Cosmic death hovers at the far edge of reality, so remote that the long shadow it casts barely reaches into our present moment of evolution. Taken together, personal death and universal death pose a shattering blow to human hopes. That is because, if accepted at face value, these forecasts of our fate would destroy the wellsprings of all human motivation, demonstrating that nothing, in the final analysis, can last.

This twofold denial marks the pivot-point of this book, for at this point I break ranks with my fellow scientists and offer a new vision of life, one that draws its strength not from a refusal to face death but from a clear-eyed recognition of what death is. To do this, I will not abandon science. Science has been my guide and mentor on this journey, and any philosophy that ignores science cannot claim legitimacy for its tenets. Indeed, my starting point lies in the very area of cosmology we have just reached—the new physics.

Some years ago, Stephen Hawking was elected to the Lucasian Chair of Mathematics at Cambridge University, the chair once occupied by Isaac Newton. Hawking's inaugural lecture had the ambitious title "Is the End in Sight for Theoretical Physics?" Hawking was suggesting that science was close to accomplishing its ultimate goal—the unification of all the laws of physics into one coherent, consistent framework, which would define and encompass the whole of reality. Such a unified scheme would not just "represent" truth in some abstract way, it would in an important sense *be truth*. By now, this should not surprise us. As we have seen, the homely metaphors of common sense and everyday life offer us no guidance when we look at the bewildering cosmos in which we find ourselves. Only mathematics, in whose code nature writes her secrets, can tell us what is "real."

I believe Hawking is right. This is not to say that science has run out of ideas or reached its limit, but that modern physics in particular (the other sciences are derived from physics) is reaching toward its grand synthesis right now. Once that has been achieved, science will have gone as far as logic can take it.

Science is essentially a product of man's discovery that the universe is written in mathematical code. In our time, we have perfected the tools of mathematics, from matrix theory to field theory, and have arrived at a definitive theory of numbers. Using these tools, we have been able to unify two (certainly) and three (probably) of the four forces of nature. Only gravity remains outside the fold, and there are encouraging hints that the new theories of supersymmetry may bring gravity into the same framework as electromagnetism, the weak force, and the strong force. Then the long search that began with the abacus will have ended; the quest for unity will be over, with only details to be filled in.

Mathematical reasoning seems largely a left-brain function, like language, the other symbolic code that makes us human. As we saw in Chapter 4, it is language that creates the ego-self. Mathematics reinforces the linear logic of the left brain and embeds our consciousness in time. This is not to deny the right brain role of intuition in the creative processes of science, simply to point to the deep similarities between verbal codes (speech) and numerical codes (algebra and calculus).

We can refine these linear, encoding processes further and, I have no doubt, discover new and exciting (perhaps even revolutionary) aspects of nature. However, we are close to a threshold. To progress farther, we must break a different barrier—one that lies inside the structure of our own brains. The limit we are reaching in physics is not the end result of a finished product, not the flawless glory of a perfect crystal, not the final face of God. It represents the limit of the resolving power of the tool we have been using, the average structure of consciousness at this human moment in evolution.

A parable may help. Imagine a primitive lens maker, trying to observe the teeming life in a drop of pond water, using a badly ground piece of glass with a low resolving power. Dimly, at the limit of his vision, he can see strange and wonderful creatures, but their shapes—their natures—are beyond his reach. He is totally unaware of the richness that lies at higher levels of magnification; to him this hidden microworld quite literally does not exist.

In this situation, the problem is not the sight but the one who sees, not the job but the instrument. That is our dilemma. In a fascinating sense, we have, in our time, arrived in the forbidden land. What lies before us is the final frontier, the mysterious border at which we are prevented from seeing more deeply into the nature of things, *not by the construction of the world, but by the construction of ourselves.*

8

THROUGH THE
LOOKING GLASS

Myself I must remake.
— W . B . Y E A T S

We have now reached the takeoff point for the message of this book. Recognizing that the problem we face exists inside our minds, not in the objective world beyond, we must now reexamine the structure of human mentality. If the instrument we use to see is flawed, we must understand why.

Before we jump, let us make sure we are standing on firm ground. I have attempted to show that the human longing for immortality is a direct result of the selfishness of our genes. All genes are Von Neumann machines, but each has its own self-promoting software, its own survival program. It is these idiomatic programs that relentlessly compete in the unforgiving world of nature.

Human DNA encodes its own selfish survival software. Since the central information-processing system of a human being is the brain, it is not surprising that the self-preserving feedback cycles (survival instincts) have come to be concentrated in the brain. There they remain to this day, buried in the limbic system and in the ancient reptilian brain stem, ready at any time to override the feeble objections of mere reason. Since we are seldom physically threatened in our everyday lives, the fight-or-flight chemistry of self-preservation is now sensitized to, and primed by, low-grade triggers and imaginary dangers. Anxiety, nervousness, phobia, and panic are the legacy of this emergency system in which our psyches are still rooted.

This selfish feedback loop at the root of the brain colors its thinking cap (the cortex), expressing itself in consciousness as a longing to live forever. Almost all human myths bear the deep stamp of that longing.

The evolution of language has put this urge for immortality into a uniquely human context. It is now embedded in the persona we build up from experience, the ego-self. This is especially true of our time; terms such as *ego trip, ego massage, egomaniac,* testify to the centrality of our sense of self in the way we conduct our affairs. The goal-oriented physiology of self-preservation—expressed in the drives that compel us to eat, drink, and make love—has been expanded into the goal-oriented psychology of ambition, which compels us to promote our own self-image at the expense of others. The close relationship between self-preservation and self-promotion is graphically shown in the term we use to describe the titillating, risky power games by which we seek to enlarge our ego-selves: We say they give us an "adrenaline surge." Fittingly, ours has been called "the me generation."

Me. I. Self-consciousness. We come back, from a different and deeper perspective, to the domain of the ego-self, the center from which we view the world. We have seen that the ego-self is a construction of the symbolate world that language (chiefly) makes possible. Note the use of the word "construction." I could just as well have said "fabrication," for our sense of ego is something we create inside our heads, a theory, to use Gazzaniga's expression. As such, it lacks the physical reality of a stone or a coin.

To recap the key conclusion of Chapter 4, the ego-self is a symbolic point of internal reference, a nexus created in the mind by the mind to organize the input of experience so as to preserve the coherence of the subjective realm and allow the body/self to function in a purposeful way.

To drive to the root of this issue, we must now ask not what the ego-self is, but how it comes into being. The answer is that our sense of ego arises by a process of *differentiation,* which progressively separated each of us from the rest of humanity. The net result of that process of differentiation, simplistically put, is that the ego becomes the sum of our differences.

This may seem obscure, so let me work it through. Look first at the way many ego-self differences are defined by differences in age, i.e., in time. The boy who looks at me from a faded photo of myself taken thirty-nine years ago is in one factual sense not me despite the fact that I am genetically and physically continuous with him over time. The sum of later memories, stored layer upon layer across the 14,235 day/night cycles that have intervened since then, has added a new persona to the child I was. If the present "I" existed in that faded image, it was only as one singular possibility, slotted among millions of options. For example, if I had not decided in 1978 to emigrate to Australia, the person I am would differ significantly from what I might have become.

Many people look back nostalgically at their youth and long to return to what they see as an age of lost innocence and vigor. What they unconsciously want to do is return to their youth with their cargo of adult memories intact. If a man were actually faced with the possibility of going back in time to the person he was thirty years ago, the chances are he would not be able to bring himself to do it. To obliterate the memory of the intervening years would be to destroy an essential part of himself. The feedback loop built into our brains recognizes *all its memories* as self, i.e., as things to be preserved. It is not possible to erase elements of stored experience without damaging the self-sense, without flawing and distorting the "I" of the "I am" statement.

The process of differentiation that creates ego begins before birth. Each ego is given a strong weighting by the genes it inherits from its parents, which predisposes mentality to grow along certain predetermined lines. Each ego also has to undergo a common rite of passage into being, emerging from a sense of primal unity with the Mother (its genesis universe) into a sense of precarious independence, when it feels fearfully on its own. But once in the world, what builds ego are the differentiating processes that involve human choice.

Choice. We return to a key point that, as I warned the reader, has now returned to haunt us. Remember the camel driver who came to a fork in the road of the space-time landscape. His choice of route created his future. The fork in the road corresponds to what I shall henceforth call a Y node, a point of decision, preceding action. In the well-known words of Robert Frost:

Two roads diverged in a wood and I—
I took the one less traveled by,
And that has made all the difference.

Y nodes are not mere metaphysical abstractions. They may, in a deep sense, correspond to processes that take place in our brains, processes that underlie the machinery of memory and the very nature of reality.

The human brain has many operational similarities to a computer. The memory of a computer is an electronic device that uses a binary code; i.e., it contains elements that can exist in either of two states. Before an item is entered in the computer's memory, either state is equally probable. This corresponds with the bottom junction of the Y node before a choice is made. After the item has been entered in memory, the system is definitely in one state or the other; it has "flipped" to either the left or the right arm of the Y node.

As we saw in Chapter 2, Y nodes occupy a more central position in any story of reality. They are the point at which the quantum wave, the ripple of possibility, collapses into the existential certainty. To use the language of the many-universes theory, they are the points at which reality bifurcates, at which the human mind, by its own choice, creates two parallel universes that thereafter go their separate ways, forever apart.

To say that the ego is the product of choices is thus not merely a psychological statement. Initially, however, those choices are not its own. When we are children, we usually cannot dictate the choices our parents make. As we grow up, it is the effects of the many Y node choices made by our parents and others around us that, increasingly and progressively, differentiate us from our fellows; in this process, the ego-self emerges. It is not until that ego-self has acquired its own personality that we begin to take on responsibility for our own decisions.

Individual decisions, then, are important, but less so than we might think. Overwhelmingly, our ego-selves result from accidents of time and place that determine that we are born here rather than there, speaking this language rather than that, thinking these thoughts rather than those, etc. To adapt an idea from a Somerset Maugham story, I am here only because one day, almost ninety years ago, my grandmother crossed a street in Berlin. That sounds ludicrous, but it's true. Had she not crossed the street, she would not have begun the train of events that led to her meeting my grandfather, and I would never have been born.

The point I am making is that the ego-self is largely a collection of accidents that separate our minds from those of our fellows. It is a kind of existential noise, which owes its being in large part to the chiefly random character of the events that create it. As such, the ego-self—the identity tag that our survival loops guard so carefully—*has absolutely no value as a window to the world.*

Experience has taught me that few people get the point of that statement, in most cases failing to see how completely the truth it encodes can change their lives. They will say, "But you should meet so-and-so. He has the most wonderful personality. He is one of the wisest human beings I know. How can you say that his personality has no value when it is that very personality that makes him unique?" My answer is that what makes your friend unique is not his ego-self but the *quality of his consciousness,* or more precisely the point he has reached in the scale of mental evolution. (I am aware that, in making this claim, I have not yet defined "consciousness" and I ask readers to make do with their own definition until Chapters 9 and 10.)

Thus two people from the same ethnic and cultural background, born in the same street, with similar ego-self frameworking, can fail to understand each other if their degree of psychological maturity differs by too wide a margin. Conversely, two people from different sides of the globe— can meet and speak the same language instantly if their minds have reached the same growth stage, despite radically different ego-self structures.

Far from being the source of consciousness in human evolution, the ego-self is a blinder that hides the truth beneath trivia. To see through this maze, one has to be able to separate the graduated spectrum of consciousness from the variable sense of self. Any human being who has reached a certain point in his psychological development will be able intuitively to "identify with" (telltale term) any other person at the same stage of growth. The stage is what matters, for each grade of consciousness is the same for all the human beings who reach it.

The ego-self is the sum of the differences, trivial in the main, that separate each human person from others. Confusion arises because people do not distinguish the trivial differences due to accidents of time and place (the ego-self) from authentic differences on the road to growth, i.e., different levels on the scale of consciousness. If you can separate these two modalities of the human personality, you will have made the critical jump needed to carry you through the rest of this book. You will understand that our survival compulsion is built into and around the ego-self, *not consciousness itself.* Indeed, growth can be achieved only if the ego-self dies. That is the deeper meaning of death. In this sense, death is not the end but the beginning, the doorway to the new world. Once that doorway has been opened, physical death loses all terror because the mind is liberated from its bondage to time.

I realize this must sound like occultism or a relapse into religion. I assure you it is not. Let me demonstrate why it is the ego-self that causes human beings to hunger after immortality. The ego-self is a composite of personal differences. If you feel inclined to challenge this statement, just try to describe your individuality in a way that does not involve comparisons with others. You will soon realize that identity is entirely relative; in the absence of some universally accepted standard of comparison, it can be defined only in relation to another person or, more likely, a mixture of people.

In the world of nature, differences matter. They are the crux and pivot of evolution. Suppose I grow several hundred million germs in a tank of broth. Examination of their DNA would show that their genetic codes, their encoded self-images, are virtually identical; any one germ taken at random would, on a probability basis, share over 99.9 percent of its sequences with any other. The other side of this statement is that, in any germ population of 100 million, tens of thousands of germs will differ very slightly from the norm.

If I now add a trace of an antibiotic like streptomycin to the germ population, virtually the entire original population will be wiped out. However, among the few survivors are the tiny subsection that, by pure chance, happen to manufacture a protein that makes them resistant to the antibiotic. Those few survivors now multiply in the runaway fashion that characterizes exponential growth. The end result is that when the new steady population of 100 million has been reestablished, over 99.9 percent will conform to the resistant type.

Therefore, in nature, differences, no matter how small, can be a matter of life and death. Differences define fitness to survive. By continually adjusting the fitness of all living systems, natural selection has, across three and a half billion years, honed the survival software of genes, indelibly imprinting the survive-at-all-costs imperative on cells and psychologies.

Differences drive evolution. I cannot stress too strongly that natural selection acts on differences among individuals, not populations. The differences can be trivial in a strictly numerical sense, as the above example showed, but their effects can be profound. This principle carries over directly into human psychology. We are sexually reproducing creatures, so our genes are a fifty-fifty blend of those from each parent. This mixing of genes makes each of us a physically unique individual. Experience builds on these genetic differences, differentiating us increasingly from our fellows as we grow up. By the time we are thirteen years old, we normally have strongly developed ego-selves—we are recognizable individuals, labeled by society with identity tags called names.

As parents, we feel strongly for our young. Fifty percent of their genes are ours, so when we look at them we are looking at a partial mirror of ourselves. Significantly, our feelings of protective love tend to be strongest when our children are just that—children. After that, their evolving ego-selves start to differentiate them from us and erect the distinctions that so bruise interactions among ego-conscious adults.

Manifestly, then, evolution still works on and through individual differences among people. Some do well, others fall by the way. However, our culture has changed the rules. Success is no longer measured in terms of reproduction but (usually) in terms of achievement—often measured by indicators of "status," such as the accumulation of material wealth and power. Differences retain their significance, however, because, in our society, at this ego-conscious phase of its evolution, differences fulfill the same competitive me-versus-you function they had in the animal phase. Up to a point, the dynamics of human life are based on the fact that each individual has a different sense of separate ego, of "I am" as opposed to "You are."

Thus human society experiences a manner of natural selection based on competition among ego-conscious individuals. What this process selects for is, in the main, what one might expect of such a system: greed, survival at all costs, a killer instinct in business, a massive emphasis on goods that reflect enlarged ego structures, wealth, power, indifference to others—in short, selfishness. Selfish egos replace selfish genes.

The basic nature of the ego-self shows up in the way it is constructed within each individual brain. The ego-self is an expression of the learned layers of memory stored in the cortex but—and here is the crucial point—*the ego-self remains inextricably locked into the survival software permanently written into its genes.* The genes of every human being create in the physical brain a robot, the limbic/reptilian complex, which houses the survival instincts. This robot is the same in all of us. Blindly, it pegs each emerging layer of the ego-self to the ancient feedback loop of self-preservation. The process is one-way. Once an experience has been added to memory, it becomes part of the ego-self, to be conserved along with everything that went before.

Thus the robot—something we all share as part of our evolutionary heritage—becomes the unwitting agent by which our emerging personalities—the source of our differences—become hostage to foreverness. The chemical loop of self-preservation takes into itself the psychological ego-self.

Let us now take the next step. According to its program, what the robot must do is *maintain the status quo.* That has a far-reaching consequence. Once a strong sense of ego-self has developed during the later years of childhood and the teens, the new (and mostly unimportant) day-to-day experiences of life usually serve to reinforce (or at worst only slightly modify) the current status-quo structure of the ego-self. We cling fanatically to our sense of identity, of me-ness, because it has become our lens of life, our window to the world, our personal guardian of the universal survival imperative of the selfish gene.

Because selfish egos spring from selfish genes, the desires built into the ego-cage are open-ended. It is the nature of the ego to reinforce its own self-image by always wanting more of those things that strengthen its definition—more money, more power, more time (whence springs its open-ended urge to last forever).

To put it another way, and so make my next point, what we dread above almost all else is *change*. By that, I do not mean the simple addition of ordinary day-to-day experiences, which are easily accommodated within the existing ego-self structure: I mean changes that profoundly alter the ego-self, reshaping and remaking it. The reason for this is fundamental. If we change the "I" self-image too deeply, we create a new creature; the "me" that emerges from a profound personality change is, in a real and factual sense, *no longer me*—it is a stranger, it is other.

For this reason, I believe that the defining feature of human growth is contained in the transformative experiences of life, those that involve suffering and pain, "shake us to the core," and are innately resisted by the self-preserving robot whose task it is blindly to maintain the status quo. Human psychology is inherently self-protective and conservative.

Evidence of this is everywhere. There is a strong community dread of genetic engineering. Why? Because gene technology has the potential to break down the barriers that separate one species from another. We must never lose sight of the selfish-gene perspective here. Genes are exclusive. Sex in nature acts as a discriminator, keeping different DNAs apart and ensuring that like breeds only with like. Any scientific advance that threatens to dissolve these boundaries threatens the separate ego-sense as much as it threatens the selfish genes that create these boundaries.

When genetic engineering goes to work on man himself, this subliminal dread is sharpened and focused. Man, like any creature, has a fierce loyalty to his own genetic model. In mythology, man is made in the image of God. Whatever threatens the stability of this form threatens man's innermost identity, his species' self-image, which is the collective counterpart of the ego-self. It is no accident that experiments on human embryos are banned by law in almost all Western nations.

This current hostility toward gene technology is a lineal descendant of a long-held hostility toward evolution itself. When Darwin published *On the Origin of Species* in 1859, the reaction it provoked was extraordinary—so extraordinary that, to explain it, one has to look beyond the conventional clash of science and religion and deep into psychology. The cause was the fear of change. In the God-given codex of the Judeo-Christian credo, all species had been divinely created in their present forms; i.e., they were immutable. This sense of unchangeable permanence was in perfect resonance with the limbic brain with its innate genetic instructions to maintain the status quo. Evolution was a shattering challenge to the psyche, because it revealed a universe in flux, in a state of constant and unremitting change.

The discovery of evolution, more than anything else, heightened an age-old tension that has always existed between the conservatism of our subconscious (the seat of instinct) and the flexibility of our cerebral cortex (the seat of intelligence). I once described man as a machine that dreams. The machine is the robot in the limbic brain, fixed in form and programmed by genes to maintain what is as it is. The dreamer is the cerebral cortex, a freewheeling adventurer whose software programs are written not by genes but by experience. A dreamer dreams of things that are not yet. He dreams of change. And change is what the ego-self fears.

We are literally at war with ourselves, the robot in the limbic brain struggling to keep the status quo while the adventurer in the cortex toys with novelty. This war within our psychology, like the day/night cycle, has become externalized in our myths. Almost every human culture has developed a folklore that shows the universe polarized between warring opposites: God versus the devil, good versus evil, light versus darkness, Osiris versus Set. The pleasure/pain centers of the limbic cortex act as ordering foci for these opposites of experience. Now we see that the struggle between the pleasurable (good/bright/day) center and the painful (bad/dark/night) center is also interwoven with an unresolved conflict between the bottom story of the mind, where instinct dwells, and the upper story, where thought lives.

The fact that our personalities are divided against themselves points to a profound evolutionary paradox. Whenever a better adapted form of life appears during evolution, the old form of life from which it arose is doomed. In a sense, a superior variant is a traitor to its own kind for, given time, it will eliminate its own antecedents. What that means is that we fear the light as much as we fear the darkness; i.e., we can be just as hostile toward deep changes for the better as for the worse. I suspect that if Jesus returned to earth today, the very people who most emphatically espouse Christianity would be the first to crucify him again, because they would sense, and be suspicious of, his otherness.

There is a famous legend about an immortal called Prometheus, who stole fire from the gods and gave it to mankind. To me, what is significant about this myth is not that Prometheus' fire was a gift to man, but that it was a theft from the gods—as if what enlarged man diminished them. The meaning of this myth, I believe, is that any advance in knowledge that strengthens man's power weakens the fit between man and the natural order from which he arose. The gods of mankind were born of that old secure world, that Paradise Lost toward which man's eyes still turn in backward yearning, even as the engine of his intelligence propels him forward.

This widening breach between man and nature is at the same time the essence of human uniqueness and the source of the deep anxieties that destabilize the ego-self. There can be no doubt that, ever since he embarked on the human adventure, man has been mortally afraid (another telling term) of its consequences. That is why so many human myths contain a recurring theme that links knowledge with retribution. When Prometheus gave fire to mankind, he was tortured by the gods. When Eve ate of the Tree of Knowledge, she and Adam were expelled from the primal jungle of animal innocence and committed to an uncertain quest in a world made painful by a sense of good and evil.

Note the message of all this, for it goes to the heart of the matter. From the point of view of the status quo, our fear of change is perfectly justified. Deep changes in personality can kill the ego-self, i.e., cause the sense of separate self to die. Unlike physical death, however, a significant ego-death is a rite of passage. Through ego death, the old "me" is destroyed, and the circuits of the mind spontaneously rearrange themselves into a new stable state, centered on a new but different "me." (The robot will now work with equal dedication to preserve the new norm, the new status quo.) If ego-death is total, a radical and novel situation arises as I will discuss shortly.

Primitive cultures have always understood the transformative power of a rite of passage. Puberty rites among aborigines mark the end of boyhood and the taking up of adult status. They recognize the necessity for pain in these rituals, using the agony of circumcision and the terror of the unknown to rework the consciousness of the initiate, "burning out" the outgrown psychology of boyhood to lay the ground for the new psychology of manhood.

In primitive cultures, the terror evoked by a rite of passage is offset by the group context in which it takes place. The boy initiate is not alone in the night of his fear. The symbolic rite of initiation takes place safely within the tribal Dreaming of the group. Modern man, however, has no such safety net of ritual and shared experience. With a few rare exceptions, we must face our rites of passage alone. That is one reason why, for the most part, we fail to enter any transformative process. We dread deep, non-pleasurable experiences that could transfigure our personalities more than anything else in life. We sense their power to destroy us, which they can. We see them as death, which they are.

Yet, it is only through experiencing psychological death that we can lose our fear of physical death and break free of time, or, more precisely, see reality at last. I said at the end of Chapter 7 that the foreknowledge of (physical) death meant that for the first time in evolution, improved awareness of "reality" was life-denying, not life-promoting. I can say now that nature does not lie or deceive. Any authentic improvement in the quality of consciousness can only benefit its owner. It follows that death, the death we so fear, is illusionary. Death, remember, is the alter ego of the ego-self. *It is not a feature of consciousness.*

This point is central to this book. It is developed fully in Chapters 9 and 10. However, to reach it with understanding, we have to delve still more deeply into the nature of ego.

Let us go back again to the way the ego is built. Consider a situation in which a young person still building a strong ego-self comes to a Y node and chooses one option. He therefore commits himself to one track, ignoring the other. To make the point clear, suppose that this decision permanently influences the character of his ego-self. It may have been the choice of a job. By electing to become an automobile mechanic, for example, he ensures that the ego-self that develops over time is very different from the ego-self that would have evolved had he become a sales rep. This choice gives shape to his ego. The choice translates possibility into actuality. Our self-conscious egos are the direct result of millions of such choices that are made through life. In the many-universes perspective, each choice at each Y node creates a separate world with which we can no longer communicate, even though one of our alter egos still inhabits it. Jean-Paul Sartre summed this up when he said, "We invent ourselves by virtue of the multitude of our choices."

I believe there is a significant similarity between choices that lead to action, like the example just quoted, and the unconscious Y choices that lead us to formalize our thoughts in words. Remember the way I described the pivotal role of speech in the development of self-consciousness: "We create self-consciousness by giving unrealized mental options a concrete symbolic structure." A large part of our personalities consists of verbal structures, which are our mental record of the billions of choices by which we fix the pattern of our thoughts. It is the words, the finished "shape" of the thought, not the preceding random walk among possible options that enters memory and becomes part of us. To return to the computer analogy, it is only after the system has selected one of two initially equally probable states that an item actually enters memory as a permanent record.

It is obvious, however, that most of the choices we make limit the universal quality of consciousness. By definition, when we opt for A, we turn our backs on B. Over time, after many choices have been made, after we have fixed the structure of our thoughts in words through tens of years, we emerge with a lens on the world which is tightly defined and narrowly focused. Over time, gradually, irresistibly, inevitably, the ego-self becomes a trap for consciousness, a prison in which our vision becomes increasingly ensnared and enmeshed. To use the language of the many-universes theory, each choice separates the emerging ego from the composite reality of the superposed quantum waves of possibility that preceded it, repeatedly fragmenting the self-sense into an indefinitely escalating number of uncommunicating ego-selves.

This is the prime quality of the ego-self: It is a house of limitations, a darkling mirror that has been so fractured and shattered (as a result of the millions of choices that shape our minds) that it correctly reflects only tiny chips of reality and prevents us from seeing more than a few images at one time. To use the alternative imagery, of the millions of universes in which "I" exist, I know only one.

Without wishing to belabor the metaphor, one could say that each choice at each Y node chips a different refractive "face," like the face of a crystal, in the mirror of consciousness. Millions of chips splinter the mirror so badly that incoming light is deflected, reflected in different directions, split into varying colors. The reality image we see in the mind's mirror is thus increasingly distorted as the ego-self differentiates during development.

Passing from the metaphorical to the real, we note that modern brain research shows us that long-term memories actually alter the physico-chemical structure of the brain. Long-term memory seems to be associated with changes that take place at the junctions where nerve cells meet—the synapses. Brief bursts of nervous impulses can cause recognizable changes in the number and the nature of synaptic contacts, and those changes in some way seem to "fix" pathways among cortical cells. Thus the mirror analogy may be more apt than it seems. If each deep memory imprinted on the mind alters the organization of the brain, over the years of life the mind must be increasingly trapped by the changes that occur in its own physical structure, resulting in an increasingly "personal" vision of reality.

Albert Einstein captured the essential quality of the ego-self when he said:

A human being . . . experiences himself, his thoughts and feelings, as separated from the rest—a kind of optical delusion of consciousness. This delusion is a kind of prison for us, restricting us to our personal desires and to affections for a few persons nearest to us.

The present chaotic state of Western society is a direct result of the proliferation of these personal, ego-self boundaries. That is why life in the affluent West is beset with limits and pettiness, barriers and greed. Our religious life is full of sects; our social life, of class distinctions; our psychological life, of prejudices. Each of these things is a limitation, a narrowing of vision, a further strengthening of the delusion of which Einstein spoke.

We wall ourselves off from each other. That is the living tragedy one sees every day on the streets of a big city—thousands of lonely strangers in irrelevant togetherness.

*   *   *

My case can now be summarized. When man invented language, he invented a system of labeling and classifying the world. During the process, he developed an internal representation of his own mental states, largely as a result of writing. From this came the modern dilemma, a verbal ego-self that acts as a barrier to, not a vehicle of, consciousness.

The verbal, ego-self phase of evolution was probably inevitable. It is difficult to see how intelligence could have evolved without passing through a phase based on the development of codes, like speech and mathematics. However, ego-self consciousness is, by its very nature, a passing phase. While consciousness is trapped in the ego-self prison, humanity remains perilously at risk from the destructive consequences of its own fragmented vision.

More important, while humanity is locked into self-consciousness, it is, in an important sense, sick, its aspirations clouded and shadowed by the fear of death. That puts the phase 6 (midlife) crisis into the only perspective in which, I believe, it makes sense. To liberate consciousness, we must destroy the ego, the sense of separateness that sunders each self from its fellows. That means that, in a real sense, *we must all experience death.*

This is the greatest challenge the psyche ever faces. The robot in the brain will fight bitterly to preserve the ego; it has no choice, being a blind automaton whose program has been written by our genes, a legacy of our selfish past, of our original sin. To destroy the ego, we must fight ourselves, pitting a higher part of our minds against a lower. That is supremely difficult; it involves genuine pain and authentic suffering. It also requires courage of the highest order, for it requires us to overcome the primal terror that death in any form inspires in beings who know they are mortal.

For 99 percent of humanity, the pain and fear involved in ego-death is sufficient to stop the processes of authentic growth at the midlife crisis. Stalled and thwarted, the psychology of people in their forties and fifties often turns to displacement or outright regression. The biggest market for teenage prostitutes is middle-aged men; the biggest market for elective surgery to "restore youth" is middle-aged women. As the clock ticks on, people of both sexes increasingly look to the past, not the future, and life takes on a retrospective "if only" flavor long before the effects of aging start to take their toll.

Left to itself, humanity would remain trapped in the ego-self phase until it would, I believe, destroy itself, either through war or through the ecological consequences of its runaway technology. However, by a flawless irony, humanity cannot remain stalled where it is. The reason brings the problem back to its own cause—death itself.

To see how death reenters the picture, we must take one last look at the character of the feedback loop. The robot in the brain is what makes us cling so tenaciously to the ego-self structure we build around consciousness. A feature of ego-consciousness is the awareness of physical death. However, as we have seen, the mind has blocked out death in our time, refusing to face the fact of its own finality and weaving webs of distracting trivia to hide the daylight self from the shadows that sometimes reappear, disturbingly, in dreams.

The fear of death can only be buried or displaced; it can never be removed while the ego-cage lasts. It thus remains potentially the most powerful negative force in psychology, because it threatens the lifeline that ties the psyche to the future. Experience and history combine to show us that man will go to any lengths to "cheat death." The pyramids stand as mute and crumbling testimony to both the strength and the futility of this longing for immortality.

Therefore death itself becomes the one power that can force man to confront mortality in midlife, because it is then that he sees that the grinning skull is his own. Only the fear of physical death—the primal terror—can drive him to enter the painful process of inner transformation from which he can emerge free and unafraid. Only the certain threat of physical death, advancing ever closer across life's landscape, can engender the crisis of confidence and conscience that prepares the receptive human mind for possible transformation, for the loss of its familiar signposts, its comforting walls of habit, its backward-looking focus.

However, it is a transformation few ever undergo (as I will discuss shortly). We cling to our egos, holding fast to the very cage that traps our real natures, because this is how biology has made us. We cling to the ego-self literally "until death." What few people see is that we have a choice between the death of the self, which means liberation of consciousness *from* time, and the continuation of the self, which means entombment of consciousness *in* time. It is cruel but somehow "just."

When I was young, I was deeply moved by Goethe's play *Faust*. In a memorable passage, Faust, the seeker after truth, is disturbed in his study by Mephistopheles disguised as a wandering scholar. After a few exchanges, Faust asks the devil, "Who art thou?" And receives the enigmatic reply, "I am part of that spirit *which always wills evil and always creates good*." I have never forgotten that interchange for it solved for me, once and for all, the problem of pain, of why hardship and suffering exist. Suffering is the agent of transcendence—it is because of rather than in spite of suffering that men are driven to "rise above themselves," to realize those hidden potentials of creativity that, in the absence of hardship, might remain untapped and ignored. I develop this point further in Chapter 11.

I now see that it also explains the midlife confrontation with death. Only something as final, as absolute, as utter extinction could force the human psyche, halfway between its dawn and its dusk, to venture beyond its ego-prison, forsaking the familiar mold of habit to try to reach the unknown shore whence comes the far-off music.

I have described the ego-self as a house of limitations, a prison for consciousness. Yet most of the information we receive from the environment around us is the common property of the human race. We all see the same sun, breathe the same air; we come into the world the same way, and so on. How do these universals become constricted into ego, narrowing our focus and distorting "reality"?

The answer is that information in itself is neutral; it is the impartial ground stuff of experience, anonymous clay containing only potential images. It is what we do with it, how we react to the common inputs, what we mold the clay into, that builds our prison.

What we do with it brings us back to Y nodes, to choices. So far, I have looked at choices as though they were equivalent in both quality and effect. That is manifestly not true. A profound distinction exists between Y node choices that are made *for us* by circumstance and those that are made *by us* by choice, i.e., by conscious selection between options. Remember how the ego-self is built: As we go through childhood, millions of Y node choices made by others give an unsolicited but increasingly definite shape to our personalities. This process eventually starts to set up a psychological feedback loop in which the "circumstantial" ego starts to take conscious charge of its own destiny. Initially born from accidents of time and place, the ego finally crystallizes into an independent (or semi-independent) structure that, by its very nature, biases the mind to prefer one branch of each Y node over the other. This is a self-accelerating process; after the ego has firmed into a recognizable "I am" image, most later decisions have the effect of merely reinforcing this idiosyncratic ego-structure, of focusing its "shape" ever more strongly.

What does this mean? Consider an extreme case, that of an affluent, middle-aged businessman who is experiencing problems with his marriage. One night, drunk, he visits a prostitute and takes out his pent-up aggression through sex. Vaguely he senses that the girl is still in her teens, and he has a blurry feeling of guilt, but his biology overrides his conscience, and he proceeds with his commercial rape. The next day, he feels a strong sense of self-loathing as he recalls details of the affair; he remembers the girl's parting look, the shoddy room with its cheap scent and the smell of sex. He is terrified he might have caught AIDS. In the following weeks, his sense of guilt deepens. He becomes depressed, sees a psychiatrist, but cannot bring himself to tell the truth and so receives an inappropriate diagnosis. His family notices the change in him—he has become a different person.

A different person, a changed person, one whose old self has been reworked. Is this not a classic example of ego-death? No, it is just the reverse. Guilt invariably strengthens ego-boundaries, centering the victim's fears and anxieties on himself, reinforcing self-contempt, building the ego walls to new and unhealthy heights. The final outcome can be a true psychosis in which the ego boundaries become so strong that the patient is out of reach, screened off from help or hope by the self-created prison of his obsession.

This is what insanity is—the terminal outcome of the process of isolation by which we shut out otherness and look only inward. It is the mummification of the ego-self, the final suicide by which the psyche carves its failure into stone. It is characteristic of insanity that the individual no longer exercises choice (which is why the criminally insane cannot be condemned for their actions, because they are not legally responsible for them). The final fate of ego, the ultimate hell, is thus to be trapped in the one reality, the one doomed, frozen universe, from which it cannot escape.

I return to my earlier conclusion, that most of our conscious choices strengthen the ego-cage. They continue and reinforce the ego-creating processes by which we differentiate our consciousness from that of others. I recognize that, in our modern world, this implies that almost all Y node choices lead us deeper into our self-created trap. That is a gloomy prognosis, but I believe it is just what happens.

Some Y node choices, however, do not fit this mold. We feel intuitively that some of our choices are "good" in the sense that they make us "better" people. However, "good" is a value judgment science does not recognize. Can we define such choices more objectively in terms of their effect on the ego?

We can. Choices that by their nature we feel make us better and more caring humans, work in a way opposite to that I have been discussing up to now. Their chief effect on psychology is that they *erode ego-self boundaries.* Anyone who looks carefully at "uplifting" experiences will recognize at once that they bring us into closer communion with our fellows or with nature. They are, in the true sense of the word, *wholesome,* leading to a feeling of "oneness" with all humanity. This is the inverse of the differentiating processes that build the ego-cage.

The sayings "Do unto others as you would have others do unto you," and "Greater love hath no man than this, that he lay down his life for his friends" contravene directly the entire self-preserving legacy of the selfish gene. They are a new thing in evolution, a turning inside out of the rules of natural selection, which require genes to promote self-interest, not self-sacrifice. This back-to-front novelty is summed up in the word we use to describe such behavior—*un*selfish.

Unselfish action reverses the character of evolution; no longer driven by competing differences, it is driven by cooperative wholeness. Significantly, competitive behavior is tightly focused on the immediate environment (in terms of space) and the present moment (in terms of time), since its purpose is to promote self-survival. It is myopic and reactive. By contrast, cooperative behavior is usually directed toward some future vision, since truly unselfish acts, by their very nature, put "other" ahead of "self." It is wide lens and pro-active.

Scientific discoveries like relativity theory and quantum mechanics have allowed us to see deeply into the structure of reality. They do that through the self-consistency of the mathematical code, which any sufficiently ded-icated human being can learn by concentration and discipline. I now wish to suggest, as a serious scientific hypothesis, that those "wholesome" proc-esses by which the ego-self is dismantled constitute another kind of learn-ing, which also allows consciousness to "see" the inner nature of reality. This raises two questions: *How* do we see? and *What* do we see? Let us first consider how we see.

9

THE SINGER AND THE SONG

Have you heard the music
that no fingers enter into?
— K A B I R

The eye is the biological organ of sight. It receives a narrow band of electromagnetic radiation and transmits this incoming data into the brain. It is the most important of the senses, our primary window to the world. However, as any biologist knows, we do not actually "see" with our eyes, but with our brains. Patients with extensive damage to the visual area of the cerebral cortex of the brain (scotomas) can be completely blind even though their eyes are fully functional.

This is only part of the story, however. To appreciate how totally the process of sight is bound up with the dynamics of the brain, we have to examine the process by which we learn to see. We reach here a counterintuitive area of science that bears directly on the question, What is reality? What do I mean when I make the apparently absurd statement, "We have to learn to see inside our brains"? Take the case of a blind person who recovers sight in his teens. Several cases have been documented. We might think that such a person would experience a wondrous awakening from a world of darkness into a world of light—the world we sighted people take for granted, the world of blue sky and green trees, of soaring buildings and varied faces. In fact, what he experiences is chaos, a jumbled confusion of shapes and impressions that make absolutely no sense. His brain has no preformed pictures of anything (a car, a beach, even his mother's face) and thus cannot relate the images falling on the retina of his newly functional eye with any prior models drawn from experience. Moreover, his brain cannot integrate the images into patterns—he does not "know" (how could he?) that the noise of the wind in the trees arises from the movement of leaves and branches, because he has never seen a branch or a leaf or a tree. Slowly, and painfully, he has to learn to construct a model of the world inside his head. *It is our brains that create the reality we see.*

Our minds tend to resist this. What we see in the outside world seems to have an objective reality of its own. We feel that if we were to vanish, that outside world would still go on, that it exists separately from us.

Well, doesn't it? No, or at least certainly not the way we think. Consider this: The eye of a bee can see ultraviolet light, which we cannot. When a bee sees certain kinds of flowers, it sees strange markings invisible to us. Those markings map out a guidance grid, a landing track, to steer the bee toward the source of the flower's nectar.

So what the bee sees is not what we see. Which picture of the flower is "true" then? The bee's or ours?

With our Western either/or way of thinking, we may be tempted to answer neither. The correct answer is *both*. The flower is something far richer than any of the images that flicker into being in the eyes of the creatures who see it. The "real" flower exists as an infinite bundle of mathematical options, a spectrum of possibilities. Each of those "possibilities" can become "real" according to the structure of the organ that perceives it. We may think that our particular image of the flower is special, but this merely reflects our own arrogance. No one image has a privileged status.

This insight lies at the heart of a remarkable but (as yet) little understood revolution that quantum mechanics has wrought in our perception of ourselves and the world. Our deep-seated feeling for reality is that we are spectators of something fixed and tangible that exists "out there."

However, the insights of modern physics say unequivocally that we cannot separate what we see from the act of seeing itself. This paradox is dubbed "quantum observership."

Cosmologist Brian Swimme captures the essence of the issue by asking the (superficially) absurd question: "Before eyes evolved on earth, was the sea blue?" The automatic instinctive answer is "Yes, of course. The blue color of the ocean exists as a real parameter that is independent of human observation of it." But quantum theory tells us that the blue color of the ocean is created by the eye that sees it. As with the flower example, another kind of eye would see another kind of reality, and both would be "true." As Swimme puts it; "Reality blooms in the encounter."

This does not mean that we can create our own reality simply by willing it, as many New Age writers seem to think. The idea of *encounter* implies a twofold dialogue between us on the one hand and something on the other. That something is the quantum world. What physics says is that that quantum world does not exist in a fixed and determinate form. Consider again the flower example. According to physics, there is "flower power" in the world. We are not imagining flowers or dreaming them into being, but we can never know their fullness. The reality of a flower is a limitless range of options, hovering at the edge of being, outside time. Which of those options reveals itself to an onlooker depends on the nature of the eye that sees it. Reality blooms in the encounter. It is the act of seeing that calls up a specific image from nature's picture book, actualizing the quantum possibility and trapping it in time.

Our whole picture of reality is woven in the same way. We assume when we are born that there is an external world out there and that all we have to do is see it. That is quite false. Our model of reality is entirely our own, much of it contributing to our ego-self boundaries. The fact that so much of our reality model overlaps with and coincides with those of others must never blind us to the fact that it is, at root, a necessary convenience, a convention, a magnificent lie.

The way we visually "decode" the world in our brains has much in common with the way we decode language in our minds, and language serves us as a useful metaphor in our struggle to find meaning in all of this. When you read the words on this page, what is happening is that a particular pattern of electromagnetic (light) waves is exciting the retina of your eyes, and the brain is translating that pattern into meaningful images on the basis of past experience. You can read these words, not because your eye is physically transmitting encrypted messages to your mind, but because during childhood you learned to recognize sets of symbols and to understand the grammatical relationships among them. *It is this learned "structure" in the brain that is actually doing the "seeing."*

In their book *The Matter Myth,* Paul Davies and John Gribbin discuss in some detail the way the human brain deduces the correct spatial alignment of objects in its neighborhood. They use the example of a broomstick, noting that when the stick is viewed at a right angle to the viewer it will present its true length, while if it is viewed end-on (parallel to the viewer, and perpendicular to the ground) it will have no length at all. Observing that the "true" length of the rod can be mentally computed from three projected lengths along three perpendicular axes (by a generalization of Pythagoras' theorem), Davies and Gribbin comment: "The human brain evidently achieves this computational feat without explicitly performing any mathematical calculations, and we regard the result as intuitively obvious."

When we look out a window into a garden, we see a picture, which we unconsciously assume represents what is there. But, as with the broomstick example, what we see is the result of a complex computational feat by the brain, a feat that deduces, for example, height from length of shadow, relationship to other points of reference, etc. This sophisticated process of computation creates the world we see. We cannot separate the world out there from the computational program by which we see it. Our perception has, in a deep sense, evolved by way of this programming.

The issue of what we really see is further complicated by a well-known psychological phenomenon called *projection.* By that, psychiatrists mean (among other things) our tendency to project onto external objects qualities and attributes that have their origins and their reality in our inner selves. For example, when we are furious with someone, we tend to find fault with almost everyone and everything we meet and see. Conversely, when we are in love, we tend to view the world through rose-colored glasses, and we do not see the weaknesses and flaws that all too often become glaringly apparent later on.

My point here is well captured by a lover's poem to the object of his adoration: "When I look at you I do not see you;/All I see is the dream my own necessity has fashioned out of longing."

Thus the world within paints itself across the world without. To put it another way and advance our argument another step, some of the things in our environment we label as real are not real in any verifiable sense. They are projections. Those projections include elements of experience as basic as our perception of moving time. Chapter 4 demonstrated that the sense of passing time is a mental fiction that was created, and that endures, solely because the symbolate world of conceptualization needs an ordering principle to create a coherent structure, a subjective "phase space" within which purposeful action is possible. That ordering principle needs a point of reference, a center, from which to operate; that center is ego, our sense of self.

There is a familiar quotation that goes: "Oh, what a tangled web we weave, when first we practice to deceive." It is an apt metaphor for the dilemma of the ego-self in the world. The ego-self is a deception, magnificent in its achievements, awesome in its power, but flawed in its essence. By its very nature, the ego-self cannot help projecting two deep-rooted elements of its "dreaming," its sense of passing time and coming death, into and onto the fabric of the symbolate world that mind creates and inhabits. The most commonly heard lament of the ego-self is its sadness at the brevity of life, and the most often seen shadow in the ego-self's world is the specter of death.

The incompleteness of the present human condition lies in the fact that, as long as the psyche operates within the nexus of the ego-self, it is fighting a battle it cannot win. It can never know "what is" because it cannot see "what is" through ego. Ceaselessly, using fictional symbols in the restless inner domain of conceptualization, ego invariably projects these fictions out onto the world and thereby blocks communion with that world at its root.

Thus we can argue with conviction that the ego-self's "reality" is a self-created "optical delusion of consciousness," to return to Einstein's phrase. The delusion goes deeper than the tricks our brains play on us or our ingrained tendency to project outward that which is inside us. As we saw in Chapter 2, our choices summon forth real events from the ripple of possibility that is the quantum wave. For the most part, our choices trap us in an ever-tightening reality noose that limits vision in the precise measure that it strengthens ego. That is the price, the terrible price, that ego demands of us in return for its life-preserving ability to organize conceptual experience coherently.

The last chapter showed, however, that some choices reverse this process, clearing our vision of reality in the precise measure that the existential noise that is ego is filtered out. It is time now to look at the faculty in our minds that apprehends unfragmented reality. That faculty is usually fogged by the bustling conceptual world in which ego lives. Hence it is strongest in those persons in whom the ego-self is undeveloped (as in children) or diminished (as in adults who have undergone some form of ego-death). This faculty is both familiar and mysterious; it is called consciousness.

I know of no word (apart from "God") that generates so much confusion and has such a slippery quality. To make matters worse, *consciousness* is often used interchangeably with such words as *mind, awareness, intelligence, cognitive faculty,* etc. Everyone will say they know what consciousness is, yet, if pressed to explain themselves, will soon run into quicksands of verbal ambiguity and logical inconsistency.

What is consciousness? We all tend to think of consciousness in terms of our awareness of what is going on around us now—we say "I'm conscious of my surroundings" or "I'm conscious that it's now three-forty P.M." etc. That means that we often identify consciousness with the mental reaction we have to incoming information from the senses. This approach does not carry us very far into the problem. Many land vertebrates have senses that are, on average, as good as ours: Indeed, the technology of perception of a creature like an eagle is significantly better than ours, due to its extraordinary distance vision. However, no one would claim that the eagle has attained the same level of consciousness as a human being.

This last sentence advances our argument a little because it focuses attention on a key point: Part of the problem with any definition of consciousness lies in our reluctance to recognize that consciousness is not a single or uniform state, but a *progressive scale of different degrees of awareness.* That scale forms a continuum in time, but tends to fracture into a graduated sequence of stable states—discrete levels at which consciousness "settles" because it has attained a coherent quality of knowing. An animal like a fish occupies a relatively lowly level in the broad scale of consciousness, while an average human being occupies a much higher level. The evolutionary process thus tells us that the quality of consciousness usually improves as one ascends the ladder of biological complexity.

This concept of a scale of improving states of consciousness focuses the problem, because it follows from basic principles of genetic and psychic variation that not all members of the human family are—or can be—at the same stage in their growth. Far from it, humans differ widely in the character of their consciousness. The average mode of human consciousness is different in kind and quality from the nonordinary states that some highly evolved human beings have reached.

Thus, when we attempt to analyze human consciousness, we are examining a confusing mixture of states, an amalgam of overlapping and intermingling degrees of awareness. To simplify my treatment, I will adopt the unusual approach of looking at the upper stratum of the present structure of human consciousness rather than the lower, i.e., I will focus on states of consciousness that are in their formative, emergent stage, rather than the still-existing but outgrown states we share with animals. In other words, I will use the cutting edge of consciousness as the reference line of my analysis.

What is this evolving quality, this cutting edge of consciousness? My definition may seem strange at first, but it will, I hope, gain in plausibility as we proceed. The emergent tip of evolving consciousness is that deep sense of *knowing* that unfolds when the ego-self is dismantled. From many points of view, unfolding consciousness is what limiting ego is not. It is timeless where ego is time-obsessed; it is deathless where ego is death-haunted; it is beautiful where ego (at least in its conspicuous mode of selfishness) is ugly. Perhaps most tellingly, it sees—and is—wholesome-ness and oneness where ego sees—and is—separateness.

In discussing consciousness in these progressive and dynamic terms, it is difficult not to confuse subject and object, the one who sees and sight, singer and song. A highly evolved consciousness can access a timeless state only if reality is timeless; it can feel that death is an illusion only if reality

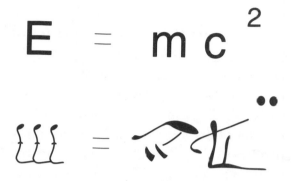

FIGURE 9.1

Symbols and the Tower of Babel. These two equations are exactly equivalent and we recognize the top version over the bottom only because its symbols are familiar. In other words, the symbols we use have no virtue in themselves—they are merely conventions. The "reality" embodied in the equation is the relationship among the symbols since this relationship is the "truth structure" that remains invariant irrespective of the conventions we use to encode it.

knows no death; it can sense that "beauty is truth" only if that is indeed the case; and it can apprehend unity only if all things are indeed one. Thus, to truly understand consciousness, we have to look at the nature of "reality" itself.

After these preliminary remarks, let us see if we can get a handle on the essential feature of consciousness as it is represented in many human beings at this moment in evolutionary time. In Chapter 2, we saw that consciousness can summon forth particular configurations of reality from the complex ripples of possibility that derive from interacting quantum waves. Consciousness is the faculty in the mind that *creates reality*. This process is not arbitrary. Only realities that are self-consistent can survive as viable dreamings. In the language of the many-universes theory, ego-creating choices split off quantum worlds that grow farther and farther apart. By contrast, ego-diminishing choices act as attracters that link separate universes, contact junctions that receive information from many sources simultaneously.

This sounds obscure until we relate it to our own mental processes.

Think about the word *know.* Ask yourself, "When do I really know something?" When you have learned it and can repeat it? Is that knowing or memory-recall?

There is a story that the Greek philosopher Archimedes got so excited when he discovered the law of hydrostatics (which states that a body immersed in fluid loses weight equal to the weight of the fluid it displaces) that he ran naked down the street shouting "Eureka!" ("I've found it!"). Archimedes had experienced that instant of revelation, that flash of unitive understanding, that underlies all creative insight. Suddenly the pieces of the puzzle—things that seemed unconnected, fragmented—fall into place. A pattern emerges. A truth is known.

This is what I call "deep knowing." Its signal, its ever-present companion, is precisely the sense of *integration,* of bringing into union things that were previously separate. Like going from two dimensions to three dimensions (Figure 2.1) and seeing suddenly that the "force" linking A and B was a consequence of the fact that *A and B were the same thing.*

Consciousness is a reality laboratory that takes us from one (limited) level of being to another (less limited) one. It is a bringing-together mechanism, an integrator, a focus on the universal. Integration is its prime evolving function and its evolving chief feature.

To explore what this means, let us look at mathematics in the light of what I have just said. Mathematics is often described as a "universal" language, but the truth this statement embodies obscures the confusion it hides. In Figure 9.1, you will see a mathematical representation of Einstein's famous equation relating energy and mass. Underneath is what seems to be a set of Egyptian hieroglyphics. In fact, they are different representations of the same law—all I have done in the bottom version is to substitute Egyptian symbols for the letters of the alphabet, and a dot-style numbering system for our standard 1, 2, 3, etc.

What this tells us is that symbols per se merely divide and confuse us (they are exactly like ego-self differences); what matters is the relationships among them. It is the relationships that spell out the syntax of reality, the underlying code of truth in which the rules of nature are written. That is a deeper level of reality than the existential configurations of certainty created by our own choices because the syntax of truth that underpins mathematical self-consistency constitutes the universal scaffolding of physical law within which the whole evolutionary process unfolds.

From this perspective, we can return to the distinction between ego and consciousness. We can see yet again how deeply and subtly the walls of the ego-self have been built, using the all-pervading symbols of speech to create the mental house we all inhabit: the house that bears our name, our identity, our sense of I am. We may also be able to see that there is a universal reality beneath and behind this ego-self fragmentation, consisting (to use misleading words for they are all I have) of relationships, integrated into a common code—a unity, a oneness.

This is not wishful thinking or mysticism, because mathematics has shown us that nature has this oneness. Beneath the confusion of detail are universal laws and those laws can be gathered together into one coherent theory of reality. My point, then, is that consciousness—the seer—accesses universal truth—the sight—directly, without hindrance, and that the variations we take for granted as essential parts of the perceived world are mere divisive shadows thrown by ego-self walls. To hardened skeptics, what I have just said probably sounds metaphysical and unconvincing. They will point out, correctly, that if consciousness is real, it must have some physical basis in the human brain. Moreover, they will insist that the faculties it embodies must have evolved through the mechanism of Darwinian evolution by way of natural selection. That means that consciousness must, during the biological phase of its evolution at least, have had some selective advantage.

I have no difficulty with this attitude, and indeed, up to a point, I share it. Let us look at consciousness from the hard-nosed, empirical point of view. What brain capabilities underlie consciousness? To answer this, let us return, briefly, to speech. The human brain contains physical centers in its left hemisphere (chiefly Broca's area and Wernicke's center) that comprise key elements in our innate language-creating hardware. These speech centers do not encode speech itself but a capability, a predisposition, which enables us (unlike all other life-forms) to learn a developed language. It seems likely that a different (but interlocking?) system of elements allows us to learn to read man's greatest symbolic code—mathematics.

I believe that there is another faculty in the brain *whose function it is to recognize unity*. That faculty does not exist as such at birth. We build it up over time in much the same way we build language skills, by evolving a structure of experience in which various elements integrate with each other until they form a neural recognizer, a kind of inner eye. Where is this faculty? It would be easy to fall into the trap of saying that it resides in the right hemisphere of the brain, just as language resides in the left hemisphere. As most brain biologists recognize, this kind of distinction is artificial and simplistic and overlooks the rich variety of dynamic connections that integrate the two halves of the brain into what is, in normal individuals, one coherently operating multipurpose organ. Nonetheless, one does an equal disservice to the facts if one goes too far the other way and asserts that there are no verifiable specializations between the two hemispheres.

Two brain biologists summarize their views as follows:

The right side is more concerned with analyzing the spatial arrangement of things in the world, recognizing objects, appreciating music and, perhaps, in determining emotional reactions. But the left hemisphere, in the vast majority of people, is dominant for speech and, indeed, for most aspects of language.

—Colin Blakemore

Instead of thinking that the left hemisphere is specialized for language, it may, more accurately, be specialised for symbolic representation. The right hemisphere, by contrast, seems to deal with representations that mirror reality more directly, those large chunks of experience that don't employ language.

—Richard Restak

Taking these summaries as broadly representative of modern brain research, what one can tentatively say is that the left brain seems preeminently involved in the functions of symbolic processing that are conspicuously associated with the ego-self, while the right brain seems preeminently involved in recognizing patterns in the environment. Significantly, the right brain seems to be able to access relationships between things in its environment directly, without relying on language.

In the context of this chapter, it is interesting to note the apparent connection between the right brain and the ability to "appreciate" music. Thus, people whose ability to speak has been damaged by strokes in the left side of their brains can often sing songs they can no longer recite.

Perhaps the best way to define the faculty that apprehends unity is to attempt to map the way it evolved. The right brain, according to neuropsychologist Elizabeth Warrington, may contain (in Colin Blakemore's words) a file of "structural descriptions" of objects, "allowing things to be recognized when seen from different directions, at different distances or under different lighting conditions." To put this another way, it may allow the individual to recognize the same object from different perspectives. The faculty that does this—wherever it is and whatever it is—is thus dedicated to sifting through relationships to detect commonalities.

It is not difficult to see why the possession of such a faculty would give its owner a marked selective advantage in the struggle for existence. Predators such as lions often seek to camouflage their approach to prey by crouching down and blending into the concealing grass or vegetation. It is often only the flickering movement of the grass that alerts the animal to approaching danger. Clearly, the ability to recognize the underlying form of a predator against a background of subtle, ever-changing variation gives the predator's target a much better chance of taking to its heels in time to save its skin. There has then, throughout vertebrate evolution, been a strong adaptive incentive to recognize common patterns in variable circumstances, to see the one in the many.

The human species has inherited this pattern-recognizing faculty from its ancestors. However, man has developed it much farther. Indeed, man has done for this faculty what he has done for language—he has carried it through the "phase transition" that transfigures reality by readjusting the way he views it.

What does this mean? In the thirteenth century, an Italian named Leonardo Fibonacci discovered a sequence of numbers that still bears his name:

1, 1, 2, 3, 5, 8, 13, 21, 34, 55, 89, 144, etc.

These numbers have some curious properties. Each succeeding number is the sum of the preceding two; every third number can be divided by 2, every fourth number by 3, etc.

Fibonacci ratios are widespread in nature. The arrangement of leaves and petals in many plants has a rotational symmetry that corresponds strikingly with a Fibonacci spiral. That is probably a result of natural selection. In the unique configuration mapped out by the Fibonacci spiral, each leaf is optimally positioned to harvest the maximum amount of sunlight. Evolutionary principles may also explain why some shells trace out Fibonacci spirals as they grow. However, evolution cannot explain why Fibonacci ratios appear also in the physical world, in certain electrical networks, for example, and perhaps in the structure of subatomic particles.

What gives these numbers their fascination is that they also occur in artworks across the spectrum of creative human activity. They occur in architecture (for example, in ancient Minoan buildings and in Gothic cathedrals); in art (for example, in Greek vases); in poetry (for example, in the stanzas of Virgil); and most especially in music. The most celebrated musical examples occur in the works of Stockhausen, Bartók, Krenek, and Nono. In Bartók's *Allegro Barbaro* for piano solo, the measures containing only an F-sharp minor chord activated in eighth notes are grouped into Fibonacci durations of 5, 8, 5, 5, 3, 13, and 8, respectively. Tellingly, the ratios of successive Fibonacci numbers also closely approximate the golden mean. By that we mean that when a line segment, for example, is divided according to the golden mean, the whole is to the larger part as the larger is to the smaller. The special quality (approximately 1.618) has been known since at least the times of the ancient Greeks and is widely found today in the proportions of our books and cereal cartons. Something about it evidently appeals strongly to our sense of order and harmony.

What the Fibonacci example shows us is that a common thread, a common pattern, runs through a diversity of different phenomena. One can discover this commonality in two ways: through mathematical reasoning, in which case we are using the time-structured, symbol-based logic of the (left) brain to deduce relationships; and through direct recognition. When one sees a golden section or hears a Bartók symphony, one is, in an important sense, intuiting the Fibonacci harmonies in a non-time-structured (right brain), instantaneous way, in a sudden flash of knowing.

I believe that the faculty in the human brain that senses this commonality is an extension of the pattern-recognizing ability common among animals, but so enormously reworked and extended that it constitutes the major instrument of sight in the present structure of human intelligence. In an article I coauthored with mathematician-musician Jeff Pressing in 1982, we explained the situation thus:

> If this is true . . . then our perception and our imagination have been strongly influenced not only by ecology and by the events of our individual lifetimes, but also by our species' evolution in a world predisposed to certain kinds of structures and processes. In other words, art and nature are so strongly linked because they have evolved in tandem. If Fibonacci spirals fill our surroundings, will they not come to be encoded into our way of seeing, and hence have the power to guide our sense of proportion in sound or movement as well?

We can see this same principle at work in the way we may "see" in certain kinds of music the symmetry principles on which crystals are based. Crystals are highly regular shapes that groups of atoms assume under defined circumstances. Using a mathematical treatment of symmetry called group theory, one can work out all possible ways to pack atoms in three-dimensional space to give crystalline patterns. In other words, there is a limited number of solutions to the packing problem that allow atoms to come together in ordered arrays.

These space-filling symmetries all turn out to be based on the numbers 2, 3, 4, and 6. Consider what seems a totally unrelated situation—the rhythmic structure of West African drum ensemble music. Much of that music is in a 12/8 meter, and the patterns used in it may be elegantly derived from the mathematical group C12. The same patterns appear in the scale structure of our own twelve-note based music. The number 12 is significant in both musical examples because it is rich in the factors 2, 3, 4, and 6. Thus, as with the Fibonacci harmonies, the inner eye seems able to "see" in song the way(s) nature builds her crystal symmetries in frost and mica.

These examples give us a vital clue to the evolution of the brain mechanism that has grown into "consciousness." What I am suggesting is that evolution has trained a specific brain faculty to pick out special regularities from the confusion of sense impressions that enter the brain. The insights that result from the use of that faculty are immediate and spontaneous. When we react strongly to a piece of music, we may be "seeing" a set of relationships—a unity—that undergirds the structure of a molecule or the distribution of petals in a flower or the crystalline arrangement of atoms in space. It matters not that this "seeing" is nonconceptual—indeed, that is its special virtue for it prevents its meaning from being trapped in words and thus avoids the limitations of the ego-cage. This is part of the liberating quality of intuition.

We call the camera eye in our heads an organ of sense, and we also speak of a sense of symmetry. What I am saying is that the faculty that intuits symmetry is analogous to an organ of perception, except that it operates on a higher level. The developed brain structure that "knows" commonalities is, in my view, our evolving eye to reality, enabling us to see more deeply than ever before the inner structure of the universe. This faculty, freed of the fragmenting confusion of ego and unshackled from the ceaseless motion of conceptual processing, is what constitutes evolving consciousness. This is the second way to escape the bondage of psychological preconditioning that I foreshadowed at the beginning of Chapter 7.

Thus it is the unique function of consciousness to recognize patterns, but they are patterns of a particular type. They are in the vast majority of cases characterized by *symmetry*, to use the physicist's term, or *rhythm*, to use the dancer's term, or *harmony*, to use the musician's term, or *beauty*, to use the most general and most meaningful term of all.

The number 3.1415926 . . . is a transcendental number (it goes on forever). Mathematicians will recognize it at once as pi, the constant value obtained when the circumference of any circle is divided by its diameter. When we look at a circle, we are seeing one of the fundamental constants of mathematics. Is it a coincidence that the circle is regarded as perhaps the most beautifully flawless symbol in the myths of so many cultures?

Indeed, Carl Jung picked the mandala (a Sanskrit word meaning magic circle and encompassing all motifs based on circles or centers) as the most fundamental of man's religious symbols.

Thus beauty, something we often think of as a romantic abstraction, is just the reverse. Unlike the sense of time passing, which is a mental fiction created by the ego-self, beauty is an innate feature of the real world. That is why highly evolved states of consciousness recognize it.

The French mathematician Poincaré caught the essence of this realization in his fascinating description of the creative process, of the way the mind selects true insights from trivial ones. Listen to his words:

> The useful combinations are precisely *the most beautiful.* I mean those best able to charm this special sensibility that all mathematicians know, but of which the profane are so ignorant as often to be tempted to smile at it ... among great numbers of combinations blindly formed by the subliminal self, almost all are without interest and without utility; but just for that reason they are also without effect upon the aesthetic sensibility. *Consciousness will never know them;* only certain ones are harmonious, and, consequently, at once useful and beautiful. They will be capable of touching this special sensibility of the geometer of which I have spoken, and which, once aroused, will call our attention to them, and thus give them occasion to become conscious.

Science may be just beginning to understand how consciousness manages to "focus" reality. Susan Blackmore has examined the possible ways in which meditation (mindfulness) may influence our state of mind. She comments provocatively:

> Mindfulness means living in the present moment, every moment, constantly alert. In meditation, this skill is practiced in quiet sitting. Any thoughts that arise are let go again ... but there is no clinging, no leap into the building of fantasies. They just come and go until eventually the mind is still ... being mindful means not following every association; not stacking up ideas to be completed; not re-

hearsing, planning, or even selecting. The models become simpler and all processing capacity is not immediately used up.

These words aptly describe the processes by which the "noise" of the ego can be filtered from consciousness. Blackmore then goes on to analyze the way the mind may access reality in the absence of this "noise":

> More and more can be linked into one model because there is less and less being modelled. And what would it be like to be the models in such a system? Obviously very different. Is this why everything seems brighter and more "real" during meditation? . . . In the end it is not even necessary for the model of self to be constructed at all. Imagine what it would be like to be a system that processes incoming information but builds no further constructions upon it, not even any self to observe. With no modelled distinction between self and other, I imagine the world would all seem one.

These words neatly nail down the point that what the egoless mind sees is unity. This, in my view, is another way of saying beauty.

Let us look more deeply at the concept of beauty. Many of us, asked to describe something "beautiful," would nominate a piece of music. There is, I believe, a sound scientific reason for that. There is a far-reaching relationship between music and mathematics that goes back to the time of Pythagoras. Pythagoras showed that the pitch of a musical note depends on the frequency of its vibration. (Figure 9.2); if a node is moved halfway along a vibrating string playing its ground note, the string plays a note an octave higher, and so on. Modern physics has adopted a similar "melodic" metaphor in its description of the hidden levels of atomic substructure. Electrons occupy discrete energy levels in atoms. Those energy levels can be thought of, and described as, vibrations or "standing waves." The basic structure of matter is musical.

Pythagoras' discovery was startling, not simply because it revealed a precise correspondence between pitch and number, but because it demonstrated that the chords that sound *pleasing* to the human ear correspond to *exact* divisions of the vibrating string by *whole* numbers.

What is it in the brain that resonates to these exact numbers? I believe

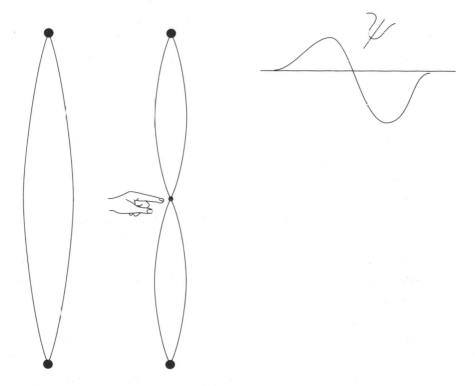

FIGURE 9.2

The musical structure of matter. The reasons why electrons can only occupy fixed positions in atomic substructure correspond remarkably with the reasons why the only notes that sound pleasing to the ear are those that correspond to exact subdivisions of a vibrating string. This is because only certain standing wave patterns allow electrons to settle into stable states. Is music more than an appeal to our sense of harmony? Is it a different and deeper way of seeing? Is the universe, in some profound sense, a song?

the answer is the pattern-recognizing faculty—consciousness. But this suggestion makes a testable prediction. If consciousness can access the deep reality of things directly, our aesthetic appreciation of music should not be just a form of psychological gratification, but a tool that can be used to delineate underlying realities in physical laws.

Modern physics seems to be reaching, hesitantly, toward some acceptance of this idea. Physicist Paul Dirac said, "God used *beautiful* mathematics to create the *world*." [Italics added] And recent attempts to unify the forces of nature depend crucially upon the use of *symmetry* principles called gauge symmetries. I believe that consciousness, the source of the aesthetic sense, experiences reality directly. And reality—the hidden structure of the universe—has a harmonic configuration. To put it another way, there is a deep, albeit subtle relationship between the harmonic structures of some moving musical compositions and the underlying musical foundation of physics, into which consciousness tunes.

If we want to describe the universe as consciousness "knows" it, we should stop thinking of it as a machine or a system or a process and start thinking of it as a song.

While we extract intuitions of beauty from the whole spectrum of experience, in the context of this book perhaps the most relevant examples are to be found in poetry. Poetry uses words—the divisive vehicle by which we create the ego-self. However, certain combinations of words have a strange resonance, a quality of "otherness." They do not simply convey information like a textbook; they cause a feeling of interruption in the normal flow; like finding a quiet moment in time, they bring the ceaseless mental activity of the verbal self to a transitory stop.

These resonances are not dependent on rhyme—blank verse can be just as effective:

> We shall not cease from exploration
> And the end of all our exploring
> Will be to arrive where we started
> And know the place for the first time.

Why do these lines of T. S. Eliot's give us pause? What is so special about this combination of a few words that makes it so memorable? The answer, I believe, is that the words evoke in us that sense of deep knowing that is the hallmark of consciousness. They are present echoes of future truth, and while we may not yet understand *why* they are true, we sense *that* they are.

Someone once said that the arts have "the past in their bones" while science has "the future in its bones." I wonder about that. Many of science's most profound discoveries seem retrospective; they retell, in mathematical code, stories of reality already encoded in poems or prose. I give a possible reason for this in the next chapter.

What I can say now is that the two access modes to reality, mathematics and intuition, are complementary sides of the same coin—different ways of getting to the same place. I believe that the left brain, handicapped by its reliance on linear codes, has, down the ages, tried to compensate for this deficiency by slowly and painfully re-creating in its own "language" that image of wholeness that the right brain has dimly "seen" for centuries. It is largely in our time that the two windows into reality have begun to come into harmony through the efforts of men like the physicists Arthur Eddington and Fritjof Capra and humanitarians like Aldous Huxley.

This reequilibration of consciousness, the rebalancing of right-brain holism and left-brain logic, is a critically important development. Many New Age writers have suggested (covertly or openly) that the aim of personal growth is to return to the Edenic level of consciousness, to recapture the innocence of the childhood of the human species, before the emergence of ego. That implies that we can go forward by going back. In considering the evolution of consciousness, it is essential to distinguish clearly between *intellect* and *ego*. Contemporary human awareness is hugely deeper than that of Stone Age men, partly because the mathematical insights of science have given sharp definition to the fuzzy insights of intuition. Left-brain reasoning and right-brain globality are equally important in the balanced development of consciousness. It is, in my view, no accident that some of the greatest scientists who have ever lived— Einstein, Eddington, Heisenberg, Schrödinger, Pauli—have had a strong mystical bent; Einstein in particular.

This puts the role of language in a deeply paradoxical light. Language is, from many points of view, what makes us human, gives us our rich and varied ability to describe the world and to analyze its features. It is (from this perspective) an evolutionary pivot. But language is also a trap, which ensnares and confuses the latent faculty of intuition. It is (from this perspective) an evolutionary pitfall. Thus speech is our most valuable tool at the same time that it is our greatest handicap.

Einstein recognized the "language dilemma" in a letter to the mathematician Jacques Hadamard:

The words or the language, as they are written or spoken, do not seem to play any role in my mechanism of thought. . . . Conventional words or other signs have to be sought for laboriously only in a second stage, when the mentioned associative play is sufficiently established.

Einstein here is clearly using "thought" in the sense that I mean "consciousness," as will become obvious in the next chapter.

Over two thousand years ago, the Chinese philosopher Lao-tzu put it even more succinctly: "He who knows does not speak. He who speaks does not know."

It is time to relate these scientific arguments to ourselves in a personal way, to touch the human in all of us. How do we react to beauty ourselves? When we listen to a song that we find beautiful, we lose ourselves in it—we forget ourselves. The reason music gives us this sense of uplift is precisely that it allows us to escape, however briefly, from the ego-self cage. For a fleeting moment of clock time, we see a different vision, sense another world.

I can now bring the various strands of my argument together. The self-forgotten state that music can engender and the unselfish gratitude that friendship can beget are, from the point of view of the inner eye, identical. They are both a fleeting and a superficial form of ego-death. Fleeting in the sense that they last only a few moments (typically), and superficial because the uplifting experience is usually followed by a relapse into a strong ego-conscious mode.

What, then, of more lasting forms of ego-death? Some people find it hard to get any feeling for what ego-death means, so let me give two examples, one from fiction and one from experiences that are the common lot of most adults. My use of a fictional example does not mean that the concept at issue is fictional. Rather, by picking a case history known and loved throughout the English-speaking world, I hope to get the point across to a large number of people.

The example I have chosen is Ebenezer Scrooge from Charles Dickens's *A Christmas Carol*. Scrooge is an archetypal ego-self—greedy, hard-hearted, walled off from humanity by his infatuation with capital. He is haunted by three ghosts:the first recalls his past, the second shows his present, and the third foreshadows his future. In a symbolic way, each of these spirits forces Scrooge into a confrontation with his unconscious, to use Jung's language. The first haunting loosens the boundaries of his ego-self by taking him back to his childhood and young manhood before his obsession for money developed. The second builds on this by allowing Scrooge to contrast his own self-imposed exile from humanity with the open-hearted jolliness and charity of the burghers of London on Christmas Day. However, it is the third that brings about the transformation of Scrooge's personality, because it brings him face-to-face with the fact, and the consequences, of his own death.

Dickens describes the moment of realization and change:

"Spirit," Scrooge cried, tight clutching at its robe, "hear me! *I am not the man I was.* I will not be the man I must have been but for this intercourse."[Italics added]

And its consequences:

He became as good a friend, as good a master and as good a man as the good old City knew, or any other good old city, town or borough, in the good old world. Some people laughed to see the alteration in him, but he let them laugh and little heeded them: for he was wise enough to know that nothing ever happened on this globe for good, at which some people did not have their fill of laughter in the outset.

In real life, most of us know at least one person who has emerged from a midlife crisis a very different individual from the one who began the process. Many men who have devoted their energies single-mindedly to success in business typically walk out of their jobs and take up an activity unrelated or less related to money. They may buy a farm or write a book or take an interest in voluntary charity work. The variations are endless; the pattern, similar.

Talk to such people and what strikes you is the suddenness with which the ego-boundaries collapse. The old ego-self remains firmly in place during the years leading up to the change, while beneath the surface its axioms are repeatedly challenged and weakened. Finally, some catalyst, some trigger, sets off that mysterious process of inner transformation by which the components of personality are rearranged into a new configuration. A new self is born from the destruction of the old.

Perhaps the most dramatic illustrations of ego-death in today's society can be seen in group-therapy sessions, where emotionally damaged people are forced to confront their anger or their hurt. In those rare cases where the group facilitators are loving and caring people, whose wisdom comes from the heart and not the head, these confrontations can lead to changes that quite literally have to be seen to be believed. Such encounter groups represent one of the few rites of passage that occur in adult life, and they offer a rare window into the nature of human transformation. I have been to such groups and watched distressed individuals retreat into themselves, working back toward the core of their problem. As they approach the block that is preventing their growth, they typically become highly emotional, displaying the kind of extreme behavior our culture suppresses— violent anger or unbearable grief. After a struggle in which, through some strange alchemy of compassion, the whole group shares, they come through in a healing catharsis that flushes the pain or the anger out of their systems. The moments that follow can be described only by that inadequate word, *beautiful.* The sufferer and the group enter a fellowship of trust in which differences die and tensions dissolve. Just as the group provided the safety net that allowed the sufferer to enter his personal darkness, so it provides the communion that restores wholeness.

From the point of view of this chapter, what impresses me about these group-therapy sessions is the way people, initially, refuse to let go. As I have said before, they cling to their hurt or their anger because it is part of them. Even when they know that the resentment or agony they have carried for years is poisoning their lives and blocking their growth, they still refuse to surrender it, because it is an entrenched element of their ego-selves. Sometimes they must be coaxed and pushed and almost bullied to step over the brink into that unknown space where the old map is discarded and the healing begins.

In today's world, we use psychological jargon to describe the problems these people experience, tagging emotional blocks as "neuroses," "fixations," etc. In the Middle Ages, people saw things in a different and simpler way, against the all-pervading background of their faith. They said that such people were possessed by a demon or devil, and it was the function of the priest to "exorcise" that demon and release the individual from his or her bondage. Despite its connotations of superstition, I prefer the ancient symbolism to the modern. A person whose growth has been arrested by some deep-seated emotional block is indeed "possessed by a demon," but that demon is his or her own terror of change, that imprisoning reflex by which the ego-self seeks to maintain its status-quo structure by denying the restorative processes their chance to operate. Then, as now, it required both faith and love to shepherd the sick personality through ego-death into the new life beyond, where they meet a stranger—themselves without their pain.

I mean no disrespect, however, when I say that most of these changes in our modern world are fairly superficial. The reworked ego that emerges from transformation may be gentler, more willing to listen, more loving, but it is seldom changed in its fundamentals. Obviously, this is a matter of degree, as some people change more than others. This leads me to the key question of this chapter: *How far can this process go?* Is it possible to find individuals in whom these transformative processes work their way down to the bedrock of identity, burning out the old ego definitions so completely that the entity that emerges is childlike (as opposed to childish), a new creature, seeing a new world for the first time?

To put it symbolically: If most Y choices fracture the mirror of consciousness, creating the ego-cage, then total ego-death would restore the mirror and make flawless its surface. What would that mean? What would we see in the mirror of consciousness if the "I" self-image were to vanish utterly?

Last century, Walt Whitman wrote a little-quoted but remarkable poem entitled "To Him That Was Crucified." It goes as follows:

My spirit to yours dear *brother,*
Do not mind because many sounding your name do not
    understand you,
I do not sound your name, but I understand you,

I specify you with joy *O my comrade* to salute you, and to salute
   those who are with you, before and since, and those to come
   also,
That we all labor together transmitting the same charge and
   succession
We few equals indifferent of lands, indifferent of times,
We, enclosers of all continents, all castes, allowers of all theologies,
Compassionaters, perceivers, rapport of men . . .
Yet we walk unheld, free, the whole earth over, journeying up and
   down till we make our ineffaceable mark upon time and the
   diverse eras,
Till we saturate time and eras, that the men and women of races,
   ages to come, may prove *brethren* and *lovers* as we are.

It is impossible to judge a poem like this dispassionately. On one level, it
sounds like religious mania, a delusion of grandeur. On another level, it
rings true. Readers must judge for themselves. What one can fairly say is
that Whitman (as the records of his life testify) was an exuberant, gutsy,
life-affirming person whose writings reveal none of the fixated narrowness
of a strong ego-self. Indeed, they show just the reverse, for the wide winds
of freedom and openness blow through Whitman's words as through the
words of few other poets in any age.

I have quoted Whitman's poem to highlight the strong sense of "identity" that Whitman felt for Jesus. Earlier, I said that any two human minds
on the same stage of conscious evolution would recognize each other at
once despite differences of time and place. I believe Whitman and Jesus
exemplify this unity of spirit. I use Whitman because, whereas the authentic records of Jesus' life are lost in history (and have been hopelessly
muddied by theological wrangling), those of Whitman's life are recent
and well documented.

Specifically, I suggest that in Walt Whitman, the inner eye had reached
a stage of development that has few modern peers. Like Jesus, he was
ahead of his time, embodying in his level of consciousness a universal
vision that the bulk of the human species may take hundreds of generations to reach. In particular, Whitman, in my view, had undoubtedly

experienced a genuine ego-death in (early) midlife. He passed through a transforming experience that so strongly diminished his sense of ego-self that, again like Jesus, he was able to identify with all humanity.

I cannot "translate" Whitman, and the only thing to do is let Whitman tell the story of this transformation in his own words. His idiom is hard to follow in places for he addresses his soul as a separate person, almost a lover ("you"), but the thrust of his message is clear, fresh, and unmistakable.

I mind how we lay in June such a transparent summer morning,
You settled your head athwart my hips and gently turned over
    upon me,
And parted the shirt from my bosom-bone and plunged your
    tongue to my bare-stript heart
And reached till you felt my beard, and reached till you held my
    feet.
Swiftly rose and spread around me the peace and joy and
    knowledge that pass all the art and argument of the earth
And I know that the hand of God is the elder hand of my own,
And I know that the spirit of God is the eldest brother of my own,
And that all the men ever born are also my brothers . . . and the
    women my sisters and lovers,
And that a kelson of creation is love.

People reading this will react according to the nature of their own ego-self structures, but to me it sums up the joyousness that follows ego-death, the dissolution of littlenesses and limits, the sense of fellowship and oneness in which sorrow dies along with separateness.

Whitman's whole life was transfigured by experiences like this, which have much in common with the moment of illumination that Guatama (the Buddha) experienced under the bo tree in India. In Whitman's own words:

As in a swoon, one instant
Another sun, ineffable, full-dazzles me,

And all the orbs I knew, and brighter, unknown orbs,
One instant of the future land, Heaven's land.

However, words alone are inadequate to describe the experience:

When I undertake to tell the best I find I cannot,
My tongue is ineffectual on its pivots,
My breath will not be obedient to its organs,
I become a dumb man.

This is a recurring theme in the writings of those whose consciousness has reached the universal quality that follows a significant degree of ego-death. The inner eye sees unity and beauty, but it cannot tell the story of its vision in words that make sense to the left-brain, verbal self.

Perhaps most significantly, Whitman declares on rousing himself from the ecstasy of his experience:

I cannot be awake for nothing looks to me as it did before,
Or else I am awake for the first time and all before has been a mean sleep.

Here is encapsulated the liberation that ego-death achieves. During deep transformation, *it is not the world that changes but our perception of it.* After ego-death, we see reality truly for the first time. I mean that literally, not symbolically.

This is the message of this book. The universal reality is there now, open to the universal consciousness that is latent in all of us. However, the ego cages it in, shutting out the light as surely as grilles of iron or walls of hewn stone.

Whether we live within the cage or strive to break free of it is up to us. This is a Y node choice.

The most important in life.

10

LOOPS IN TIME

On the earth the broken arcs:
In the heaven, a perfect round.
— R O B E R T   B R O W N I N G

The conclusion to the last chapter brings us close to the end of our quest. Close but not quite. I have chosen to introduce the concept that an evolving consciousness accesses reality directly by using those aspects that work best for me, namely music and a sense of the beautiful. Many people will feel that this interpretation of consciousness is unsatisfying and incomplete. They are quite right.

The whole focus of this book has been on time and death. What the last chapter failed to do was to interpret consciousness in terms of time. It did not seek to explain unresolved problems raised in earlier parts of the book, like the startling statement, "Death is not a feature of consciousness." Moreover, it did not address the wider issue of the death of the cosmos. These omissions were deliberate. The interknotted issues of time and death, the linking threads of this book, are central to the deepest of all deep questions, the nature of reality itself. Only when we have looked at this, the secret "face of God," can we truly see the dual role that consciousness plays, both in our lives and in the world. It is to this, the final paradox, that we now turn.

Let us quickly review what we have learned about time. In Chapter 2, we saw that, from the standpoint of physics, time has no verifiable status: It is a fictional map we draw on the seamless space-time fabric so that we can find our way around. Chapter 4 showed how our peculiar sense of moving time arises. In order to cohere the conceptual flux of symbolic images that exploded into being when the ego-self was born, the mind needed an ordering principle and a nexus of reference. That ordering principle was time, and that nexus was self.

In gaining self, man took upon himself the responsibility for his own actions. That burden is with him still. In gaining self, man stepped out of the Dreaming and into time. That sadness is with him still. This is why the emergence of the egoic-conceptual mind—an upward step in evolution—is given the paradoxical title of the *Fall.*

The first half of this book stated the problem that time poses to the human psyche. The thrust of my argument in Chapters 1 to 7 was to show that time is the greatest barrier that nature has erected between the average structure of the human mind and reality. To paraphrase a favorite saying of the late Joseph Campbell: "History [time] is a nightmare from which I hope some day to awaken." The German mystic Meister Eckhart (1260–1327) echoed the same thought when he said, "There is no greater obstacle to God than time."

In Chapters 8 and 9, we began to feel our way toward the beginnings of a resolution of this time problem. In Chapter 8, we saw that the differentiating processes that build ego can be diminished effectively (as we now understand) by filtering out the ego-based existential "noise" that jams the input and output channels of consciousness. Chapter 9 focused on the unifying quality of consciousness, showing how it integrates information, seeking always the one in the many, the hidden oneness of things.

The unanswered question in all this is: What happens to our fallacious sense of tick-tock time when the ego-self collapses? How does deep consciousness "see" time? That question can be meaningfully answered only if some human beings have evolved sufficiently to "see" the reality behind time. I think one can confidently assert that such individuals exist. According to the idea of the "mutant minority," there are always, in each generation, a few individuals who are ahead of their time, whose consciousness has evolved far beyond the species norm. Who are they? And what do they tell us?

Who they are is easy to answer; they are the great religious teachers, the mystics. And what they say is a matter of record:

Verily, I say unto you, *before Abraham was, I am.*

—Jesus

One moment holds eternity.

—Goethe

To see a world in a grain of sand
And heaven in a wild flower,
Hold infinity in the palm of your hand
And eternity in an hour.

—William Blake

Yet the timeless in you is aware of life's timelessness,
And knows that yesterday is but today's memory and tomorrow
is today's dream.
And that that which sings and contemplates in you *is still dwelling*
within the bounds of that first moment which scattered the
stars into space.

—Kahlil Gibran

Or say that the end precedes the beginning,
And the end and the beginning were always there
Before the beginning and after the end.
And all is always now. [Italics added]

T. S. Eliot

These poetic sayings must be read in the spirit of a koan—a paradoxical epigram used by students of Zen to focus the mind on hidden depths of meaning that are not obvious from mere surface inspection; i.e., they are not logical statements born of reason but insights of the inner eye. The meaning they carry is below the level of the words themselves. And that meaning is, I believe, that pure consciousness is *freed of time.* To the highly evolved mind, which has filtered out ego noise, reality appears as a *timeless* continuum.

In the light of what I have said in this book, this should not be taken as a cop-out, a retreat into spiritualism or religion. Let me remind the reader that this "in-sight" corresponds remarkably with the portrait of space-time depicted by contemporary science. Since I have used the words of others to convey this sense of being out-of-time, I will use the words of a scientist to paint the relativistic picture of space-time that science sees. The quote is from mathematician Clement Durell's book *Readable Relativity*:

> The universe is to be regarded as a collection of events anywhere and anywhen, an entity which mathematicians call a continuum, and the difference between A (one observer) and O (another) is simply that they slice it up differently. The universe as an entity is timeless (and spaceless). What each individual perceives is merely his own time-section. History records some of the time sections of our ancestors and H. G. Wells forecasts time-sections of our descendants. With neither group have we the power to make direct acquaintance, merely because we cannot put ourselves in the position in which the desired time-cleavage would be the natural one. *But all events, past, present and future as we call them, are present in our four-dimensional space-time continuum, a universe without past or present, as static as a pile of films which can be formed into a reel for the cinematograph.* [Italics added]

Quantum mechanics approaches the issue from a different perspective, but its conclusions can be remarkably similar. As Fred Allan Wolf says in *Parallel Universes*:

> The past, present, and future exist side by side. If we were totally able to "marry" corresponding times each and every moment of our time-bound existences, there would indeed be no sense of time and we would all realize the timeless state, which is taken to be our true or base state of reality by many spiritual practices.

The point of this book is that true consciousness, free of the ego-cage, "sees" this timelessness without travail or trammel. To be free of time is to be free of death. This is the same message as the poet William Blake's when he said, "If the doors of perception [the existential noise of the ego-self] were cleansed [by ego-death], everything would appear to man as it is, infinite [timeless]."

I can sum up and, as it were, round off this point by looking at the evolution of consciousness from the point of view of a creature's awareness, not of its physical or biological environment, but of its dimensional environment. Start with the kind of creature many biologists believe gave rise to the whole vertebrate supergroup, a small, odd-looking, wormlike animal whose modern representatives include the filter-feeding sea squirts and acorn worms. The free-swimming larvae of these creatures have a rudimentary brain, a barely developed "eye," and a special organ called an otocyst that serves as a simple ear.

The picture of the world that any brain builds up can be only as good as the information it receives from its sense organs. Even if this ancestral creature had a highly evolved brain, its impression of the world would be limited to the information supplied by the "eye" and the otocyst. The eye at this stage of evolution is so primitive it cannot resolve elements of information—it cannot perceive objects, it merely registers changes in light intensity. The otocyst does not hear; it simply aligns the animal with respect to gravity. Therefore the reality experienced by this creature is merely a vague impression of brightness or not-so-brightness and a sense of up and down. For it, the star-frosted night sky, the deep blue of pelagic ocean waters, the green of waving banks of sea kelp, *literally do not exist.*

Because sight is so rudimentary in this creature, the only strongly developed sense of dimension in the animal's "mind" is the up/down axis supplied by the otocyst; that means that its consciousness is effectively one-dimensional.

Now, jump to the evolutionary level of a bony fish. This animal has well-developed camera-type eyes, internal ears, and a fairly sophisticated smell apparatus. The eyes in particular provide a rich and varied image of external reality. However, the eyes of a fish look sideways out of each side of its head; its field of vision is planar and there are two nonoverlapping visual fields to its right and its left. Its consciousness thus exists in two dimensions.

In man and higher primates, the eyes have rotated to the front of the head. That gives us stereoscopic vision and expands our consciousness to three spatial dimensions. This whole book, however, bears witness to the fact that our consciousness is singularly flawed in respect to the fourth dimension, time. Through mathematics and experiment, we have deduced the existence of a fourth space-time dimension, but we do not experience it as it is. We see it in glimpses, strangely fractured into ever-dissolving, nondimensional planes called "now."

We know this is a less-than-perfect condition because our reality is locked into a fiction—this Daliesque now-you-see it-now-it's-gone trick-state called the present.

To understand the nature of our trap, imagine a line segment of, say, 10 inches (25 centimeters). Move it an equal length at right angles to itself. That gives us a square (two dimensions). Move the square an equal length at right angles to itself, and we have a cube (three dimensions). It is mathematically possible to repeat the process another time, moving the cube simultaneously at right angles to all three dimensions of familiar space into an imaginary fourth space dimension. This gives us a four-dimensional structure called a hypercube or tesseract. We cannot see or experience a hypercube because our brains cannot see or experience a fourth dimension of space. But we can see the three-dimensional shadow cast by the four-dimensional object, just as we can see the two-dimensional shadow cast by a three-dimensional cube on a sheet of paper (it looks like a nested pair with a small cube contained in a bigger one).

At this stage in the evolution of our minds, our experience of reality is like that of the shadow, a limited, impoverished ghost-image projected into the three dimensions of our present (average) mode of consciousness by the invisible (to us) four-dimensional truth structure that lies beyond and behind it, extended in time as we are extended in space. I cannot stress too strongly that it is this four-dimensional truth structure that is the universe's reality. What we call objective reality, our everyday common sense world, is only a dim phantom construct of the timeless hyperstructure that exists, in or, perhaps as, the "mind of God," to use religious imagery. Yet just as our present three-dimensional state of consciousness evolved from the one-dimensional mode of our remote ancestors, so there is abundant evidence that the four-dimensional mode is struggling to be born in the *Homo sapiens* species at this human moment in the cosmic story. We are almost there.

Whether a four-dimensional state of consciousness is the ultimate truth of the universe, or whether beyond it lie higher states of being that extend into an infinitely rich, multidimensional hyperspace and hypertime, we do not know. One day our descendants may.

This seems to bring us to the end of our quest. Yet one problem remains, and, like all final problems, it is the greatest one of all, sticking like a thorn in the vision of hope the inner eye holds out to us. The cosmos is a space-time continuum, and in this regard the poet's intuition of a timeless state of consciousness merely reflects the facts of the physical universe as science depicts them. However, timelessness implies *foreverness,* and the same science that reveals space-time to us also tells us that the universe will one day *end,* in fire or ice.

The death of forever. The fact that the very cosmos in which we live is mortal. That was where this journey began. At the finish of the race, we seem to run head-on into one last, unresolvable paradox, something that seems to make our intuition of timelessness as insubstantial as a lovely vision, dreamed by a dreamer in a quiet time but dissolving like a snow-flake at first contact with brute fact.

Is this really the case? In Chapter 7, I discussed a recent model of space-time put forward by Stephen Hawking (Figure 7.3). I had to seem to be dismissive of the model at that time because I had not yet focused the reader's attention on the way our flawed, ego-conscious window to the world distorts the structure of the world we see. Now, however, we can return to Hawking's idea from a new and different and, I believe, truer perspective.

Hawking built a model of the cosmos that he called the no-boundary model because, in his theory, time does not begin at a point, nor does it end in one (Figure 7.3). From the earlier perspective of Chapter 7, this model seemed, from many points of view, unsatisfactory, because it used imaginary time, not real time. Chapter 9 gives the model a new source of credibility, for it is characteristic of the inner eye that it can disregard the commonsense aspects of experience and penetrate to the inner logic of nature.

Thus, when the inner eye "sees" a circle, a mandala, and recognizes therein some impression of flawlessness, it is, at a different level, seeing the endless number 3.1415926 . . . It may be significant that we call such numbers transcendental. Indeed, science builds its deepest truths using numbers that are, in an important sense, "illogical." The square root of −1 is imaginary (it is, in fact, part of the number system Hawking uses to build his model). The square root of 2 is irrational. And so it goes.

Moreover, the word "imaginary," like all symbols invented by the conceptual mind, confuses the issue by implying that such numbers are in some way unreal. This is fundamentally false. As Hawking's colleague, mathematician Roger Penrose, says cryptically:

> It is important to stress the fact that these "imaginary" numbers are no less real than the "real" numbers that we have become accustomed to. . . . The relationship between such "real" numbers and physical reality is not as direct or compelling as it may at first seem to be.

We find a similar situation in particle physics where the so-called ultimate building blocks of matter (quarks) are given such mythic names as "strange," "charmed," etc. At this deep level of reality, the false distinction between scientist and poet breaks down, and scientists use the language of song and parable in their intuitive attempts to seek out the basic structure of the world.

To return to my point, I find it fascinating that Hawking himself recognizes that his use of imaginary time, far from being a ruse or trick, may in fact be a door to a higher order of insight. Listen to his own words:

> This might suggest that the so-called imaginary time is really the real time and that what we call real time is just a figment of our imaginations. In real time, the universe has a beginning and an end at singularities that form a boundary to space-time and at which the laws of science break down. But in imaginary time, there are no singularities or boundaries. *So maybe what we call imaginary time is*

really more basic, and what we call real is just an idea that we invent
to help us describe what we think the universe is like. [Italics added]

This goes to the heart of the matter, for the defining quality of the inner eye in its most highly evolved forms is that it can "see" the deepest hidden structures of reality without impediment. If timelessness is an authentic feature of consciousness—and the evidence I have summarized in this book very strongly suggests that it is—then consciousness may just as well "exist" in what the mathematicians call "imaginary" time as in "real" time. Indeed, it may be precisely because the ego-self lives in real time that it "knows" death, while it may be precisely because consciousness lives in imaginary time that it "knows" eternity.

I want to build on Hawking's model, but in a particular way. I want to use it in the poetic sense of a metaphor, not in the rigid sense of a mathematical model. There are three reasons for this: First, Hawking's model presupposes that the universe is closed (that space-time is positively curved), and this is, as yet, unproven. Second, I do not believe Hawking's model (despite the credentials of its creator) is science's last word on this subject. Third, we are, by any definition, crossing into uncharted psychological territory by thinking about human hopes for the future in terms of imaginary time, or any other mathematical representation of time that science may discover.

The key feature of the Hawking metaphor is that time *closes back upon itself to form a loop.* That is why in this metaphor we cannot talk of a beginning or an end to time, for a circle has neither, except for the arbitrary points we choose to mark on it. It may be no accident that the inner eye has for long sensed that reality is eternal, for in this higher-order understanding, foreverness is restored to its ancient position as the foundation of consciousness.

The most fascinating consequence of the loop-of-time metaphor is summed up in Figure 7.3. There, we see evolution starting with the "north pole" (the big bang) and progressing around the circle to "now," represented, say, by the 18th line of latitude. From this "now" perspective, we can look "back" at our past, hidden behind the "southward" space-time rim, or forward into our future, hidden behind the "northward" space-time rim. Yet that is illusionary, a hangover of the flawed way we look at time through the ego-self window. The loop-of-time metaphor shows that when we look forward into the future, we are also looking back into the past because the arrow of time traces out the full circumference of the circle, eventually coming back to itself.

In this "song of reality," the distinction between past and future vanishes. The process of "seeing" is then symmetrical in both directions. In T. S. Eliot's apt words:

> Time present and time past
> Are both perhaps present in time future,
> And time future contained in time past.

If this is what consciousness "sees," it is timeless in a deeper and different sense than we ever dreamed possible. In real time, such a closing of the loop would play havoc with our notions of causality, cause becoming effect and effect cause. However, that may be a superficial view, as I will try to show in a moment.

The unexpected feature of the loop-of-time metaphor is that a signal from the future becomes a signal from the past. Nothing is wholly new, for information is always travelling where it has been before. This is why I find the loop-of-time parable so satisfying. It resonates deeply with a poem cited earlier—T. S. Eliot's "Little Gidding":

> We shall not cease from exploration
> And the end of all our exploring
> *Will be to arrive where we started*
> *and know the place for the first time.*
> Through the unknown, remembered gate
> When the last of earth left to discover
> Is that which was the beginning. [Italics added]

The famous line "and know the place for the first time" is critically significant in the context of this book. Relate this message to your own moments of growth—those times you look back on as marking some kind of quantum jump in your understanding—a leap forward. One key characteristic of those moments is that we suddenly understand something we feel we have, in a dim way, understood all along. Hence such sayings as,

"I've known that all my life but I've only just realized it's true," or "Now I see—I understand it." This shows up a deeper layer of meaning in the way we use the words discussed in Chapter 5: recognize (know again) and remember (recall to mind).

It is said of the Renaissance artist Michelangelo that he approached a block of marble believing that the perfect sculpture he sought to create already existed in the unhewn stone. The artistic act was thus an act of discovery, not creation, and the long hours of painstaking work were devoted to revealing what was already there.

A scientific colleague once (in a moment of not entirely complimentary frankness) described me as a "prophet, not a scientist." One of my most successful papers was a short article published in the science journal *Nature* in 1979. In that paper, I made a specific prediction about the way cells process genetic data. That prediction was confirmed shortly after. The interesting thing is that I knew the moment I had the idea on which the prediction was based that the idea was right. There was in some hard-to-define way a certainty about the insight that put it beyond doubt. This is, I believe, the stamp of an authentically creative act: *One discovers what is already true.* When a human being "sees" a preexisting truth, already known to the cosmos, in a very deep sense, the universe recognizes part of itself, comprehending it at a higher level of understanding. This kind of incremental knowing is the self-realization of the cosmos.

In other words, there is a deep knowing about consciousness that is utterly distinct from mere intellectual comprehension. This deep knowing is a remembering of what is already there. One becomes, in the full sense, conscious of what one has always subconsciously been aware of. In terms of Eliot's poem, the "gate" is remembered, even though it is unknown. We arrive where we started and know the place for the first time!

We do not create the future, we discover it.

Roger Penrose captures something of the flavor of the mode of knowing in *The Emperor's New Mind,* when he says:

> Recall my proposal that consciousness, in essence, is the "seeing" of a necessary truth: and that it may represent some kind of actual contact with Plato's world of ideal mathematical concepts. Recall that Plato's world is itself timeless. The perception of Platonic truth

carries no actual information and there would be no actual contradiction involved if such a conscious perception *were even to be prop-
agated backwards in time*! [Italics added]

The loop-of-time metaphor goes a long way toward explaining a puzzle
that many readers will have picked up as they worked their way through
the pages of this book. The argument I put forward in Chapters 8 and 9,
that ego cages consciousness, is not a novel one—it is an ancient tenet of
many religions. In particular, much of what I said in those chapters could
be described as a scientific interpretation of a set of beliefs mapped out
in the Hindu *Upanishads* thousands of years ago. Hindu belief, for example, sees the ego as a deception (*maya*) that separates the "I" from the
Ultimate. When the mirage of ego is dissolved, the underlying union is
made plain—Thou art That (*tat tvam asi*) is the illuminating recognition
of this oneness. This is essentially the message of Chapter 8.

Even the metaphor of the ego-smudged mirror of consciousness that I
have used repeatedly (Chapters 8 to 10) has a Hindu parallel. Yoga teaching uses the simile of wind blowing across the surface of water to describe
the relationship between self and reality. While the wind blows, the water's
surface—the mirror—is fragmented, shifting, the reality it reflects continuously disrupted into half-truths and confusing images. However, *when
the wind stops,* the surface of the water, like that of the mirror, becomes
still and perfect, reflecting the wholesome majesty of God, beheld in mo-
tionless serenity. Hence, the origin of the much misunderstood word *nir-
vana* (*nir*, "beyond"; *vana* "wind").

Moreover, Eastern religions seem to have arrived by mystical contemplation and insight at an understanding of the deep structure of physical
reality that Western science has only recently been able to formulate in
empirical mathematical terms. Consider these two descriptions of the nature of time, as quoted by Fritjof Capra in his well-known text, *The Tao
of Physics:*

It is believed by most that time passes; in actual fact it stays where
it is. This idea of passing may be called time, but it is an incorrect

idea, for since one sees it only as passing, one cannot understand that it just stays where it is.

—Zen master Dogen

This passage captures the essence of the relativisitic picture of time. A further insight into time comes from a Buddhist text:

It was taught by the Buddha, oh Monks that . . . the past, the future, physical space . . . and individuals are nothing but names, forms of thought, words of common usage, merely superficial realities.

This passage not only encapsulates the modern scientific view of our subjective sense of time with its false tense structure (past-present-future); it also aptly summarizes the formative role of language in the creation of the ego-self.

Is all I have done in this book to retell, in the imagery of science, a story of reality that has been known to mystics for centuries? In one sense, the answer is no. I have tried to derive my argument entirely from known scientific premises, attempting at all times to keep my logic internally consistent. However, in another sense, the answer is yes. I have already said that the linear logic of the left brain has, from one point of view, been compelled to create science so that it could "see," in its own conceptual way, the image of unity that the right brain had, through intuition, glimpsed aeons ago.

This leads me to an adventurous speculation. The time when many of the deep myths of our species crystallized out—about 5,000 to 3,000 years ago in the West—corresponds remarkably with the period of the Fall, the emergence of the ego-self. At this transition stage of human evolution, consciousness was, by the definition of my argument, stronger in highly evolved individuals because the confounding distractions of the still-evolving ego had not yet hardened into their final form. It is not surprising that the visionaries or prophets of that period possessed a more powerful insight than we do today, submerged as we are in the fallacy of our tick-tock time.

What I am suggesting is that the prophets who formulated the deep intuitive insights common to the major religions of humanity were in some sense tuned in to the future, "seeing" the dim and far-off image of knowledge still unborn, listening perhaps to the holistic message of a science thousands of years away, in the twentieth and twenty-first centuries of the modern era. I propose that this is not a rare or a strange thing; it is precisely what consciousness recognizes, not just a premonition of the past but a memory of the future.

A memory of the future. Is that scientifically possible? The answer is quite emphatically yes. Many scientists, including Paul Davies and Fred Hoyle, have noted that electromagnetic waves, for example, can propagate in both time directions. Radio waves spreading outward from a point source define an arrow of time because they get farther and farther from their origin, moving from past into future. The field equations that govern electromagnetic radiation work just as well the other way round; they describe mathematically valid waves, which converge back to a point, reversing the direction of time from future to past. Past-to-future waves are called "retarded," since they arrive after they have been sent; whereas future-to-past waves are called "advanced," since they arrive before they are sent.

While physicists acknowledge that advanced waves exist as a theoretical possibility, most would deny them any existential reality. This majority view is being increasingly challenged by scientists such as John Wheeler, John Cramer, Yahir Aharonov and others. Among the scientists who take the idea of signals from the future seriously, Fred Hoyle stands out. In his book *The Intelligent Universe,* he poses this question about electromagnetic waves that are reversed in time: "Is it conceivable . . . that the possibility of a reversed time-sense, future-to-past, is an exception, pretty well the only exception to this general rule of natural parsimony?" He then gives his own answer: "I have for long considered that the answer to this question must surely be no, and I have for long puzzled about what the consequences of such an answer would be."

Acknowledging that communication from future to past appears to lead to "logical inconsistency," Hoyle, significantly, also invokes the idea of a loop in time. To solve the old paradox of what would happen to a person who goes back in time and prevents his own parents from marrying, i.e., stops himself from being born, Hoyle proposes what seems at first sight to be merely an ingenious stratagem:

So the reader [time-traveler] hesitates, trying to make up his mind [about his parents], which he eventually does through an individual quantum event in the brain, an event *which takes the form that preserves logical consistency.* In short, the reader proceeds to arrange the marriage believing himself to be acting voluntarily, whereas he is really acting through a control from the future which always preserves consistency.

Here, I believe, Hoyle has hit upon a fundamental insight. In Chapter 5 (on self-consciousness) and in Chapter 8 (on the ego-self), I hammered the point that we create our ego-selves largely through the verbal structures in which we encase our thoughts. Each act of speech definition, however, is preceded by a "readiness potential" or something analogous to it. During this brief interval, something happens in the mind that translates the unrealized option into the realized choice.

We come back to choice, to the Y node that has been a pivotal point of this book. The readiness potential phase corresponds with the Y node ambivalence, the moment before choice. Before a decision is made, both possibilities are open. After it has been made, one is shut (decided), the other still open (not used). As I have noted before, a system like this corresponds closely to the binary system on which computers operate. I find that significant because I have been impressed by analogies that link the brain with computers; from many points of view, the two mechanisms of information storage and processing seem to have much in common.

The point is, we imagine that our conscious choices are our own—that they reflect some essential us-ness. Yet, the fact is that we do not know what happens during that split second that precedes choice. Do *we* decide, or is the decision something we automatically own "after the event." In the latter case, the actual deciding factor could have little (if anything) to do with us; it could be partly or wholly a result of quantum uncertainties in the brain.

Can we link this speculation with brain research? Perhaps we can. Nerve cells typically end in a bunch of minute, treelike "feelers." As mentioned briefly in Chapter 7, the gap between the feeler of one nerve and that of another is called a synapse. A nervous impulse is transmitted across a synapse by special chemicals called neurotransmitters.

Synaptic gaps are extremely short, about 200 to 300 angstroms across (an angstrom is one hundred-millionth of a centimeter), which means they are approaching the atomic scale of dimensions at which quantum effects become important. It does not strain imagination unduly to believe that a synapse teetering on the brink of its "firing threshold" could be triggered into activity by an event from the quantum realm. The instrument used to measure radioactivity, a Geiger counter, may provide an analogy. The Geiger counter can detect the disintegration of a single atom, something that is firmly in the quantum domain, by amplifying the initial signal into an avalanche of further disintegrations (in this case among gas molecules), which results in a detectable electrical pulse. In this example, a single quantum microevent can set off a chain reaction that results in a measurable large-scale result.

The father of the so-called Copenhagen interpretation of quantum mechanics, Niels Bohr, speculated as far back as 1958 that key points in the regulatory mechanisms of the brain might be so delicately balanced that they could be affected by quantum mechanical events. Significantly, eminent brain biologist John. C. Eccles seems to agree. As Eccles has observed:

> If one uses the expressive terminology . . . the "ghost" (the quantum mechanical event) operates a "machine" (the brain), not of ropes and pulleys, valves and pipes, but of microscopic spatio-temporal patterns of activity in the neuronal net woven by synaptic connections of ten thousand million neurones, and even then only by operating on neurones *that are momentarily poised close to a just-threshold level of excitability.* [Italics added]

This means the Y node choices that are almost evenly balanced between two outcomes are most likely to be susceptible to quantum influences, because it is only in these near-equipoise situations that the quantum fluctuations are the feather on the scale that tips the balance one way or the other. In psychological terms, such equipoise choices may correspond to those decisions we find hardest to make because we are almost equally pulled in both directions. It would be interesting if that were to prove to be the case, because it is these extremely difficult choices and the decisions that arise from their resolution that often have the greatest influence on our lives.

Quantum fluctuations could also explain those thoughts that come to us "in a flash" or "out of nowhere." I wonder what role, if any, they play in intuition. It is possible that the neural center that "sees" unity, no matter how much it is perfected by unselfishness, is incapable of determining when it will have its deeper insights. That may well still be a matter of complete chance, or, on the above hypothesis, of quasi-chance and non-causal cross-linkaging.

If some Y node choices were quantum in nature, a profound and enduring link would be established between the dynamics of consciousness and the structure of the cosmos itself. It is not in the sense of a presently available scientific theory that I intuitively sense a rightness in Hoyle's idea but in the sense of a song of truth, an insight. It may take science years to formulate such a concept in a mathematically consistent way that will win it acceptance.

However, one prediction does seem to be possible now. The constraints placed on quantum events by the need to maintain consistency in the loop must constitute one of the great ordering principles of nature. Such an ordering principle could require a profound modification of the laws of quantum mechanics, which are rooted in and dependent on the statistical principles of probability and randomness. (It was this indeterminate character of quantum mechanics that caused Einstein to declare that God "did not play dice with the world.") To maintain consistency in the loop, many quantum events could not be random; they would have to be linked in the nonlocal way so characteristic of quantum mechanics. Could that linkage correspond to (and explain) the principle of *synchronicity* formulated by psychologist Carl Jung and quantum physicist Wolfgang Pauli and others?

Synchronicity refers to the apparently inexplicable coincidences that crop up from time to time. We all have experiences of this type. For no apparent reason, you may suddenly think of a friend you have not seen for years at the very moment when the phone rings and you discover that he/she has just landed in town and wants to visit. The quantum event that caused you to think of the person at the very instant he/she was thinking of you may result from the need to preserve the internal consistency of a quantum world closed back upon itself to form a loop of time.

The self-consistency concept may also help to explain what scientists call the anthropic principle. That refers not to the coincidences of human life, but to cosmic coincidences. When Hoyle describes the universe as a put-up job, he is referring to the almost unbelievable way in which the cosmos seems to have been tailor-made to permit the evolution of creatures like ourselves. If the fundamental constants of physics were readjusted by a tiny fraction, the universe would become inhospitable to life. For example, if the gravitational constant were just a fraction bigger, the instabilities that cause stars to explode as supernovas could never have developed. That means that there would have been no way to seed space with the ash of heavy elements essential to life. The gravitational constant, in other words, is very finely tuned to create just the right kind of universe in which life can evolve.

Physicists from Paul Dirac to Paul Davies have also pointed out that the cosmos seems to be sensitively built on a number of quite amazing coincidences. In particular, the large number 10^{40} crops up in some of the most basic relationships in physics.

$$x_G^{\,1} \sim 10^{40}$$
$$N \sim 10^{80} = 10(^{40})^2$$
$$N_* \sim 10^{60} = 10(^{40})^{3/2}$$
$$t_H/t_N \sim 10^{40}$$
$$t_N/t_P \sim 10^{40}$$
$$S \sim (10^{40})^{1/4}$$

The letters and numbers on the left refer to qualities or relationships that have fundamental importance in physics; their meaning need not concern us—it is the fact that the number 10^{40} crops up so regularly in the context of the parameters that determine the structure of the universe that is so remarkable.

The anthropic principle says that all these "coincidences" create the special kind of cosmic conditions needed to produce us. The puzzle that this presents dissolves, however, if consciousness interacts with matter by means of quantum events in the brain, because the space-time loop can only maintain its self-consistency by creating and preserving just those conditions that permit consciousness to flourish. Consciousness, in this context, does not mean the average mode of human consciousness at this moment in evolution; it means whatever completed limit consciousness may reach in future time. *The cosmos then emerges as the ultimate feedback loop, and consciousness is a created product of its own antecedent activity.*

This idea has many similarities to the bootstrap principle formulated by physicist Geoffrey Chew, which defines all basic constituents of the real world in terms of their mutually self-consistent relationships. It is also a cousin of John Wheeler's concept of the universe as a "self-excited circuit" in which the cosmos is called into being by retroactive causation, that is, by events in the future propagating backward in time to cause events in the past.

This is a very bold, almost rash speculation, and it invites the obvious criticism from a scientific cynic: If these synchronicities that underpin consistency are real, if they exist, they must show up somewhere as mathematical regularities. Okay, where are they?

To explore this issue, we must look at the mathematics of randomness. And, up front, we encounter a surprising fact. It is difficult, if not impossible, to say with confidence that a given number sequence that appears random in any one context is in fact random in an absolute sense. Most seemingly random numbers when compared, for example by adding or subtracting, would give further numbers that themselves would seem to be random. Consider this sequence: 31415926535897(1). It passes all currently available tests for randomness. Now compare it with the sequence 20304815424786(2), which also qualifies as a wholly random number. On the face of it, we simply have two random numbers. However, if we subtract the lower sequence (2) from the higher (1), with the wrinkle that if we get a negative number we add 10 to the result, we obtain the sequence 11111111111111. This is strikingly nonrandom. These two random numbers thus have a special property. Heinz Pagels, who gives this example in his book *The Cosmic Code*, draws from it a conclusion that goes to the heart of my argument about synchronistic cross-linkaging. He says: "This illustrates that two random sequences can be *correlated*—each is individually *chaotic* but, if properly compared by using some rule, then a *nonrandom* pattern appears." [Italics added]

If I am right, analogous nonrandom cross-linkages at the quantum level may be the fine gossamer threads, fragile in themselves, but indestructible in their collective strength, that hold the cosmos in a self-consistent loop of becoming.

Y nodes, choices, thus emerge as the determinants of the pattern of our psychological development. Because of them, we create our own heaven, our own hell, we create ourselves, we create the very fabric of the world.

We are getting into very deep waters where ordinary experience cannot guide us. So again, I will let a more eloquent voice speak for me. Not the voice of a scientist, but of a poet-writer. In her remarkable retelling of the legend of King Arthur, *The Mists of Avalon*, Marian Zimmer Bradley makes her heroine, Morgan le Fay, say, "For this is the great secret, which was known to all educated men in our day, *that by what men think, we create the world around us, daily new.*" [Italics added]

With this discussion of synchronicity and self-consistency, we have arrived at the point where we can begin to see the strange relationship between consciousness and the universe, between the thought within and the thing without.

We have established that consciousness cannot be treated separately from the reality it observes. We can assert this confidently. It is now a (virtually) unchallengeable axiom of quantum mechanics that each act of observation causes the ripple of possibility of the quantum wave to concretize into entities with an observable and measurable existence.

In Chapter 9, I postulated that consciousness is that unifying activity in the brain that "sees" one in many. However, consciousness is not just a passive receiver. By its choices, it creates unities. Indeed, its very essence is that it acts as a nodal integrater between the quantum ripples of possibility that emanate from both past and future. It is, if you like, the "reality slit" into which multiple ripples of possibility enter, leaving the temporally symmetric quantum world and "falling" into the one-way world of matter that decays with time.

Wolf has summarized this viewpoint admirably:

Our minds [i.e., consciousness] are thus tuned . . . to multiple dimensions, multiple realities. The freely associating mind is able to pass across time barriers, sensing the future and reappraising the past. Our minds are time machines, able to sense the flow of possibility waves from both the past and the future. In my view, there cannot be anything like existence without this higher form of quantum reality.

All this sounds highly abstract, remote from the kind of consciousness you and I experience now. So let me bring the message close to home. Think back to a moment when you suddenly felt you really understood something you had not understood before. It may have been a mathematical problem you had been wrestling with for days. Suddenly, after hours of frustration, the answer was there—complete and perfect.

This is the essence of insight. Things hitherto separate and unconnected suddenly click together. The pieces of the jigsaw slide into place. As I have stressed, this *integrative* faculty is the hallmark of consciousness. The understanding that follows a Eureka moment is not a surface comprehension; it is a deep knowing that will stay with you for life precisely because it is part of a wider multiform consciousness, of which your mind is but a single unit. In deep knowing you become part of the self-unfolding of the cosmos.

Think about this in terms of time. The answer you sought existed *prior to your discovery of it.* What happened in your flash of understanding was that your individual consciousness suddenly caught up with a truth already known. It tapped into the completed, unitive consciousness that underpins the closed feedback loop of becoming. What you experienced was a faint foretaste of the final act in the evolution of consciousness, a memory of that magic future moment of total togetherness, when the distinction between observer and observed vanishes completely.

One of the founding fathers of quantum mechanics, Werner Heisenberg, said of his subject: "The common division of the world into subject and object, inner world and outer, body and soul, is no longer adequate." In saying this he, a scientist, found himself using the language of mysticism. Compare Heisenberg's words with those of the Dominican monk Meister Eckhart: "The knower and the known are one." Or the words of the Indian philosopher Krishnamurti: "Consciousness is its content" and "There is neither the outer nor the inner but only the whole. The experiencer is the experienced . . . the thinker is the thought."

Here then is the longed-for end of the age-old road. Here science and religion speak with a single voice, each subtending and validating the other. Here confusion ends and contradictions cease. All things *are* one. Even the distinction between inner and outer, singer and song, fades in the full light of completed consciousness.

Even now, today, here, still trapped in time, if we strain our ears to their limit, we can hear the strains of that distant music "from some far shore the final chorus sounding," as Whitman put it. A whisper of to-morrow, reaching into today. More than a beacon of hope, more than a promise of better things, a commitment from our higher selves to their lowlier foundations, a conviction that the creative evolution that fashioned man from microbe will fashion God from man, no, *has* fashioned God from man. From around the closed arc of time, the time-free God speaks to his time-trapped children, who are both his parents and his heirs.

What then of the arrow of time, forever pointing toward decay and death? Hoyle gives us an interesting clue. Speaking of the ability of elec-tromagnetic waves to propagate in both time directions, Hoyle notes that the propagation of radiation in the familiar past-to-future time sense leads inevitably to loss of information. However, over evolutionary time, or-ganisms have gained in complexity (such a gain being powered by the energy of the sun's radiation).

He then goes on to suggest, as I have outlined above, that life uses information *from the future*. In real-time science, such a suggestion would run afoul of the second law of thermodynamics. However, if time is closed into a loop, a relentless decay of order into noise is impossible because at some point in the circle, the situation must reverse itself so that noise becomes order. Again, in a metaphorical sense, the idea of a loop in time seems to resolve a paradox. In this metaphor, life and intelligence can draw, not only on information in their past, as "remembered" in their DNA, but on information in their future, which is their past once re-moved.

Where does consciousness fit into this global picture? My problem here is a perfect example of the thing I have emphasized over the past few chapters—of the way the words we choose, by trapping (defining) our thoughts in words, confuse the reality we are trying to reach. I have now implanted two models in the reader's mind, Hawking's space-time loop and Hoyle's idea of choice as a resultant of quantum uncertainties translated into conscious action (even if that action is only the fixing of a thought in words). These two models do not readily mesh together. As always happens with language, I have brought clarity in one case only by muddying the waters in another.

From this perspective, we can now map out an evolution of consciousness in terms of the space-time globe. In Figure 10.1, I sketch out a mandala, a mythic symbol in the form of a Hawking space-time globe, a loop in time. Each pole is dark, symbolizing undifferentiated simplicity in a physical sense and total ignorance (zero consciousness) in a psychological sense. From this darkness, gradually, through evolution, light is born and increases in strength. That light is information, the data stored in DNA code, and, in us, expressed as consciousness. At this stage, we are low on the scale of consciousness. Beyond the "now" point occupied by man at his present stage of evolution, the light of consciousness continues to brighten, reaching a maximum for reasons of pure symmetry at the equator of the space-time globe, after which it fades away again to reach another pole of darkness.

The "pure symmetry" of the "equator" is not just a turn of phrase. The point at which the cosmos reaches its maximum size has a special property because it is unique, marking the exact moment at which growth transmutes into decay. As such, it has something of the quality of a phase transition or a symmetry breaking. If consciousness reaches its full flowering at its point of maximum strength, its very perfection may, for reasons beyond our present comprehension, require a dissolution into darkness in order to realize itself again on the other side of the space-time rim.

This idea has its own poetic logic, for the definition of something *perfect* is that it has reached finality—it has fulfilled its dream, it has realized the most sublime expression of beauty that the cosmos is capable of. In a real sense, therefore, it can evolve no farther, because it has nowhere to go. If the structure of the cosmos is such that nothing can stand still, the only thing a perfected structure can do is undergo a symmetry-breaking effect that reverses the process that brought it into being. At this climactic point of flawless and absolute perfection, the laws of physics may require that evolution invert itself, unbuilding what has been built, unlearning what

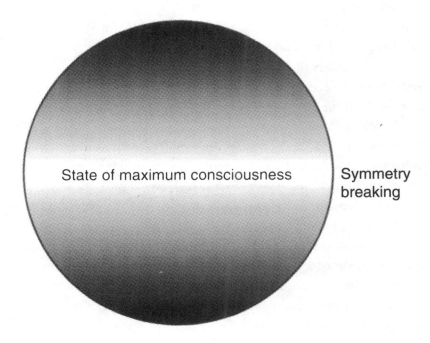

Zero consciousness

State of maximum consciousness   Symmetry breaking

Zero consciousness

The universe

FIGURE 10.1

A highly speculative representation of the evolution of consciousness in a self-consistent, cyclic universe. At the beginning of the cosmos (the big bang), matter is in its simplest physical state and intelligence does not exist. As space-time expands, matter begins an adventurous evolution that will lead to the development of life systems. Out of that evolution grows the ability of the part to mirror the totality of the whole (consciousness). At this human moment in evolution, consciousness is fragmented and rudimentary, handicapped by ignorance and confused by ego. However, beyond the "line of latitude" represented by the average level of human understanding at this point in time, consciousness continues to flower, attaining its maximum power at the exact point that the cosmos reaches its maximum size. At this unique point of perfected flawlessness, the cosmos may undergo a "symmetry breaking" operation, which reverses the process that brought it into being. All modes of consciousness, however, continue to exist in this "eternal" space-time structure since the lowest and the highest levels are continuous with each other and the degradative process that leads to noise is seamlessly connected with the creative process that leads to music.

has been learned, forgetting what has been remembered, destroying created order to regenerate creative chaos.

If this idea still feels vaguely unsatisfying, remember that we are using a metaphor to try to convey some feeling for a concept that is beyond our power to conceive or formulate at this stage of our evolution. As usual, poetry gives us a sharper insight. Listen to what T. S. Eliot says in "Burnt Norton":

> At the still point of the turning world. Neither flesh nor fleshless;
> Neither from nor towards: at the still point, there the dance is,
> But neither arrest nor movement. *And do not call it fixity,*
> *Where past and future are gathered.* Neither movement from nor
>   towards.
> Neither ascent nor decline. Except for the point, the still point,
>   There would be no dance, *and there is only the dance.* [Italics
>   added]

And later:

> Words move, *music moves*
> *Only in time;* but that which is only living
> Can only die. Words, after speech, reach
> Into the silence. *Only by the form, the pattern*
> *Can words or music reach*
> *The stillness,* as a Chinese jar still
> Moves perpetually in its stillness.
> Not the stillness of the violin, while the note lasts,
> Not that only, but the co-existence,
> *Or say that the end precedes the beginning,*
> *And the end and the beginning were always there*
> *Before the beginning and after the end.*
> *And all is always now.* [Italics added]

In a symbolic way, this new mandala solves many of the paradoxes that have bedeviled our quest for meaning through the course of this book. In Chapter 2, I painted a grim picture of the future in a cosmos destined to move to a state of maximum entropy, i.e., of death. In the mandala, the chain of cause-and-effect is continuous—maximum entropy is linked to and continuous with maximum order for the arrow of time points not only to the dark node but inevitably to the brightness beyond. This may be the final darkness-before-the-dawn image.

The mandala also shows—clearly—how consciousness can be universal while at the same time being fractured into different reflecting crystals by ego-boundaries. In this representation, the lines of latitude on the space-time globe represent levels of consciousness, progressing from the pre-conscious minds of animals to the various levels of human consciousness and beyond. A thousand different human minds may reach a given line on the scale by any one of a million different, meandering "worldline" routes (resulting from billions of different Y node choices), but, once there, the quality of the consciousness they experience will be identical. There are a million roads to the same place, a million roads to Avalon.

What is true of man is also true of extraterrestrial intelligences, if they exist. Whatever the physical basis of its mentality, an alien life-form would experience exactly the same quality of understanding at any given line of latitude as a human; universal consciousness admits of no exceptions.

In this mandala, there is no need for God to create (cause) the cosmos, since the act of creation is itself a result of its own prior effects.

Perhaps (only perhaps) the mandala metaphor allows us to see why ego-death can free consciousness from time even at our present, far-from-perfect stage of evolution. Consider the line of latitude that the average human consciousness has almost but not quite reached on the space-time globe as a breakthrough point at which ego-death occurs for most humans. Today, we are somewhere short of that threshold, and all we can do is strive for the small ego-deaths that lead to those rare moments of insight so treasured by those who have experienced them. These may be enough to allow us to escape our bondage to real time. One has only to break the time threshold fleetingly to make a permanent contribution to the evolutionary process, for that breakthrough, once it has happened, is indelibly imprinted into the fabric of space-time. We must never lose sight of the fact that our past thoughts are as real as our past bodies. They do not cease to exist just because our awareness is locked in the present. This is true not only of those things we remember, but of the millions of forgotten Y node choices through which we fixed the pattern of our minds.

The universe remembers them even if we do not. In this sense, the poet's intuition may be right: One moment may hold eternity.

So, finally, the pattern emerges. Through the haze of ego, through the limitations of ignorance, we of this generation begin to see something no other generation has ever seen. At least, not with such precise, mathematical detail, and not in such depth.

What we see for the first time is truth; the truth of what we are and whence we came. We know the scale of deep time: fifteen billion years. We know the evolutionary sequence: big bang → formless clouds of hydrogen (and helium) gas → galaxies → first generation stars → supernovas → second generation stars and planets → life → mind. We are beginning to feel in our bones just what this means. We see that from hydrogen, the simplest atom in the periodic table, has come symphony orchestras, diamonds, the sound of starlings at sunset, *Voyager* spacecraft, the glitter of dew on spiderwebs at dawn, fractal images on computers, the laser light of cognitive awareness. That is a creative act of staggering proportions. We are the products of this evolutionary process. We are also its heirs and its trustees.

So here we stand at this human moment in evolution, sentient stardust looking back at its origins with eyes that see for the first time a universe made conscious of itself. Poised in the present, we look forward to the future—in both senses of the term. For here is the most intimately awesome realization our science has bequeathed us—the creative process that fashioned the human mind will not stop with us. We know that consciousness will continue to grow in strength until it is as far removed from the present human mentality as our minds are from the rudimentary nervous systems of the slipper animalcules that swarm in a drop of pond water, until its creative power is so great that it can *realize itself*, making its own unbegun splendor explode into being in a supreme "instant" of consciously retroactive causation. In 10 billion years, or 10 million, or . . . ?

What is the climax of consciousness toward which the whole evolutionary process draws, the point of paradox where beginning and end meld? Is it God? I have already used the word God, but I must caution that "God" is only a word, a label. The reality is beyond our comprehension. If we could foresee the fulfilled cognition our minds will evolve into, we would perish in an instant. It is a law of life that understanding comes only to a mind that is ready to receive it. If cosmic consciousness were to flood into the present structure of the average human mind, if today's thought pattern were unpreparedly to "know" tomorrow's consciousness, simultaneously aware of being at the fine scale of atoms and the colossal scale of stars, mind would self-destruct. Such premature insight would fry our brains.

In his wonderful prose poem "Deep Time," physicist David Darling maps out the future path of consciousness in words I cannot improve upon.

Even now, at the close of the twentieth century, we sense it. You and I are the infant cosmos, still only dimly aware, still only conscious of things immediately around the reality generators that are our minds. We perceive only dully, over a small range of wavelengths of light and sound, and we comprehend structure over only a narrow range in space and time. But, eventually, we will see X rays and gamma rays, radio waves and gravitational waves. And subatomic particles. And whole galaxies in their most intimate detail. We shall see and understand all there is to know. What we are today will evolve to become a single universe-wide mind, so that every particle in space will be within this cosmic consciousness—free, but aware. Every particle of which you and I are made will ultimately be reconstituted in this universal mind, along with everything else. Given such a prospect, we need hardly fear our own personal deaths. For nothing ever dies. And in Deep Time we shall be as one.

This map of future evolution allows us to remove the last fracture in our understanding, the final fissure that stops us from seeing things whole. In order to carry my argument through Chapters 8–10 in logical order, I allowed the impression to develop that consciousness was largely a right-brain function, and ego largely a left-brain function. In so doing, I preserved the very dualism I was trying to demolish. Let me therefore repeat a point I raised briefly in Chapters 8 and 9—that completed consciousness melds together right-brain holism and left-brain logic. It is not a sufficient function of consciousness that it simply sees the oneness of things. The cosmos is a *creative* process, a stupendously generative *act*. That act demands work, the work that comes not from contemplation but from action. In the final analysis, the Western tradition of science has been as necessary for the evolution of consciousness as the Eastern tradition of mysticism. Far from being set against each other, these differing approaches support and enrich the complementary yin/yang oneness they create.

The insights of science—monuments of unaging intellect—are part of the deep knowing of consciousness. We must not confuse ego with intellect. While prescientific societies could intuitively sense the oneness of things, the cosmos could never realize itself without the detailed mathematical definition that science brings about. In a more profound sense, the self-realization of the cosmos required—and requires—the ongoing collapse of temporally symmetric quantum waves into matter, the transfiguration of possibility into actuality, the Fall from Eternity into Time. It is this endlessly repeating metamorphosis that produces in the static space-time world of *being* the dynamic adventure of *becoming*, that generates in us the sense of *motion* that so confuses us when we apply it to time. For this Fall is the heartbeat of the cosmos—that which keeps it "real" by making it whole. Without this Fall we and the world we inhabit would be only virtual quantum possibilities, shapeless dreams in the Mind of God.

This mandala sings to us that consciousness will continue to evolve into a truly supreme state in which it will be fully timeless and creatively free of all limitations. In this state of divinity, it will have the capacity to build a world from what Paul Davies has called structured nothingness. In this continuum, the individual human brain is not simply a passive receiver, tuning in to information from both past and future. Rather, it receives data from the past and then, by reworking it in consciousness, creates the data that will go forward into the future. Consciousness is not just a mirror (another confusing image) that receives the light of truth with clearer definition as its ego-barriers go down. Consciousness is also an amplifier, a generator of the light that brightens beyond itself to reach the transcendent radiance of the center, the still point.

Giver and receiver, consciousness is both, its ability to take and to give being handicapped by the level of growth it has reached and by the confusing noise of the ego-cage. A highly evolved mind free of self receives fully and gives fully. In both senses, it "sees," it "knows."

The message of this chapter, and this book, is, to me, flawlessly captured in my favorite poem, by the English poet Siegfried Sassoon:

I am that fantasy which race has wrought
Of mundane chance-material. I am time
Paeaned by the senses five like bells that chime.

I am that cramped and crumbling house of clay
Where mansoul weaves the secret webs of thought.
Venturer—automaton—I cannot tell
What powers and instincts animate and betray
And do their dreamwork in me. Seed and star,
Sown by the wind, in spirit I am far
From self, the dull control with whom I dwell.

Also I am ancestral. Aeons ahead
And ages back, both son and sire I live
Mote-like between the unquickened and the dead—
From whom I take, and unto whom I give. [Italics added]

11

THE PURSUIT OF
HAPPINESS

Fool! All that is, at all
Lasts ever, past recall;
Earth changes, but thy soul and God stand sure:
What entered into thee
That was, is, and shall be:
Time's wheel runs back or stops;
Potter and clay endure.
— R O B E R T   B R O W N I N G

The pages of this book have taken us on a journey to far-off places. We have looked around the rim of space and time to the ultimate beginning and end of things, and we have looked at our dread of death and the misty genesis of faith. We have shared a journey of exploration. However, exploration is a poignant metaphor of the human state, for what explorers seek in the outside world is often that which is missing in themselves. The brave pioneer is sometimes the lost child, looking for home.

So at the end of our story, inevitably, we come back to our point of origin, to the frail, perishable constructions of blood and flesh and bone that are you and I. In the light of where we have been, we ask a final question, a simple, almost plaintive question: *What is happiness?*

What do we mean by this strange, paradoxical, sad word? To make sense of the question, we must phrase the answer in terms of evolution. We have seen how the human brain preserves, in its present structure, the history of its past development. The newer layers are built on top of the older layers, just as younger strata in a geological formation lie on top of—and conceal—the more ancient strata that preceded them. In particular, we focused on the ancient reptilian core and the next-oldest rind wrapped around it, the limbic brain, because those are the seats of the so-called instincts.

Let us quickly review these, ordering them into a hierarchy based on the character of the emotions they generate in our ego-awareness.

1. The instinct that drives us to eat and drink. It is hardwired into our brains because it is the means by which the body/self preserves its own structure. As parts wear out, they must be reconstructed as water that is lost through sweat and urine must be replaced so that the concentration of key chemicals like salt in the blood remains at the constant level needed to sustain life. Associated with this instinct are the most primitive emotions, hunger and thirst, barely capable of being called emotions and hardly distinguishable from physiological states. These emotions tend to be prolonged, and their gratification may be delayed without endangering life; thus we can "feel hungry" for hours before we are driven to eat.

2. The instinct that drives us to defend the integrity of our body/self in the face of danger. This is the fight-or-flight reaction we discussed in Chapter 1 and elsewhere. When life is threatened, the mind-computer has to make a rapid choice between two options—to avoid the danger by trying to escape from it, or to confront the danger by engaging in real or mock combat. Associated with this instinct are the emotions of rage (fighting) and fear (fleeing). These emotions correspond to a sense of crisis, which means that they are rapidly aroused and demand an immediate response. Where we can ignore or suppress feelings of hunger and thirst, rage and terror dominate the psyche until the threat that engendered them has been dealt with.

3. The instinct that drives us to reproduce. Reproduction is unique among the instincts because it involves not one individual but two. Associated with this instinct of sex is the emotion of lust, by which

I mean simply the direct expression of sexual urge without taking into account any of the complicating value judgments that arise when the biological drive is viewed through the distorting prism of the symbolate mind. Those value judgments color the underlying instinct so deeply that the sensation of love, which we normally associate with sex, is seen as the highest of all human emotions.

These instincts conform to a common pattern. In cases studied in animals, the instinct is often triggered by a specific signal, which behavioral scientists call an innate releasing mechanism, or IRM. In the case of the male stickleback fish (which has been the subject of many studies), the color red on the belly of another male during the mating season acts as an IRM, setting off an attack reaction aimed at driving the intruder from his territory.

The role of hormones in instinctive behavior is often misunderstood. Hormones are responsible for the state of arousal, the turn-on that accompanies the instinct, but they do not trigger it. That is the role of the IRM. What hormones do is determine the threshold of response. Thus, during winter, a male stickleback can see a red-bellied male and remain indifferent—because he is not hormonally primed to respond. It is a different matter in spring when the concentration of reproductive hormones reaches its maximum; now the mere sight of the color red, even on a bit of wood, will provoke the male to attack; hormones have so lowered his excitatory threshold that the prime feature of the signal, not the signal itself, is enough to set the aggressive/defensive response in motion.

There has been an enormous controversy over the question of whether IRMs exist in humans and, if so, whether they are learned or inherited. The controversy need not concern us. There is no doubt that we share the instincts of the four Fs with our vertebrate relatives (for example, the chemical changes in the blood of a terrified man are identical to those in the blood of a terrified cat), and it seems hard to dispute that these instincts are activated by powerful stimuli or signals. When a man is hungry, the succulent smell of roast lamb makes him want to eat; when he feels sexy, the provocative sight of well-formed female breasts or buttocks makes him want to make love.

Once an IRM has set the scene in an appropriately primed individual, the final step is the carrying out of a specific action pattern that leads the animal to engage physically in the particular behavior that the specific hormone has prepared and the specific IRM triggered. Behavioral scientists call these selective action patterns consummatory acts because they remove the source of their own motivation.

The pattern common to all instincts is thus encoded in the following paradigm. Hormones raise the level of arousal and thereby diminish the barriers that inhibit the action pattern; the IRM triggers the action, and the consummatory act completes the sequence. Instinctive behavior is fundamentally goal-driven and goal-oriented. That is why it conveys such a strong impression of purpose.

To bring out the inner nature of instinct, we can recap it thus:

eating and drinking = *self*-maintenance
fighting or fleeing = *self*-preservation
reproduction   = *self*-continuation

Readers will recognize at once that what I am describing here is a mechanism of negative feedback or homeostatic control (see Figures 1.1 and 1.2). In all cases, a stimulus (the IRM) provokes a response (the consummatory act) that restores a stressed system (the body/self) to its original nonstressed condition.

What has all this got to do with human happiness? On one level, almost everything. We possess all these instincts; they are, as we have seen, our original sin—the genetic memory of our animal ancestry. However, the selective action pattern of each instinct does not, in the human case, take place in a mindless mechanical automaton like a thermostat. The chemical states associated with each instinct register in our conscious awareness as *feelings*. Thus we experience any move away from the equilibrium condition of the bodily status quo as a *need* or urge, and we experience the reestablishment of equilibrium following the consummatory act as contentment or *happiness*.

"Happiness is a full stomach" is an old adage that captures this point neatly. Consummation of any instinct takes us back into the state of body-bliss where our physical machinery is running smoothly, all components oiled and functioning in perfect harmony. This is the warm inner glow of satisfied appetite.

The gratification that follows consummation of an instinct means that the demands of the body/self no longer intrude into the realm of mentality: The psyche can sink back into the easeful slumber of semiconsciousness.

Thus we reach the first key conclusion of this chapter: *consummatory pleasure is the basic archetype of human happiness.* However, the instinctual paradigm is heavily overlaid by the complexities of the ego-self. So much so that we may fail to see the ancient groundwork beneath its modern superstructure.

This is important, so let us work it through. Think back to the ego-self. The world of the ego-self is a symbolic world, generating a subjective life that has a reality all its own. In that world, we create new constructions through imagination. Most material in novels deals with situations that, from the point of view of the "real" world, do not exist. This is the domain of the symbolate mind, where action consists of constructing constellations of symbols (thoughts), not carrying out physical movements involving the body. This is the domain of predicative awareness—"If I do this, then that will happen," a continual testing of options in the light of the likelihood of a preferred outcome.

Here is the clue. Whereas an aroused animal will simply carry out a consummatory act in the eternal present of its now-centered focus, the symbolate mind often interposes sets of intermediate actions between the archetypal urge and its archetypal fulfillment. Most humans work. Why? To earn money. Why? To enjoy the good life. It is in the definition of the "good life" that the ancient consummatory patterns reemerge. To come at this from a different angle, most people in the West would be ecstatic if they won a lottery worth a million dollars. Why? What are the typical ego-constructed fantasies associated with such a dream-come-true? While the variations are enormous, they tend to cluster around a limited set of common themes—good food, a holiday in the sun, indulgent sex with all its embroidery, absence of stress, and so on. In other words, they would use the newfound money to gratify the old compulsions that lead to the state of body-bliss.

The ego-self may disguise the old paradigm in a coat of many different colors, but it remains, for the most part, the motivational foundation of psychology. Remember that consummatory behavior is, by definition, goal-driven. The goal-oriented archetype of instinctive behavior has become the model for almost all purposeful mental activity. Indeed, the fundamental quantum of human behavior could be described as the creation of a goal that is triggered by signals, empowered by motivation, and consummated by action. Note the use of the word "creation." Here is where the human individual rises above his animal past. The consummatory instincts of the four Fs were created by natural selection, and the predisposition to act them out is hard-wired into our brains by our genes. Conceptual human goals are created by the symbolate mind, and they can be as many and varied as the rich tapestry of human experience itself. However, the drive that motivates the individual to realize these mind-generated goals remains, long-term, pegged to the legacy of instinct. To a surprising degree.

This comes about because the symbolate mind with its enormous capacity for flexible cross-linkaging and association fixes on the mind-generated intermediate goals; most of the end-oriented tension stems from the biological urge to final consummation. In many circumstances, those intermediate goals, intended as means to an end, can become ends in themselves. Jobs are a prime example. How many men get hooked on their job? In these cases, the halfway mark becomes a motivational substitute for the finishing line. However, the force that draws behavior through complicated sequences of conscious actions all too often comes from the ever-powerful magnet in the subconscious realm of the limbic brain, where the pleasure/pain nuclei lie. No one should underestimate the influence of this magnet; one has only to think of the laboratory rat, which self-stimulates its own pleasure center until it drops from exhaustion, to recognize that consummatory happiness has an open-ended capacity to entrance the psyche.

The goal toward which this open-ended drive is directed must, however, never be forgotten: It is to eliminate the destabilizing influences that upset the body/self's equilibrium. To advance matters we must examine what that equilibrium means.

* * *

In Chapter 2, we saw that one of science's most basic theorems, the second law of thermodynamics, encodes a universal tendency for order to decay into disorder, for information to degenerate into noise, for complex systems to move back toward a state of inertia or equilibrium. Analogous processes operate in human psychology, and there is in all of us a tendency to psychic laziness, a desire to say "it's all too hard" and opt out of the struggle. Lord Tennyson once wrote a poem about the victors of the Trojan War. On their journey back to Greece after their ten-year battle, these wanderers chance upon a charmed isle inhabited by mythic beings called Lotus Eaters. The Lotus Eaters offer the war-weary warriors the opium poppy of forgetfulness, whereupon they sink into a state of drowsy happiness, turning their backs on the pain-racked, strife-bedevilled life of the outside world:

> Hateful is the dark-blue sky,
> Vaulted o'er the dark-blue sea.
> Death is the end of life; ah, why
> Should life all labour be?
> Let us alone. Time driveth onward fast,
> And in a little while our lips are dumb.
> Let us alone. What is it that will last?
> All things are taken from us, and become
> Portions and parcels of the dreadful Past.
> Let us alone. What pleasure can we have
> To war with evil? Is there any peace
> In ever climbing up the climbing wave?
> All things have rest, and ripen toward the grave
> In silence; ripen, fall and cease:
> Give us long rest, or death, dark death or dreamful ease.

I quote this poem because the urge to succumb to this siren call is present in all of us. Religion has symbolized it as the Great Tempter (the devil or Satan) whose voice forever whispers to us to prefer the shortcut to the long journey, the easy answer to the hard question, to choose the safety of the inn and forsake the challenge of the road. "Rest," the voice whispers. "Sleep."

In the context of the quest for happiness, one has to ask the obvious question: Is not this return to Eden, to the lost Paradise of the instinctual psyche the end of the search? Why should we not eat the opium poppy and, forsaking pain, slumber in dreamful ease? To answer this, we need to go back to the exchange between Mephistopheles and Faust, for that epitomizes the very crux of the evolutionary process: "Who art thou?" asks Faust, to which Mephistopheles replies, "I am part of that spirit, *which always wills evil but always creates good!*" [Italics added]

I can now give a deeper explanation of what this interchange means. In the metaphorical imagery of religion, the devil is not merely the Tempter who whispers to us to lie down in easeful slumber; he is also the mythic embodiment of the very hardships that make us suffer and, in suffering, transcend our present limitation. The things we see about us that seem so cruel, so unfair, so tragic, are the very things that prevent the human psyche from falling back into the state of equilibrium, the inertia of indolence, toward which it always tends. It is precisely *because* Beethoven was going deaf that he was driven to write some of his greatest music; precisely *because* Demosthenes had a speech impediment that he went on to become one of the greatest orators in ancient Athens; precisely *because* Helen Keller lost sight and hearing as an infant that she was able to see the inner workings of human sorrow in such clear outline.

I can put this point into a scientific perspective by using a biological analogy. What I have been trying to say in the last few pages is that an animal can enjoy instinctual happiness only if its body/self is in perfect equilibrium with its surroundings with no demands being made on it by hunger, fear, or illness. There is a profound similarity between this condition of psychic equilibrium and the process of adaptation that occurs during biological evolution.

If you dig in the sand of certain beaches, you may come across a variety of worm that has remained virtually unchanged since the Precambrian period some 600 million years ago. As the physicist Lecomte Du Nouy has noted:

The pre-Cambrian sandworms were probably not very different from those of our own shores. Their adaptation was remarkable and very superior to that of Man. Having attained equilibrium, living under only slightly changed conditions, they have had no reason to transform themselves further. . . . One of these worms, however, continued to evolve because it was less well adapted than the others. . . . This worm, *less perfect as a worm*, may have been our ancestor. [Italics added]

The evolutionary line that led from microbe to man has thus been precisely defined by just those creatures that did *not* equilibrate to their environments. Throughout evolution, it has always been the misfit that has been the vehicle of creative change.

The misfit is the biological and psychological embodiment of Mephistopheles' principle; by creating maladjustment (in religious language, by willing evil), misfits continually cause the present to be transcended (in religious language, they create good). The happiness that comes from an achieved equilibrium situation lives only in the now; it is the unhappiness of an unstable, nonequilibrium state that thrusts awareness into time.

To understand this principle better, we should go back to Chapter 2. The arrow of time is defined by the direction of increasing entropy, i.e., by the direction a system spontaneously adopts as it tends to equilibrium. At equilibrium, time literally loses all meaning. Without some asymmetry in the system to make one part different from another, the very concept of time evaporates.

Thus it is the nonequilibrium situation, the unstable state, the misfit condition, that *creates time.* That is why the birth of the ego-self, the Fall, was, in the longest perspective, an upward step in humanity's journey toward higher consciousness. By creating the time sense, the ego-self put mind in an unstable, misfit situation where it cannot remain, where it has no choice but to go on. Only by transcending the fallacy of the time sense can mind climb into a state of true timelessness, not the non-time of equilibrium (where neither past nor future exists), but the universal time of consciousness (where both past and future coexist together).

To summarize simply, when a creature fits its environment, it has no cause to change; it exists in a nontime state of being; when a creature does not fit its environment, it has no option but to change; it exists in a time-trapped state of becoming. That is why Gerald Heard captured the essence of evolution when he said: "Indeed, life's development, the evolution of awareness, may best be rendered into three attitudes towards time; then, we see successively the time-unaware animal, the time-haunted man and the time-understanding mind."

The unpalatable aspect of this is the inevitable requirement for hardship as a precondition of human growth, of the evolution of consciousness. Most people, obedient to the psychic pull of entropy, want salvation in six easy lessons. That is not possible.

The point of the devil's message to Faust has been captured, for me at least, in a simple poem by Angela Morgan, which highlights the essential and utterly unavoidable role of ordeal in human transformation:

When Nature wants to take a man
And shake a man
And wake a man;
When Nature wants to make a man
To do the Future's will;
When she tries with all her skill
And she yearns with all her soul
To create him large and whole . . .
With what cunning she prepares him!
How she goads and never spares him,
And in poverty begets him . . .
How she whets him and she frets him
How she often disappoints
Whom she sacredly anoints,
With what wisdom she will hide him,
Never minding what betide him. . . .
Bids him struggle harder yet.
Makes him lonely
So that only
God's high messages shall reach him,
So that she may surely teach him
What the Hierarchy planned.

Though he may not understand
Gives him passions to command—
How remorselessly she spurs him,
With terrific ardor stirs him
When she poignantly prefers him!

Is this then the meaning of life? To struggle, to bleed in silence, to grow through suffering? Is comfort the necessary adversary of growth? Others may think differently, but my answer has to be yes. We live in a society that has elevated the cop-out to the level of an art form. We live in air-conditioned buildings, drive heated cars; above all, we hide and deny death. This hiding of death—the final and absolute agent of change—is the epitome of our contemporary Western civilization, just as I believe it will be its epitaph.

The problem of death should be familiar by now—it has been a key theme of this book. We fear nothing so much as change. Why? Because change, deep change, *is a form of death*. A system of any kind, mechanical, biological, or psychic, that operates on the principle of negative feedback has, by the definition of its being, to adjust to change in such a way as to restore itself to its original state. In its perspective, change is a disturbance to be eliminated. If a self-preserving feedback system absorbs rather than resists change, it loses its self-sense, its identity—it dies.

This is why the little deaths of life, the losses that result from divorce or the death of people with whom we have shared much of our lives, create in us a terrifying sense that everything is breaking down, a sense of being adrift without familiar anchors, in extreme cases, a sense almost of going mad. We invest so much of ourselves in those we love that their departure takes with it a large chunk of us. There is a simple reason why the familiar saying "To part is to die a little" has become a cliché. It is true.

People in grief often express their feelings in two familiar phrases: "Nothing matters anymore because my life is over" and "I can't go on." These are giveaway indications of what is going on in the psyche. And they are accurate: The old I cannot go on because it is in the process of restructuring itself; the former (stable) homeostatic controls are too altered simply to return to their prior state.

Professionals in grief-counseling are often confronted with people who are visibly struggling to keep control. When they present for therapy, the old, familiar self is still in position, but it is perilously poised on the edge of breakdown in a metastable equilibrium from which it can be dislodged by the slightest push. That push is usually no more than the presence of a safe place and the chance to externalize their hurt by talking it out. As Shakespeare said in *Macbeth*: "Give sorrow words. The grief that does not speak whispers the o'erfraught heart, and bids it break." The rush of release that follows is cathartic. With this release, the knotted tension that held the old self together is unwound. The old self dies.

The result of that ego-death is almost invariably a lessening of the self-sense, at least in the short term. The psychic vacuum left when people let go of the focus of so many of their own projected hopes and longings is not refilled, at least not in the same way. The psyche has unlearned many of the differences that separated itself from its fellows. The lowered ego-sense that remains is more open to and tolerant of grief in others because it recognizes them as its own. The barrier between "self" and "other" weakens. This is a pivotal point, and I will return to it later.

It is impossible to describe scientifically the changes that occur during grieving, because we have no neurophysiological or psychological models to guide us. Perhaps chaos theory will one day open up the issue, showing as it does how ordered patterns can arise spontaneously from disordered turbulence. However, the point remains. The death of the old is the birth of the new, and the new self, the new stable state into which the lessened ego-sense settles, is simpler, one is tempted to say more beautiful. Out of death comes more perfect life.

This sentiment, that a higher state of being emerges from death, takes us into a crucial area of human activity, that of creativity. In one of the very few (to me) authentic analyses of creativity, the psychologist Rollo May notes:

Anxiety is understandably a concomitant of the shaking of the self-world relationship that occurs in the encounter [between the creative mind and the new insight]. *Our sense of identity is threatened;* the world is not as we experienced it before, and since self and world are always correlated, we no longer are what we were before. [Italics added]

This deep insight puts death into an entirely different perspective. It is the hallmark of any truly creative thought or act that it generates novelty; something that was not present before emerges from the chaos of creation, is caught by the memory of the universe. This new insight, this unexpected music, inevitably has to destroy the old thought forms, which it replaces because new symmetries are almost invariably molded from the broken-down modules of old assumptions. Death is forever present at the cutting edge of consciousness, for death is the midwife of creative change, of transcendence. Always.

We seem to have moved a long way from the notion of happiness. We are now talking about evolution, and that, by definition, means change, death, and rebirth, genetic or psychic. In this context, the question of happiness remains pegged to an issue that has bedeviled students of evolution since Darwin; i.e., Does evolution move toward a goal?

Benjamin Disraeli once said of the present condition of humanity: "This is no place to stop, halfway between ape and angel." In the terms of reference of this book we can see that the bulk of the human species at this point in time is trapped in a halfway no-man's-land, an existential nightmare in which it is divided against itself by ego and ensnared in tick-tock time. This condition is, from the perspective of physics, *unreal* at its root. It is a function not of the world but of the present state of the human mind, of human limitation, a projection onto the world of fictions and fallacies evolved by the processes of mental natural selection that occurred as the conceptual mind struggled to make sense of the symbol-rich domain it was creating.

In this focused sense, evolution does have a goal. Biologist Julian Huxley went part way to defining it when he said: "Man is evolution made conscious of itself." In this book, I have tried to show the logical end-point of this process of progressive enrichment of consciousness. *The goal of evolution is to realize itself through consciousness,* to close the feedback loop between mind and matter. Indeed, this has already happened; otherwise space-time would not be folded back upon itself to form a circle in which past and future are seamlessly interconnected. The unhappiness of the current stage of human development stems from the fact that, for the most part, we do not yet see the reality toward which both science and intuition point. We are caught in a hollow where the fog still enshrouds us; we still have far to go on our journey toward the high place.

However, the future already exists. The visionaries who have lived the timeless state of consciousness foresaw what will one day be the common experience of mankind. The way has been mapped for the many by the few. The road to transcendence then passes through ego-death toward that unified sense of reality that is a defining criterion of unfettered consciousness. That is why mystics spoke of God (pure consciousness) as holy, the word *holy* coming from *whole*, whence also comes *heal* (make whole).

Can we flag the signposts along this road to guide the traveler on his journey? I believe we can. I have ranked these according to the criterion of the *mutant minority*. Chapter 4 suggested that change appears first in a tiny subsection of the population, a mutant minority (sometimes a single individual) and only slowly spreads through the population until it becomes the norm. This principle may not apply so constrainingly to psychological change, because the power of one individual to transmit his enhanced awareness to others is greatly amplified by teaching and by the written word.

In seeking signposts for change, I start with indicators that are, first, common to all humans at this stage of evolution; second, found only in a minority of advanced members; third, so rare that they are, in an important sense, waiting to be born.

I AND SHE ARE ONE

Sex has a special role in human interaction; in order to escape the doomed bodies they inhabit, male genes (in sperm) and female genes (in eggs) unite to form a child, a new generation. Sex is clearly linked to the future as well as the past; this is one source of its uniqueness.

As we have seen, the true axis of human growth lies along the road that leads to the lowering of ego-boundaries. That is what sex achieves—for a while. When two individuals fall in love, they surrender, to a quite remarkable degree, the me-first individualism that is evolution's legacy. In their physical union, two meld into one. In the first flush of romantic love, they quite literally lose themselves in each other, often addressing the needs and problems of the other above their own.

The problem is that in modern society the two-into-one union achieved by sex seldom outlasts the biological impulse that gave rise to it. Moreover, sex often locks both consenting parties into the backward-looking focus that is the hallmark of regressive behavior; it is often corrupted into the ego-mode by emphasizing the ego-gratifying release from sexual tension achieved by each, not the communion shared by both.

Often, but not always. Our history is filled with and illuminated by examples of human love where self is not separate from other. In the late Middle Ages, when physical love fell under the shadow of the Christian aberration about sex, Heloise could write to her lover Abelard: "I can expect no reward from God, as I have done nothing from love of Him. . . . God knows, at your command I would have followed or preceded you to fiery places. For my heart is not with me, but with thee." This pledge of love is made all the more poignant because Heloise could no longer expect its physical fulfillment—Abelard had been castrated because of her.

This ideal of romantic love, the ever-changing, ever-new story of boy meets girl, is a central theme of the human condition. Not merely because sex is the route to the future, the thread of genetic continuity, but also because sex is, for the vast majority of the population, the only significant form of ego-death we knowingly seek out. It is this communion that lifts love above lust and makes of the sexual act the most ambiguously noble of all human functions, a strange chimera of past and future, beauty and blasphemy. Sex is therefore a perfect metaphor of the processes of wholesome unselfishness that deepen consciousness. That is why the word "love" has become the preferred symbol for man's longing for communion, at any level.

Sexual love is then, a first step toward deep happiness. However, it can never be more than that, a first step. The reason for that arises from the very premise on which sex is founded—it is restricted to *two* persons. Two only. The next step toward deep happiness requires us to widen the circle of communion beyond the limits of gene kinship (parents and children) and biological partners.

I AND MANKIND ARE ONE

In looking at this statement, I have to discuss religion directly. I would like to do so without prejudicing the scientific basis on which this book is predicated. In the section that follows, I am not judging the material at issue from the standpoint of faith. Rather, I am looking at religion as a source of psychological insight, to be examined and interpreted like any other body of valid human experience.

The thing that strikes one about the psychology of religion is not the difference of dogma, over which so much blood has been pointlessly spilled, but the commonality of insight. What insight? At its root, simply that all men are brothers and that we should treat others as we treat ourselves.

Christianity: "All things whatsoever ye would that men should do to you, do ye even so unto them" (Matthew 7:12).

Judaism: "What is hurtful to yourself do not to your fellow man" (Talmud).

Taoism: "Regard your neighbor's gain as your own gain: and regard your neighbor's loss as your own loss" (*T'ai Shang Kan Ying P'ien*).

Hinduism: "Do naught to others which if done to thee would cause thee pain" (*Mahabaharata* 5.15.17).

Buddhism: "Hurt not others with that which pains yourself" (*Udanavarga* 5.18).

The unity of insight encoded in these sayings is all the more remarkable because they seem, for the most part, to have evolved independently, in different parts of the world, under the influence of different cultural traditions, at different times during history. The feeling that each of us is capable of loving the world is a common human intuition. Most of us, when supremely happy, are able to affirm, "I'm in love with all mankind." However, to let it rest there is to miss the deeper message. What these sayings tell us is not merely that we should use a common code of conduct in our dealings with our fellow creatures, but rather that, at the taproot level, we *are* our fellow humans, the distinctions that divide us are functions of ego and of differing phases of growth.

I am too young to have any memories of the Second World War, but I have a vividly etched memory of a photo I saw of the campaign in the Western desert, where my father fought. It showed a soldier, naked from the waist up, hung over the edge of a gutted tank. He looked so pathetically young and beautiful that it was hard to realize that what I was looking at was death. I mention that image because it always brings to mind the saying of the Greek dramatist Sophocles: "Who is the slayer and who the victim? Speak." And over twenty centuries later, the words of the German soldier-poet Heinrich Lersch: "My eyes deceive me, but my heart cannot; each corpse has my brother's face."

What these lines tell us is that, in those moments of compassion that reach beyond tears, the boundary between self and other breaks down. We are our victims; each act of degradation perpetrated on the body or mind of another is an act of violence against ourselves. Bertrand Russell captured another element of the same intuition when he said: "He who watches a crime in silence commits it."

Is this mere intellectual sophistry? I for one am certain it is not. In grief therapy, when someone weeps for a recent loss, other members of the group will automatically reach out and touch the person in pain. They feel the woundedness of the mourner as their own; for a brief moment of communion, the individual's sorrow becomes that of the group. In that dilution, the grief, no longer confined to the one but shared among the many, becomes bearable; healing begins.

The reality of this losing of oneself in others is unmistakable when it occurs in ordinary life. In the course of a conversation, you will often notice that the person you are talking to is only half listening. Even as you are speaking, they are phrasing their reply. Watch the difference when someone really listens, totally absorbed and self-forgotten as they focus on your story. In situations where grief is involved, this kind of loving listening is the genesis of trust. When it is present, it can make the plainest face beautiful.

Psychologist W. Scott Peck in his book *The Different Drum* discusses the mechanism by which a sense of community evolves among a group of initially separate and ego-centered individuals. I can speak from my own experience here and affirm that group awareness can indeed be forged from the reality of shared experience, and that the awareness so created seems, in some hard-to-define way, greater than the sum of its parts. One of the most hopeful signs of change in the egoic structure of Western man is the rapid proliferation of groups dedicated to exploring personal relationships in a communal setting. As is inevitably the case with any new movement, the structure of many of these groups is becoming heavily overlaid with and corrupted by a lot of New Age baggage—belief in crystals, tarot, astrology. However, the original impulse was healthy, oriented as it was to communion, not self.

Thus the collective reality of pooled human consciousness (not separate as in ego, but together as in true communion) is one and indivisible. One cannot cause pain to another without causing pain to oneself. In John Donne's famous words:

> No man is an island, entire of itself: every man is a piece of the continent, a part of the main. . . . any man's death diminishes me, because I am involved in Mankind; and therefore never send to know for whom the bell tolls; it tolls for thee.

The measure of our failure to understand this is the measure of our immaturity as a species.

I AND ALL CREATURES ARE ONE

Modern molecular biology has shown that all forms of life on earth use a common genetic language. In this sense, a truly deep unity underpins the surface diversity of life. Evolution demonstrates beyond doubt that all forms of life on earth are related, sharing as they do a common ancestry. Thus the growing number of organizations dedicated to animal welfare and the recognition that other creatures have rights are but introducing into the Western egoic structure the ancient sense of kinship that the Sioux Indians knew so well: "With all beings and all things we shall be as relatives."

The idea that the whole complex web of terrestrial life is one coherent interrelated system has now achieved the status of a respectable scientific theory in James Lovelock's Gaia hypothesis. Gaia was the Greek earth goddess. The Gaia theory points to the fact that the highly selective conditions that favor most forms of life, e.g., the concentration of salt in the sea and oxygen in the air, have remained remarkably constant across geological ages in the face of chemical tendencies that should have brought them to equilibrium. The Gaia explanation is that life has collectively created, on a planetary scale, the sophisticated systems of feedback control that preserve constancy in the chemistry of its member individuals. The human race is discovering, to its cost, that it is impossible to damage any one element of Gaia without damaging the whole. Burn coal in Britain and acid rain falls in Norway; cut down a rain forest in Brazil and the climate of the entire earth warms. Here is the principle of the preceding section writ plain, in scientific language.

I AND CREATION ARE ONE

In the symbolism of the world's great faiths, the sense of communion that begins so hesitatingly with sex finds its supreme expression in a sense of total union with the universe as a whole. "I and my Father are one," affirms Christianity. The Atman (the true Self) is the Brahman (the Supreme Being) says Hinduism. Across the ages, the voices of the world's mystics have echoed this same deep insight:

> I went from God to God, until they cried from me in me "O thou I."
>
> —Bayazid of Bistun

> The knower and the known are one. Simple people imagine that they should see God as if he stood there and they here. This is not so. God and I, we are one in knowledge.
>
> —Meister Eckhart

> When the Ten Thousand things are viewed in their oneness, we return to the Origin and remain where we have always been.
>
> —Sen T'sen

Mahayana Buddhism makes perhaps the most explicit statement of the one-in-all-and-all-in-one principle when it says, "When the one is set against all the others, the one is seen as pervading them all and at the same time embracing them all in itself." However, it is Hinduism that captures the essence of this total sense of unity when it says, simply, "Thou art that."

It might seem that ultimate union, such as is encoded in these religious insights, can have no scientific underpinning. That is fundamentally false. We have already seen (Chapter 10) how quantum physics vindicates the insight of Meister Eckhart, "the knower and the known are one." This principle, at the deepest level, holds true in all areas of reality. We can see why by going back to the genesis event, the big bang, and tracing a forward path to now.

Let us start with the just-born expanding seed of space-time. As it expanded, it cooled. A few minutes after the genesis, its temperature had dropped enough to allow the first atoms to be created. Those atoms, by a large margin, were hydrogen atoms. Hydrogen is the simplest atom in the periodic table of the elements. It is the raw material of all subsequent evolution, the very stuff of of creation. Its significance has been beautifully summed up by the zoologist N. J. Berrill, who said: "If you listen intently, you can hear the universe singing its song of hydrogen, the first and sustained note in the melody of creation."

There are trillions of hydrogen atoms in our bodies. Thus the texture of our bodies and brains—part of our very being—is still continuous with an event that took place at the dawn of creation. We are still part of that "great silent fire at the beginning of time," to use Brian Swimme's evocative phrase.

Hydrogen is the start of the evolutionary journey. In a typical star like the sun, hydrogen is burned to helium, the next highest element. This is the pattern: As the fires inside stars grow hotter, as the furnaces of creation glow more brightly, ever more complex elements can be created—carbon, oxygen, iron. Our bodies are made of star-ash. *We are children of the stars.* When we look at the night sky with its far-off lights, when we feel an aching longing for we know not what, we are *remembering.* The "now" us is speaking to the "then" us, each knowing the other in some dim way, below words.

These bones, this hand,
Star-ash.
Brain molten with genesis heat,
This quiet thought, that raging fire.

This is the message of modern cosmology. All parts of the cosmos, including ourselves, are deeply interconnected, flawlessly interwoven, one wholesome unity. Increasingly, science is coming to see that in order to explain *anything,* you have to explain *everything.*

* * *

All this seems to have led us a long way from the issue of happiness to which this chapter is dedicated. In fact, it has not; we have been approaching the question, "How can I be happy?" from the only perspective in which it makes sense, the cosmic perspective.

In the above section, I tried to show how each human individual can connect to beings and objects around him, starting with another human being, a sexual partner, and ending with the totality of all, the universe. Through these successive communions, one rule, one basic premise, has always held true. Each act of union *lessens the boundary between self and other*. That is the absolute and final criterion by which all action can be measured and judged.

To give these lessenings of self some human reality, I must bring them back from the abstract into the realm of everyday life and ordinary experience. So, let us retrace the sequence that successively links the individual with a sexual partner, then with humanity as a whole, then with life as a whole, then with the cosmos as a whole, looking at each link in the chain from the standpoint of the happiness it generates.

Let us begin once again with sex. The happiness that comes from sexual love needs no elaboration. It is part of the weft and web of all adult human experience. In the physical and emotional coupling of male and female, the "I" sense falters; the boundary between self and other weakens. Sexual union also involves a release from tension, it engenders a drowsy contentedness, a sense of peace. This is, in part, the warm inner glow of satisfied appetite—but only in part.

The happiness that comes from nonsexual communion is also a fact of human life. We all have friends whom we can truly say we "love," even though the drive toward physical consummation is absent. If we analyze our feelings toward these special people, we always find that the source of the attraction is something that fits the self/other rule: a shared interest, a feeling of trust, i.e., of being able to expose our vulnerability without being hurt.

The feeling of union between man and nature takes us into what, at first sight, seems unfamiliar territory. "Nature and I are one." Yet the urge to commune with nature is precisely what drives people to picnic in the country, take walks through the bush, climb mountains, and watch sunsets. Each of us can think back to some special moment when the feeling of peace that comes from being alone in a wilderness setting gave us a sense of being at one with the environment.

At first sight, the drive to commune with nature seems at odds with our drive to commune with our fellow humans. Most of us from time to time feel the need, not to relate to our fellow humans but to get away from them, to have our forty days in the wilderness. We think of this yearning as a desire to be alone, and yet, in the wilderness, we are not alone. We have the companionship of life in all its richness and variety. We return whence we came, to find silence in the still center, so that we may renew ourselves at the deep roots of our life.

Many of us have a particular love for the ocean. The sight of endless acres of blue, interrupted perhaps by tossing caps of white foam, seems to capture our longing for transcendence as few other visions can. In its vastness, the sea is a metaphor for infinity, and in the ceaseless surging of its breakers, ever arising and ever dying, a simile for the shortness of life. The ocean recalls our origins. Far back in the remote deeps of time, our prehuman selves slumbered, quickened but not yet conscious, in the salt waters that are remembered to this day in the chemical composition of our blood.

Am I lapsing into metaphor here? Yes and no. It is not simply that the crossopterygian fish that swam in the ancient seas were our lineal ancestors. Rather, in a perfectly factual sense, we existed then in these creatures, just as the more-than-human consciousness we will become already exists in us now. So it goes throughout the whole scale of deep time. The process of genetic evolution, which led from microbe to man, is seamless and unbroken. The process of chemical evolution, which led from the simplest element, hydrogen, to the more complex elements, is seamless and unbroken. We would not be here if they were not. Most of us, if asked our age, would say "fifteen years old," or "thirty years old," or "sixty-four years old," etc. The truthful answer is "*I am fifteen thousand million years old.*"

Many intelligent people still cannot make this jump in understanding. A man of forty-five will readily admit that he, in some sense, existed in the boy he was at thirteen, just as he will still exist in the person he will be at sixty. He admits that even though his actual memory of his past forty-five years is unconscious, something he can summon forth only at intervals, not necessarily in sequence, and usually in highly incomplete form. However, he will balk at acknowledging the oneness of his being with any of his ancestors, human or prehuman, because he cannot remember them at will.

Part of his difficulty here is the feeling of discontinuity that birth creates. Birth seems like a break in the thread of being—but is it? Suppose that our forty-five-year-old man is asked to track the worldline of his life backward in imagination, successively stripping his brain of its stored layers of memory (remembered or not remembered). For most of the time, in each year of his relived past, he will be able to recall something, some image, of what he will insist is himself as he was at that stage of his life. When he gets back to his first year, he will, most likely, not be able to summon forth any memory. He will, almost certainly, not be able to recollect any snapshot of life in the womb. Yet he will still insist that the fetus he once was was himself despite his total lack of any consciously recallable memories of that time.

Think carefully about this. Our forty-five-year-old's fetal self is a valid part of his four-dimensional being, but it is much less information-rich, relatively less being stored in the memory banks of its brain, and relatively more in the memory banks of its genes. From the standpoint of the branch of science called information theory, genes, like brains, are both recording devices and ways of remembering. Our forty-five-year-old's genes came from two prior sets of genes by direct copying, the male gene set from his father and the female gene set from his mother. These prior gene sets remember the physical characteristics and temperamental dispositions of his parents. As one winds the clock of evolution backward, across hundreds of millions of years, these ancestral genetic recording devices get less information-rich—they remember less. However, all these prior genes are still part of our forty-five-year-old's lifeline, still part of *him*. There is no break at any point.

"But," our stubborn skeptic will say, "I did not experience events that took place before my birth, along the time-track of evolution." To that I must give the only truthful answer I know: "Of course you did!" You experienced each and every phase of the long journey that has led from the big bang to now—*only you were not human in those earlier "mo-*

ments." Your consciousness was dimmer and less focused when it stirred in the ancient reptiles whose brains remain to this day as the core of your own mind. It was dimmer and less focused still when it slumbered in the mindless cells of the first seas whose oxygenless chemistry remains to this day the base of life. You were there, at every stage. There never was a time when you were not there. The vital being that is cosmos, aroused and brightened into consciousness in you, is one process, unbroken, real and ongoing.

Boy and man are one being, separated only by the stage of their growth. Cosmos and man are one being, separated only by the stage of their growth. The block in our minds comes from the separation—the sense of being dismembered into unconnected fragments. The whole thrust of this book has been to try to show how separateness is anchored in self, which is anchored in time. The message of this book, now clearly revealed, is that separateness is an illusion and the source of sorrow. In truth, in reality, nothing is separate, everything is united in the four-dimensional dance of becoming. The one exists in the all, and the all exists in the one. There is no boundary between self and other. Thou art that.

At the end of our journey, we now approach the final question. How can we understand, really understand, the inner sensation that reflects and communicates a state of near-perfect communion with all creation? The truthful answer is we cannot. Happiness is too weak and anemic a word to capture the *rapture* that pure consciousness knows and is. To see into the nature of this bliss, at our present level of evolution and in the midst of our present human limitation, is virtually impossible. It is like hearing the sound of strange music, some supreme melody whose joy is the birth of galaxies and whose sadness is the death of suns—but far off, barely audible, at the farthest limit of our capacity to hear.

Those who have attained something of this bliss, who have experienced the "thou art that" state, have enormous difficulty putting into words what is beyond the power of language to convey; thus Whitman, in a poem written with a sense of the black depths of sickness and advancing age, says movingly:

One effort more may alter this bleak sand
That Thou Oh God my life hast lighted
With ray of light, steady, ineffable, vouchsafed of Thee,
Light rare untellable, lighting the very light
Beyond all signs, descriptions, languages.

To "get inside" this "cosmic consciousness," to capture some faint impression of that yet-to-be rapture in ordinary English, I can only quote a key paragraph from Somerset Maugham's *The Razor's Edge*. In this well-known account of a young man's search for God, the youth in question, Larry, goes to India to study at an ashram. After spending some years in prayer and contemplation, he goes one morning to a high place in the Himalayan foothills, to spend his birthday in solitude. Larry describes what happens in his own words:

I have no descriptive talent, I don't know the words to paint a picture: I can't tell you so as to make you see it, how grand the sight was that was displayed before me as the day broke in its splendor. Those mountains with their deep jungle, the mist still entangled in the treetops, and the bottomless lake far below me. The sun caught the lake through a cleft in the heights and it shone like burnished steel. I was ravished with the beauty of the world, I'd never known such exultation and such a transcendent joy. I had a strange sensation, a tingling that arose in my feet and travelled up to my head, and I felt as though I was suddenly released from my body and as pure spirit partook of a loveliness I had never conceived. I had a sense that a knowledge more than human possessed me so that everything that had been confused was clear and everything that had perplexed me was explained. I was so happy that it was pain and I struggled to release myself from it, for I felt that if it lasted a moment longer I should die; and yet it was such rapture that I was ready to die rather than forgo it. How can I tell you what I felt?

Is this a mirage, a romantic's myth, a dreamer's dream? I am certain it is not. One night, many years ago, I went to a concert in Auckland with a friend. As we came out after one of the most magnificent performances of a classical symphony I have ever heard, my friend turned to me and said, "Ah well, music is all very well, but we have to get back to the real world." It has taken me half a lifetime to realize what was wrong with that statement. It was the wrong way around. Music is the most powerful alchemy we know, the magic agent of transcendence that lifts consciousness into a more perfect state. When we lose ourselves in music, *we become more real.* The return to the everyday mode, to the sad, confused world of the ego-self, is a Fall, a reversion to unreality, an expulsion from some simulacrum of eternity, back into time.

The essence of the human quest is to break free of time, to reconnect to the eternal in all of us, in that space where the past and the future interweave, the reality laboratory of our own minds. We are all explorers; we are all time-travelers; we are all lost children seeking home. We have a dim memory of home; it is a place we have been before. In the remote future.

The last signpost on this journey is now in sight. It points to what is, to me, the strangest and most revelatory part of the quest. Of necessity, this part has to be incomplete for it can be "known" only when we ourselves die.

In Chapter 6, I described the sequence of psychological states a dying person goes through, in the experience of Elisabeth Kübler-Ross. I stopped short, however, of describing the actual moment of death itself. Let me now restate a point made in Chapter 6. Our attitude to and ignorance of death is shaped by the fact that we cannot comprehend death experientially; we cannot remember something we have not yet gone through. However, this statement is, in a limited but important sense, not true. There exist in the community people who have died in the scientific definition of the term and, as it were, returned to the living state by luck or medical management. Those people can tell us what death experience is like.

Near-death experiences, or NDEs, have now been documented in many hundreds of cases. NDEs are defined by the cessation (at least to an outside observer) of some or all the normal physiological indicators of "life": The heartbeat may stop, breathing may cease, and, perhaps most important, the repetitive blips traced out on a video monitor by brain waves on the EEG may fade away, leaving a flat line on the screen (hence the term *flat-*

liners). This is not to say that every case of NDE occurs in a hospital, but rather that, to qualify as a genuine NDE candidate, a person must have at the very least stopped breathing or lost any detectable pulse, and that NDEs are most credible when the cessation of vital function is monitored by state-of-the-art technology. The period during which vital functions can no longer be measured can be as short as a few seconds, or as long as two hours.

The remarkable thing about NDEs is that they show a consistency, a common core of seemingly identical experience, irrespective of gender, religion, background, or race. This hints at the possibility that the brain experiences a more-or-less universal cognitive shift at the point of death. That is centrally important in the context of this book. The message of this book is that ego ceases with physical death, but that consciousness does not. NDEs may thus offer a window into that climactic moment my hypothesis predicts, when our human reality melts away like a shadow, when the fabricated skein of the time-trapped ego-self unravels, exposing the deep knowing of consciousness in its temporally unfettered four-dimensional state.

Before I analyze NDEs in the light of my conclusions in this book, I must address the alternative explanations for their occurrence. Are NDEs hallucinations? Does the brain malfunction in a consistent way at death? Many experts think so. Some of the key elements of an NDE experience can be artificially induced by hallucinogenic drugs like ketamine (used as an anesthetic) or "angel dust." This may be significant because, once the blood supply to the brain is diminished or cut off, the brain enters a period of anoxia, or oxygen starvation. There is evidence that that oxygen starvation reproduces some of the effects of those hallucinogenic drugs that mimic the NDE.

Against this, an impartial observer must set the following facts: At precisely the time one might expect *impaired* brain function because of the stopping or winding-down of vital life-support functions, NDEers report *heightened* cognition, a strong sense of a reality that is in a deep way more real than everyday awareness. Moreover, at least one NDEer, of whom I have heard, deliberately took a range of hallucinogenic drugs after his NDE, specifically to compare their psychological effects with those of his NDE. His verdict was quite emphatic: Where the drug-induced condition brought about sensory disorientation, the NDE was cogent, indelible, and overwhelming; the effects of the drug-induced state faded quickly, the memory of his NDE remains with him to this day.

It is neither possible nor desirable in a book like this to give a balanced discussion of the various hypotheses advanced to "explain" the NDE. Readers are referred to the detailed investigations of Margot Grey, Kenneth Ring, and others, which attempt to analyze the phenomenon using accepted scientific methodology. The only point I would make concerns the criticism that, with the virtue of hindsight, one can question whether a person who is later restored to full cognitive function can ever be said to have been dead at all. I agree with this. In my view, the significance of the NDE is that it gives us a fascinating window of insight into the actual experience of *dying*. It can say nothing about possible postmortem existence, except by inference and extension.

My attitude to NDEs has been significantly affected by a program I saw on ABC television. In that program a group of people who had experienced NDEs were brought together with doctors and other experts. One aim of the program seemed to be to try to see whether the NDE was a mental aberration induced by the loss of vital function, or whether it opened a door to a different dimension of being. The people who described their NDEs had a big impact on me. It is one thing to read about NDEs in books, quite another to watch real people struggle to find words for something that seems to transcend language.

Consider the words of a scientist whom I will call John:

It's as if everything was there and everybody was there; the sense was of absolute total fulfillment. *And yet there was no sense that I was there.* That's the most extraordinary thing; John vanished at that moment." [Italics added]

That comment fascinates me: my hypothesis predicts that ego, the sense of self, evaporates at death, but that consciousness remains. John in this instance used just the words I would expect of someone whose ego-self had dissolved, but whose deep knowing, his real self, was unaffected. The

I flickers out of existence, but integrated awareness, one in all and all in one, remains.

John expanded on this point in these words:

> The sense was of immense depth. . . . It's like having been to a space before everything was and then coming back and seeing all this from that space instead of seeing it, as I used to, from inside my head.

Other NDEers speak of retaining a sense of identity, but only as a strand of the greater whole they now feel part of:

> One of the feelings I remember most about them was the feeling of unity, of being totally a part of everything around me and about me. There was no separateness at all.

Different NDEers use different words and images to describe their experience, but the one universal factor that almost everyone reports is a vision of light. Not just any light, light that goes beyond light. A radiance that is wordlessly ineffable:

> I just found myself in this extremely bright light and felt absolute peace. I feel the light and the peace were one.

> The light is brighter than anything you could possibly imagine. There are no words to describe it.

> A beautiful light—it's like being an ant inside a large diamond.

Compare this with Whitman's words: "Lighting the very light, beyond all signs, descriptions, languages."

Another universal element in the core experience is a sense of profound and transcendent love and oneness:

> And the quite amazing thing is that I had an incredible sense of well-being—I just felt completely borne aloft by goodwill and by love . . . just the most fantastic feeling of love and goodwill.

I felt exhilarated and felt I was one with everything.

And from another ABC program on the same topic, this, to me, the most powerful description of all:

I came into the light, and it hit me all over. I stood in the light. . . . While I stood in the light, for that split second or a few minutes, whatever it was in time, I had this feeling of just total understanding. It was just being part of that universal spirit, part of what you can only describe as being all. Everything . . . and it was the most inspiring and, I guess, the greatest single experience I've ever had in my life. It was just incredible.

This can be compared to Larry's description of his illumination in the quote from *The Razor's Edge*. Although Larry is a fictional character, Somerset Maugham seems to have modeled his description of Larry's enlightenment on historical accounts of the moment as documented, for example, by R. M. Bucke in his classic opus *Cosmic Consciousness*. The point I want to emphasize is that Larry's description of his illumination could fit into a book on NDEs without changing a word.

To me, one of the most intriguing aspects of the NDE is the feeling two people reported, in which they state that their NDE was so real that living seemed shallow by comparison:

As if it's not the dying that's the problem, but the living.

I felt as though I was awake for the first time in my life.

Compare this again with Whitman's words:

I cannot be awake for nothing looks to me as it did before, or else I am awake for the first time and all before has been a mean sleep.

In the context of this book, one has to note especially the odd time-sense perception that often accompanies an NDE. As one NDEer reports of her "life-review," the replay of one's life history seems to be an integral part of an NDE:

> I can't exactly describe it to you, but it was just all there. It was just there all at once. I mean, not one thing at a time, blinking off and on, but it was everything, everything at one time.

Compare this with Goethe's words: "One moment holds eternity." I am also impressed by the strongly *nonverbal* nature of the NDE experience. Not only do NDEers find that existing language is completely inadequate to describe what they went through, but communication with the "light" (which seems to invite them to review their lives) takes place, wordlessly, in a kind of instant telepathy. As Patrick Gallagher, who had a nearly fatal car accident in 1976, reports:

> I seemed to possess a knowledge as radiant, transfiguring and ideal as the luminous light. . . . I knew that all one had to do was approach an interesting person and quite easily and almost immediately understand his essence. To do so completely required only a brief glance . . . without any speech . . . the result was a consummate exchange of knowledge. Words cannot provide a hint of such a universal knowledge.

Confronting the deep similarities between NDEs and mystical experience, "cosmic consciousness," at least one commentator, Kenneth Ring, has drawn a striking conclusion:

> What occurs during an NDE has nothing inherently to do with death or the transition into death. . . . The NDE . . . should be regarded as one of a family of related, mystical experiences that have always been with us, rather than the recent discovery of modern researchers who have come to investigate the phenomenon of dying.

In this context, it is interesting to note that the myth of the Fall, which I have used repeatedly throughout the course of this book, is not a specifically Christian phenomenon. Every human culture has its myth of a golden age, paradise, a time of innocence that man has lost through some wrongdoing. Anthropologist Richard Heinberg suggests that this golden age, this lost paradise, can be equated with the Dreaming consciousness of primitive cultures before the advent of symbolic written language:

> Perhaps our most useful new clue to this lost state of being is contained in the modern study of altered states of consciousness and in particular, the near-death experience. The essence of Paradise is . . . equivalent to what various traditions have termed, nirvana, ecstasy, union and cosmic consciousness. It is the condition of the absence of the separate human ego with all its defenses, aggressions and categories of judgement.

The concept that Eden really existed, as a paradisic state of mind, is appealing, but it can lead too easily to the facile New Age belief that the purpose of life is to go home to Eden, to go back to the Golden Age, by returning to prehistory. That is woolly-minded romanticism. Evolution never runs back along its own tracks. As Ken Wilber stresses, the Edenic mentality felt itself to be one with nature because it had not yet separated from nature; it was preconscious (infantile), not superconscious (spiritual). So the goal of personal growth and development is (in terms of the metaphor) not to go back to prehuman Eden but forward to posthuman God, to integrate nonlinear consciousness in its full depth with the self-consistent elegance of linear mathematical definition, perfecting both the intuitive holism of right-brain knowing and the mathematical logic of left-brain science, uniting and thus completing both mind modalities, finally, in the one mutually supportive, complementary, splendid synthesis.

This sense of return brings me to my final point. Carl Sagan has advanced an interesting explanation for the NDE. Noting the frequency with which NDEers report going through a tunnel toward a source of radiant light, Sagan suggests that what NDEers are doing is, in fact, *reliving the birth process*—running their lives back to their beginning. Elements of the core NDE may be consistent with this suggestion—the "life review" for example—but if Sagan is right, it is difficult to see why the sense of love and unity reported by NDEers is always linked to the light. One would suppose it would more logically be linked to the unitive darkness of the womb, which the backward-running mind records as its first memory, prior to the traumatic separation of birth.

However, Sagan's thesis does dovetail with a motif of this book, that to know the end one must return to the beginning (see Chapters 5 and 7). The key cosmological conclusion of this book is that time is closed back upon itself to form a self-consistent loop. Thus end and beginning are, in a sense, linked events. NDEs in this perspective reunite the consciousness of life's "end" with the consciousness of life's "beginning," but moved up one or more octaves in the scale of creation because of the increase in knowing that comes from a life of searching. That is, I believe, how consciousness evolves. At our present stage of evolution, we may be limited in what we can see, even after death. But the collapse of the linear-time fallacy must bring us closer to the climactic mystery of completed consciousness, which in the mythology of our past cultures we have called God.

Several times during the ABC program I referred to earlier, the camera kept panning back to one man in the front row. As others described their NDEs, he obviously relived part of his. On his face was an arresting expression, a look hard to put into words; a look that, in less cynical times, might have been called holy.

That look haunts me.

Finally, how does the message of this book help us live our lives? I believe that what is missing in our lives is a sense of the *sacred*. By this, I do not mean a return to religion in any formal sense. Religions like Christianity and Islam are, in my view, profaners of the sacred, denying in practice the very truths they profess in principle. The American historian, Lewis Mumford, summed up the failure of organized Christianity when he said:

Karl Marx once said of himself that he was not a Marxist; and of Jesus one may say without irreverence, that he was not a Christian. For little men, who guarded Jesus' memory, took him, drained off the precious life blood of his spirit, mummified his body, and wrapped what was left in many foreign wrappings; over these remains they proceeded to erect a gigantic tomb. That tomb was the Christian Church.

To see how this came about, remember that the structure of our minds, with their emphasis on negative feedback, predisposes us to resist change. Organized religion, with its bureaucratic insistence on the right way and eternal truths, denies change. Its very exclusiveness shows how tightly its dogmas are identified with its own sense of collective ego. The eagerness it displays to win converts, to bring their otherness into its own self-image, betrays its deep-rooted insecurity—the inevitable companion of ego. Christianity and Islam have been the chief examples of this unstable superego, and the consequences of their insistence that their way is *the only way* are only too evident, even today, on the streets of Belfast or Beirut.

The metaphor I have always used when confronted with the paradox of a thousand faiths, each claiming to have found "the way," each claiming for themselves a monopoly on truth, an exclusive right to salvation, is the parable of the searchers on the mountain. At the bottom of the mountain they look up, dimly sensing the high place that the intuition of their prophets see as "God." Each searcher starts from the baseline of the mountain where, handicapped by ignorance and trapped by ego, he cannot see around the corner where his nearest fellow traveler is. So each searcher thinks, and believes, that the path he has found, his way up, is the only way and the vision he glimpses is a special privilege granted to him alone. As the searchers climb higher, i.e., evolve toward higher states of consciousness, their various paths start to converge, and they see that around the edge of the hill are other roads, with other seekers. At the summit, the high place (pure consciousness), all paths unite. The sense of separateness that divided searcher from searcher and road from road is no more. They finally understand that all the seemingly different roads led to the same place in the end, the common meeting point that novelist Umberto Eco describes, where each can say:

I shall sink into the divine shadow, in a dumb silence and an ineffable union, and in this sinking all equality and all inequality shall be lost, and in that abyss my spirit will lose itself, and will not know the equal or the unequal, or anything else; and all differences will be forgotten. I shall be in the simple foundation, in the silent desert where diversity is never seen, in the privacy where no one finds himself in his proper place. I shall fall into the silent and uninhabited divinity where there is no work and there is no image.

When I began this book, I spoke of a "gap at the center" in Western civilization, due to the breakdown of the old faiths. The clear implication was that this gap needs to be filled. But with what? I repeat, I believe it can be filled only by a renewed sense of the sacred. By that, I do not mean a new set of beliefs, which will inevitably harden into dogma. I mean *an experiential sense of trust and caring, a renewed feeling for beauty in whatever form it may be found.* To give this experiential message some shape, it will, I think, be necessary to develop a new story for our time, based on science. I say "story" because science in its present form gives no human dimension to the truths it creates and illuminates. We need a parable, not a textbook, a poem of reality so rich and beautiful that its meaning will transcend the words it uses.

An example may help. The timescale of evolution is framed in numbers so vast that they literally lie beyond comprehension. Who can really get a feel for a number like 10 billion years ago? However, all of us can sense the meaning of deep time from a story I read when I was a boy, in Arthur Mee's *Children's Encyclopedia:*

> Far away, in the West of the world, there is a mighty granite rock, a mile high, a mile wide and a mile deep. Once every hundred years a little bird comes to the rock and sharpens its beak on the granite. And when the bird has worn the rock away, that will be one day in eternity.

The restoration of this sense of the sacred is the most important task of this generation. People may say, it is more important to develop strategies to combat the greenhouse effect, for example. This is only superficially true. The greenhouse effect, a result of planetary pollution, is a direct consequence of not so much a rapacious commercial culture as the attitudes and assumptions that make that culture possible. We see now whence those attitudes come. They are the direct consequences of the me-first competitiveness of the ego-self. The only way, I repeat, to reverse this planetary degradation is to break down the barriers that wall us off from each other and the world, to recognize that aphorisms like "the brotherhood of man" are not romantic, pie-in-the-sky daydreams, but practical patents for survival.

To achieve this, I believe, we need to reintroduce a cycle of rituals into life—not grandiose, self-important charades, but participatory ceremonies that have their roots in human needs, rituals that give meaning to our lives by connecting us to both the elemental simplicity we once were and the sublime glory we shall be. When a group of people gather to share a meal, they could, for a minute, link hands. Small though this gesture is, it is rich in significance. We all need that human contact, because we all need to belong to something bigger than ourselves, something that remembers our past and affirms our future. We should create new rites of passage to celebrate the phases of the human life cycle, rituals for birth, for the transition into adolescence, and above all, for dying.

Of these, the need for a ritual of dying is the most urgent. I know of no greater testament to the failure of our civilization than the fact that so many people die alone, abandoned like discards on society's junk heap. Dying must again be united with a sense of the sacred, for it is here, if anywhere, that the psyche outgrows its human limitation. The most important message of this book is that consciousness cannot be extinguished by death, for consciousness transcends time. We should learn to approach death with gratitude, seeing it for what it is, the final elimination of ego, the end of the fallacies of time and self.

In the end it can all be said so simply.

Time and self are outgrown husks, which consciousness will one day discard, just as a butterfly abandons its chrysalis, to fly toward the sun.

BIBLIOGRAPHY

All in the end is harvest.

— EDITH SITWELL

Readers interested in pursuing further some of the issues raised in this book may find the following works useful:

Blum, Harold. *Time's Arrow and Evolution.* London and Princeton, N.J.: Princeton University Press, 1951.

Bohm, D. *Wholeness and the Implicate Order.* London: Routledge & Kegan Paul, 1980.

Bucke, R. M. *Cosmic Consciousness.* New York: E.P. Dutton, 1901.

Capra, Fritjof. *The Tao of Physics.* U.K.: Wildwood House; New York: Shambhala/Random House, 1975.

Charlesworth, Max, Howard Morphy, and Kenneth Maddock, eds. *Religion in Aboriginal Australia.* St. Lucia, Australia: University of Queensland Press, 1984.

Chew, G. F. "Bootstrap: A Scientific Idea?" *Science* 161 (1968): 762–65.

Chomsky, Noam. *Language and Mind.* New York: Harcourt Brace Jovanovich, 1972.

Coveny, P., and R. Highfield. *The Arrow of Time.* London: W.H. Allen, 1990.

Darling, D. *Deep Time.* New York: Dell, 1989.

Davies, Paul. *The Accidental Universe.* Cambridge: Cambridge University Press, 1982.

————. *God and the New Physics*. London: J.M. Dent & Sons, 1983.

————. *The Mind of God*. New York: Simon & Schuster, 1992.

————. *Superforce*. London: Heinemann, 1984.

Davis, Paul, and J. Gribbin. *The Matter Myth*. London: Penguin, 1991.

Du Nouy, L. *Human Destiny*. London: Longmans, Green & Co., 1945.

Durrell, Clement. *Readable Relativity*. London: G. Bell & Sons, 1926.

Eliade, Mircea. *The Myth of the Eternal Return*. Princeton, N.J.: Princeton University Press, 1954; reprint, 1974. (Originally published as *Le Mythe de l'eternel retour: archetypes et repetition* [Paris: Librairie Gallimard/NRF, 1949].)

Faulkner, R. O. *The Ancient Egyptian Book of the Dead*. Rev ed. London: British Museum Publications, 1985.

Flood, Josephine. *Archeology of the Dreamtime*. Sydney: Collins, 1983. Rev. ed., New Haven, Conn.: Yale University Press, 1990.

Frazer, J. G. *The Belief in Immortality and the Worship of the Dead*. London: Macmillan, 1913.

Gibran, Kahlil. *The Prophet*. London: Heinemann, 1926; New York: Knopf, 1970.

Grey, Margot. *Return from Death: An Exploration of the Near-Death Experience*. London: Routledge & Kegan Paul; Boston: Arkana, 1985.

Gribbin, J. *In Search of Schroedinger's Cat*. U.K.: Wildwood House, 1984.

Grof, Stanislav. *Beyond the Brain*. Albany, N.Y.: State University of New York Press, 1985.

Hawking, Stephen. *A Brief History of Time*. London and New York: Bantam, 1988.

Heinberg, Richard. *Memories and Visions of Paradise*. Wellingborough, U.K.: Aquarian Press; Los Angeles: J.P. Tarcher, 1989.

Hick, John. *Death and Eternal Life*. London: William Collins, 1976.

Hoyle, Fred. *The Intelligent Universe*. London: Michael Joseph, 1983.

Huxley, Aldous. *The Perennial Philosophy*. London: Chatto & Windus, 1946.

Kaufmann, William J. III. *Black Holes and Warped Spacetime*. New York: W.H. Freeman & Co., 1979.

Kirkwood, T., R. Rosenberger, and D. Galas, eds. *Accuracy in Molecular Processes*. London: Chapman & Hall, 1986.

Kramer, K. *The Sacred Art of Dying*. Mahwah, N.J.: Paulist Press, 1988.

Krishnamurti, J. *Krishnamurti's Journal*. London: Gollancz, 1982.

Kübler-Ross, Elisabeth. *On Death and Dying*. New York: Macmillan, 1969.

Lord, Walter. *A Night to Remember*. London: Longmans, Green, 1956.

Lovelock, J.E. *Gaia*. Oxford: Oxford University Press, 1979.

Magouin, H.W. *The Waking Brain*. Springfield, Ill.: Charles C. Thomas, 1958.

May, Rollo. *The Courage to Create*. New York: Bantam, 1975.

Mumford, Lewis. *The Condition of Man*. London: Martin Secker & Warburg, 1944.

O'Connor, Peter. *Understanding Jung*. Melbourne: Methuen Australia, 1985.

Pagels, H. R. *The Cosmic Code*. New York: Simon & Schuster, 1982; London: Michael Joseph, 1983.

Parker, B. *Invisible Matter and the Fate of the Universe*. New York: Plenum Press, 1989.

Peck, M. Scott. *The Different Drum*. New York: Simon & Schuster, 1987.

Penrose, Roger. *The Emperor's New Mind*. Oxford and New York: Oxford University Press, 1989.

Piaget, Jean. *Language and Thought of the Child*. London: Routledge & Kegan Paul, 1926.

Reanney, Darryl. *Genesis*. Australian Broadcasting Company Television, 1982.

————. "The Molecular Evolution of Viruses." In "Viruses," part 2 of *The Microbe*. eds. B.W.J. Mahy and J. R. Pattison. Cambridge: Society for General Microbiology/Cambridge University Press, 1984.

Restak, Richard. *The Brain*. Toronto: Educational Broadcasting Corporation/Bantam, 1984.

Ring, Kenneth. *Heading Towards Omega*. New York: William Morrow, 1985.

Sagan, Carl. *Broca's Brain*. London: Hodder & Stoughton, 1974; New York: Random House, 1979.

————. *The Dragons of Eden*. London: Hodder & Stoughton; New York: Random House, 1977.

Sassoon, Siegfried. *Selected Poems*. London: Faber & Faber, 1968.

Shneidman, Edwin. *Voices of Death*. New York: Harper & Row, 1980.

Shri Purohit Swami, trans. *The Gita*. London: Faber & Faber, 1935.

Tarnas, Richard. "The Transfiguration of the Western Mind," *Revision* 12, no. 3 (1990):3–19.

Taylor, A. *Acquainted with the Night*. London: Fontana, 1989.

Thomas, Lewis. *The Lives of a Cell*. New York: Viking; London: Futura, 1974.

Viorst, Judith. *Necessary Losses*. New York and London: Simon & Schuster, 1988.

Watson, James. *The Double Helix*. New York: Atheneum, 1968.

Weinberg, Steven. *The First Three Minutes*. London: Andre Deutsch; New York: Basic Books, 1977.

Whitman, Walt. *Leaves of Grass*. New York: Modern Library, 1981.

Whyte, L. L. *The Next Development in Man*. New York: Mentor, 1950.

Wilber, Ken. *Up from Eden*. London: Routledge & Kegan Paul, 1983.

Wolf, Fred Alan. *Parallel Universes*. New York: Touchstone/Simon & Schuster, 1990.

Wooldridge, D. E. *The Machinery of the Brain*. New York: McGraw-Hill, 1963.

Zilboorg, G. "Fear of Death." *Psychoanalytic Quarterly* 12 (1943).

Zohar, D. *The Quantum Self*. London: Bloomsbury, 1990.

————. *Through the Time Barrier*. London: Heinemann, 1982.